CHILD POVERTY IN AMERICA TODAY

CHILD POVERTY IN AMERICA TODAY

Volume 3: The Promise of Education

Edited by Barbara A. Arrighi and David J. Maume

Praeger Perspectives

Westport, Connecticut
London

Library of Congress Cataloging-in-Publication Data

Child poverty in America today / edited by Barbara A. Arrighi and David J. Maume.
    p. cm.
    Includes bibliographical references and index.
    ISBN 978–0–275–98926–2 (set : alk. paper)—ISBN 978–0–275–98927–9 (v. 1 : alk. paper)—
    ISBN 978–0–275–98928–6 (v. 2 : alk. paper)—ISBN 978–0–275–98929–3 (v. 3 : alk. paper)—
    ISBN 978–0–275–98930–9 (v. 4 : alk. paper)
    1. Poor children—United States.   2. Poor families—United States.   3. Poverty—United States.
    4. Child welfare—United States.   5. Children—United States—Social conditions.
    6. Children—Government policy—United States.   I. Arrighi, Barbara A.   II. Maume, David J.
    HV741.C4875   2007
    362.7086′9420973–dc22   2007003046

British Library Cataloguing in Publication Data is available.

Library of Congress Catalog Card Number: 2007003046
ISBN-10: 0–275–98926–7 (set)   ISBN-13: 978–0–275–98926–2 (set)
         0–275–98927–5 (vol. 1)   978–0–275–98927–9 (vol. 1)
         0–275–98928–3 (vol. 2)   978–0–275–98928–6 (vol. 2)
         0–275–98929–1 (vol. 3)   978–0–275–98929–3 (vol. 3)
         0–275–98930–5 (vol. 4)   978–0–275–98930–9 (vol. 4)

First published in 2007

Praeger Publishers, 88 Post Road West, Westport, CT 06881
An imprint of Greenwood Publishing Group, Inc.
www.praeger.com

Printed in the United States of America

The paper used in this book complies with the
Permanent Paper Standard issued by the National
Information Standards Organization (Z39.48–1984).

10 9 8 7 6 5 4 3 2 1

To our children
Eiler, Elena, and Megan
and
Meghan and Allison
Our concern for their welfare piqued our interest in the
welfare of all children

CONTENTS

ACKNOWLEDGMENTS

First, we wish to thank all of the contributors to the four volumes for the exceptional caliber of their research. Their dedication and commitment to understanding the causes of child and family poverty is remarkable. It has been a pleasure to work with such a fine group of scholars. It is noteworthy, too, that more than a few of the contributors endured family emergencies and/or experienced personal crises during the research and writing phase, yet remained committed to the project. For that, we are grateful.

We are honored that Diana Pearce is the author of the Introduction for Volume 1: Families and Children. Professor Pearce has written a thoughtful essay weaving common threads among diverse chapters. She is a tireless researcher who has been a pioneer in examining the causes and effects of poverty in the lives of women and children. Not only has Professor Pearce illuminated the way for other researchers in explaining the complex factors influencing women's poverty, she has been an ardent advocate for ending the feminization of poverty.

Thanks to Rachel Sebastian, graduate student at the University of Cincinnati, who assisted with the project. We appreciate, too, the guidance of Elizabeth Potenza, editor at Praeger, throughout the editorial process, Anne Rehill who assisted early on in the project, Nicole Azze, production manager, Vivek Sood, and Saloni Jain who oversaw the copyediting. Finally, thanks to Marie Ellen Larcada, who first approached Barbara about editing the four-volume set.

INTRODUCTION

David J. Maume and Barbara A. Arrighi

People agree with everything I say. They say, yes, it is unfair *they* don't get as much per pupil as our children. Then they say, tell me one thing. Can you really solve this kind of problem by throwing money at it? And I say, you mean, can you really buy your way to a better education? It seems to work for *your* children.

Jonathan Kozol, Marx Lecture at Columbia University, Teachers' College 2002

CHILDREN AND EDUCATION

Any discussion of the educational system in the United States has to consider several factors. First, is public education in the United States sufficient to maintain a literate middle-class, a condition required for a republic? That is, are young people who finish the twelfth grade critical thinkers, able to discern logical arguments and not easily swayed or manipulated by political chicanery? Second, is public education sufficient so that young people can move onto higher education seamlessly, without remedial courses, and complete a four-year degree successfully within four years? Third, is the relationship between the educational system and the economic system synergistic so that a young person (who does not wish to pursue a bachelor's degree) can obtain a high school diploma and find a job that will enable s(he) to be self sufficient, even in a "global economy?" Fourth, does the educational system equalize the playing field between the haves and the have-nots?

Unfortunately, the gap between the lives of the children of the poor and children of the well off is glaring and well documented. Education, purportedly the "great equalizer" is part of the matrix of inequality. Children of the well off are sometimes home schooled and privately tutored, poolside.[1] Poor children who are academically behind and eligible for tutoring under the No Child Left Behind Act must wait for funding to be appropriated. While poor children struggle to pass state and federal proficiency tests,[2] well-connected parents are buying internships for their children at their private school silent auctions.[3] Middle-class and well-off parents have the means to flee public school systems for private schools. Meanwhile school systems in poor areas are finding it more difficult to muster support for school tax levies.

Employers are able to evaluate the state of the educational system by the literacy skills prospective employees exhibit when they come through the corporate doors; however, now the corporate doors can be in India or China. For example, although I.B.M. laid off thousands of employees in the United States it increased the number of its employees in India from 9,000 in 2004 to 43,000 in 2006, about 13 percent of its global workforce, and not just service workers.[4] In its India Research Lab, a hundred employees have Ph.Ds. If corporations can find whatever they need off shore—well educated, motivated, docile, less expensive labor—in order to provide the highest profits to share holders as well as top executives, what incentive is there for them to boost the education of U.S. children? As more and more corporations are making a greater share of their profits outside the United States rather than in the United States and investment gurus are encouraging investors to buy overseas stocks, how effective can school systems be in their appeal for funding? And what is left for young people in the United States? Almost half of all workers earn $13.25 or less an hour, $26,784.00 or less a year.[5] Thirty million low-wage workers earn less than $8.70 an hour.[6]

Parents of public school children who do not have the means to flee public schools might have been encouraged by the upward trend in the standardized state test scores earned by their children individually and schools collectively. However, the too-good-to-be-true test scores seemed to be just that. Evidence suggests that states have simplified the tests to facilitate high rates of passing and therefore, "comply" with the No Child Left Behind directives. For example, according to state test results of fourth graders in Idaho, 90 percent of students were proficient in math; however on the federal test only 41 percent were proficient. States in which discrepancies between state and federal testing were found include: New York, North Carolina, Alabama, Texas, and Tennessee.[7] If students are not proficient in reading and math, can they be good stewards of the republic they inherit?

Can simplified state tests be reconciled with the National Academy of Sciences' report that sagging educational standards threaten the U.S.'s "strategic and economic security?"[8] Concerns abound. At present, even the most advanced twelfth graders in the United States "... perform poorly relative to their peers on international tests." Nicholas Kristof, *New York Times*, editorial writer, showed his daughter's third grade homework to teachers in China who evaluated it as comparable to their first grade work. In China, most students take advanced biology and calculus compared to less than 18 percent of U.S. students.[9] Some argue that the state of U.S. education is related to U.S. decline in technological advances. For example, The Economic Strategy Institute, reported that in 2000 the United States was the leader of broadband internet, but now ranks 16th. And 21 percent of the world's telecom equipment is manufactured in the United States today, down from 40 percent.[10]

Self-interest could be key to motivating corporate leaders (not living abroad or in gated communities) who might otherwise think the problem isn't theirs to fix. On the one hand, Bill Gates expresses grave misgivings about the state of U.S. education vis-à-vis other countries. On the other hand, his concerns provide justification for Microsoft's outsourcing of American jobs. Statistics that are of interest to all and especially the corporate class include the following: High school graduates are less likely to commit crime; increasing high school completion rates by 1 percent can reduce justice system costs by $1.4 billion annually; a one-year increase in average years of schooling can reduce murder and assault by almost 30 percent and car theft by 20 percent; the average 45-year-old high school drop out is in poorer health than the average 65-year-old high school graduate (the former translates into higher health-care costs for taxpayers to bear).[11] Although the well-off can send their children to private schools to ensure a *quality* education and a safe environment away from poverty, at some point in time, the lives of the well-heeled and the *other* will intersect because the *other* performs the jobs the well-off don't want to do and can afford to pay the *other* to do.

If, as the evidence has suggested, the playing field is not level for children in poverty, then it isn't rocket science to understand the importance of starting education earlier for these children. Yet, while other countries are investing more in their children, the United States has been backpedaling. For example, in 1996, while the United States was dismantling decades of welfare assistance for families and children living in poverty, Quebec was implementing subsidized day care for 4-year-olds. Four years later Quebec extended its programs to infants.[12] Britain, considered somewhat of a laggard when it comes to early childhood education and child care, has instituted a program for 3- to 4-year-olds.[13] If other countries are capable of early childhood education and care, why not the United States? Some argue that early childhood education is a better investment than having kids try to "catch up" later. If a child falls behind in the fundamentals the likelihood of future academic success decreases.[14]

The Children's Defense Fund reported that 3-year-olds living in poverty knew half the words as other kids their age, but by first grade they had lost ground and knew only a quarter of words that other first graders knew.[15] In a similar study by the Economic Policy Institute it was reported that the average cognitive score for high-SES kids was 60 percent above kids in the lowest SES group.[16] There is evidence that kids from disadvantaged backgrounds suffer "summer set back"—they tend to forget what they learned in the previous academic term because of a lack of stimulation over the summer.[17] Adding fuel to the argument others have found that children who experience high-quality care have ". . . greater mathematical ability, greater thinking and attention skills, and fewer behavioral problems than children in lower quality care."[18] Sheila Kamerman, testifying before the U.S. Senate, made the point that early childhood education and care programs "enhance children's development and prepare them for primary school . . . [and] . . . are increasingly viewed as a 'public good.'"[19]

While the federal government ignores the gorilla in the room, several states have implemented universal prekindergarten programs. For example, Georgia introduced a universal, voluntary program and expanded the program to 4-year-olds. Oklahoma, Florida, and New York have all developed prekindergarten programs; however, New York's program has not been fully funded. Maryland plans a universal program for 4-year-olds in 2007 and cities, like Chicago and Los Angeles are "on board," and making preschool available for all 3- and 4-year-olds.[20]

The bottom line is: The educational system does not exist in a vacuum. It is connected to the political and economic and as such is not neutral. Decades ago, Bowles and Gintis argued that the "structure of social relations in education not only inures the student to the discipline of the work place, but develops the types of personal demeanor, modes of self-presentation, self-image, and social-class identification which are the crucial ingredients of job adequacy."[21]

In other words, children from lower socioeconomic backgrounds are intertwined in a matrix of negative physical and social factors—food insecurity, dilapidated housing, violent neighborhoods, lead paint poisoning, lack of health and dental care, asthma, perhaps homelessness—education is some nebulous thing vying for their attention. Kids living in impoverished families live in the practical world, a concrete world—their lives revolve around scrounging money for rent, food, gas, heat, water, clothing—struggling to satisfy what Maslow refers to as the basic physical needs of food, clothing, and shelter.[22] According to Maslow's perspective, humans can't achieve beyond the concrete level until the basics are assured. Children living in poverty arrive at school prepared for "concrete" thinking, not the abstract—what Bordieu calls "symbolic mastery" that children of higher socioeconomic status (SES) are prepared to tackle.[23] Because higher SES families have a surplus of resources to ensure their basic physical needs, their children are able to turn their attention to higher-level thinking. The educational system is bifurcated—one for the haves and one for the have-nots, one that reproduces Harrington's two Americas. Will it safeguard the republic?

The pursuit of diplomas is consistent with wider cultural messages that emphasize striving and hard work as the primary route to a higher quality of life. Certainly, when the public considers ways to eliminate or reduce poverty, their first inclination is to provide better schooling to those who need it most. And many social scientists have completed studies that show schools do in fact, improve the skills of the less-advantaged.

Other social scientists, however, have long been interested in how family circumstances predict educational attainment. This research agenda is consistent with the notion that schools are bureaucratic institutions that protect the interests of educators, and reproduce current inequalities. Although purportedly predisposed to prepare everyone for success in adulthood, schools instead identify students who exhibit values and behaviors consistent with the future-oriented, disciplined, and acquisitive nature sought in the labor market. Such students are rewarded with good grades and receive favorable treatment from teachers. Students who fall short of this ideal are weeded out over time, and their lack of success in school (and by implication, their lack of success later in life) is attributed to internal deficiencies that preclude them from taking advantage of the "promise" offered to them.

The diverse articles in this volume fit within this debate and extend it as well. For example, at the very beginning of the life cycle, researchers are increasingly focused on the child-care experiences of children, especially those whose families receive public subsidies for care. Deborah A. Phillips and Marcy Whitebook examined the quality of care offered by licensed, center-and home-based child-care programs operating in low- and middle-income neighborhoods in the Oakland area. They found that the standards for licensure among home-based care providers pertained more to safety standards, in contrast to licensed centers that had to meet additional standards regarding the number and educational skills of teachers. Consequently, children's literacy scores were higher in center-than home-based day care, a quality gap that interacted with the socioeconomic status of the neighborhood in which care was offered. The authors are concerned that given the cumulative nature of education, these prekindergarten differences may widen when children enter school.

Indeed, Dylan Conger's analysis shows that within-school decisions also contribute to variation in educational outcomes. Using data from New York City public schools, she found that a nontrivial 11–12 percent of the total racial/ethnic segregation of students was attributable to within-school decisions to cluster students of similar racial and ethnic background in the same classroom. The outcome of this decision is hardly benign, as Conger further shows that segregation varies positively with the poverty status of children, and negatively with standardized test scores.

Despite the fact that many classrooms are segregated by race, ethnicity, and social class, there is some evidence that schools are effective in fulfilling their mission. Annie Georges drew from the *Early Childhood Longitudinal Study*, a nationally representative sample of 1998–1999 kindergarten class, to examine students' math achievement. Although her data largely confirmed that scores on standardized math tests were lower among students from disadvantaged families, she also found that students' fall-to-spring *gain* in math skills was the same irrespective of income and education of their parents. Although Georges expected the *type* of instruction (drills and worksheets versus group-learning) to have an effect on math achievements she did not find it. Rather, she concluded that, "... children below poverty benefit more from formal classroom instruction than children who are not in poverty." Georges' research provides more evidence for earlier classroom education for children living in poverty.

Edward B. Reeves reports similar findings in his analyses of data on Kentucky schools, a state where there exists an almost "... 'iron law' linking student [social-economic status] and education outcomes." After being one of the first states in the nation to implement comprehensive educational reform in 1990, Reeves analyzed current performance data among more than 700 elementary schools to assess the impact of reform efforts. Like Georges, Reeves found that point-in-time correlations between academic achievement and poverty rates among schools were negative and significant. But, when he examined the 7-year *change* in test scores, he found no correlation with the poverty status of the school. Reeves suggested that state and federal mandates have elevated expectations of what students should know, and students in *all* schools have responded by improving their performance in the classroom.

Sandra Mathison's chapter is a treatise on state and federal mandates that focus on testing students to determine educational effectiveness. In a provocative essay, she argues that testing (at all levels of education) is a mechanism by which weak students are identified and weeded out of schools. Students who remain in school generate higher tests scores for their schools and districts, enabling educators in these districts to claim that their superior effectiveness entitles them to increased financial support for their efforts. Readers who have little memory of standardized tests in their own educational experience, will no doubt be surprised by Mathison's first table showing the typical testing experience today for children between grades K-12. Further, today's students take more "high-stakes tests" that determine their futures and those of their educators. For example, districts are increasingly relying on ninth-grade proficiency tests to determine who should graduate from high school. Students of color and those from disadvantaged backgrounds are at higher risks of failing these tests and dropping out. After doing so, high schools are composed of better test-takers producing higher school-wide scores (and greater claims to teaching effectiveness from administrators). Those who fail these tests in the ninth grade often drop out and later acquire a GED certificate, allowing educators to further claim that they are not neglecting the educational needs of the poor.

Yet, Richard K. Caputo maintains the GED certificate is not equivalent to a high school degree, and instead GED recipients are more like high-school dropouts when measured by their success in the labor market. Using data from the 1997 *National Longitudinal Survey of Youth* he analyzed the correlates of several education outcomes, including dropping out, getting a high school diploma, or attaining the GED. Like other authors in this volume, he found that socioeconomic status determined attainment; however, that finding did not hold up when he controlled for social and behavioral problems of the adolescents. Importantly, however, he found that the quality of educational experiences in elementary school had a strong effect on attainment in later years, and that these factors also varied by race and ethnicity.

The remaining authors in this volume considered links between schools and other community institutions to determine how schools might fulfill their "promise." For example, Jason M. Smith argued that extracurricular activities provided students with role models and experiences that fostered their success in high school. Using data from the *National Education Longitudinal Study*, he contrasted inactive students with those who were involved in extracurricular activities such as sports, plays, band, or other school clubs. He limited his sample to students who attended high-poverty schools and found that active students had a significantly higher graduation rate than nonactive students. This finding is particularly important given community tendencies to cut funding for extracurricular activities in tight budgetary times. Such a course of action may disproportionately affect the graduation chances of poor students thereby reproducing current inequalities in the area.

Youth employment is the focus of attention for Constance T. Gager, Jacqueline C. Pflieger, and Jennifer Hickes Lundquist, especially in conjunction with students' socioeconomic status. The authors drew on the *Survey of Adults and Youth*, a survey funded by the *Robert Wood Johnson Foundation*. They found that the youth labor market largely paralleled the adult labor market, in that employment rates are higher for white youths who come from families of higher socioeconomic status. Because youth employment fosters behavioral change and introduces youths to key gatekeepers in the community, it can potentially reinforce and accentuate the skills learned in school. Thus, it is noteworthy that these authors conclude that "... policies are needed that specifically target job training for youth, especially those in urban neighborhoods."

Finally, Judith Hennessy considers the role of education of welfare reform as it affects single mothers. After reform legislation was passed in 1996, welfare recipients were required to "earn" their benefits by developing plans to become self-sufficient. Most states defined this as requiring women to work and only a few states allow women to attend college as part of their plans to be self-sufficient. Hennessy interviewed workingwomen and those in college to determine how they made sense of their choices. She found that low-income student mothers had to wrestle with the prevailing definition that women were "successful" when they were working, but that this often conflicted with the care of children. Moreover, these women realized that education offered the "promise" of a better life in the future, but welfare officials measured their own success by the number of women who were working and no longer drawing welfare. Thus, working women got better benefits and more support from welfare offices, yet student mothers couched their choices as striving to fulfill the "promise" that linked educational attainment with future productivity.

NOTES

1. Susan Saulny, "In Gilded Age of Home-Schooling Students Have Private Teachers," *The New York Times*, June 5, 2006, A1, A17.

2. Diane Ravitch, "Every State Left Behind," *The New York Times*, November 7, 2005, A25.

3. "Internships for Sale," *The Wall Street Journal*, June 10–11, 2006, P5.

4. Saritha Rai, "A Crucial Cog in the Machine at I.B.M.," *The New York Times*, June 5, 2006, C4.

5. Thomas Geoghegan, "How Pink Slips Hurt More Than Workers," *The New York Times*, March 29, 2006, B6.

6. Beth Shulman, "Working and Poor in the USA," *The Nation*, February 9, 2004, 20–22.

7. Diane Ravitch, "Every State Left Behind."

8. Diane Ravitch, "Every State Left Behind."

9. Nicholas D. Kristof, "Chinese Medicine for American Schools," *The New York Times*, June 27, 2006, A19.

10. Thomas L. Friedman, "Facts and Folly," *The New York Times*, March 29, 2006, A27.

11. Henry Levin and Nigel Holmes, "America's Learning Deficit," *The New York Times*, November 7, 2005, A25.

12. David Leonhardt, "The Price of Day Care Can Be High," *The New York Times*, June 14, 2006, C1.

13. Tamar Lewin, "The Need to Invest in Young Children," *The New York Times*, January 11, 2006, A31.

14. James J. Heckman, "Catch 'em Young," *The Wall Street Journal*, January 10, 2006, A14.

15. "Early Childhood, Critical Years, Critical Investment," *State of American Children*, 2005, Washington, DC: Children's Defense Fund, 65.

16. Ibid.

17. Douglas B. Downey, Paul T. von Hippel, and Beckett Broh, "Are Schools the Great Equalizer? Cognitive Inequality During the Summer Months and the School Year," *American Sociological Review*, 2004, 613–635.

18. "Early Childhood, Critical Years, Critical Investment," 72.

19. Sheila B. Kamerman, "Early Childhood Education and Care: International Perspectives," Testimony Prepared for the United States Senate Committee on Health, Education, Labor, and Pensions, March 27, 2001, 3,6.

20. Anthony Raden and Lisa McCabe, "Researching Universal Prekindergarten: Thoughts on Critical Questions and Research Domains from Policy Makers, Child Advocates and Researchers," 1–4.

21. Samuel Bowels and Herbert Gintis, *Schooling in Capitalist America: Educational Reform and the Contradictions of Economic Life*, London: Routledge and Kegan Paul, 1976: 131.

22. Abraham Maslow, *Motivation and Personality*, New York: Harper, 1954.

23. Pierre Bordieu and J-C. Paseron, *Reproduction in Education, Society and Culture*, London: Sage, 1977.

CHAPTER 1

WHAT D   CHILD CARE
DOLLARS   EPENDS. . . . *

Deborah A. P   *Whitebook*

Concern about the school achievement gap between children of low-income families and other children is the focus of much research, discussion, and policy. The facts are startling. Young children just entering school from the lowest quintile of family income score at about the 30th percentile of their cohort's academic achievement, while those from the top quintile of income enter school scoring at about the 70th percentile. Disadvantages arise early in life, and poorer children do not arrive at the school door as prepared for academic learning. Because of the cumulative nature of education, moreover, children in or near poverty levels almost never catch up to the educational proficiency of their wealthier counterparts and often drop out as early as ninth grade. That fact runs to the foundations of socioeconomic inequality in America and of disparities in later life chances—for healthy living, for living wages, for secure, and for productive citizenship.

Facts of this nature have led to a virtual explosion of interest in early education. The policy response has consisted primarily of efforts to prepare 4-year-olds for school so that "no child is left behind." This includes federal initiatives to upgrade standards and training for Head Start teachers, exponential growth in state investments in pre-k programs—focused primarily on low-income children, and increasing pressures to document the long-term educational impacts of these investments. These initiatives have fueled a dramatic shift from viewing early care and education settings for 4-year-olds as part of the long-standing child care system and thus focused on ensuring an adequate supply of care to support parental employment to approaching them as a new educational environment that must be of sufficiently high quality to support the early learning of young children.

Over the next decade, it is likely that a growing proportion of 4-year-olds will move into pre-k programs given state expansion in this area. At the same time, consistently high rates of maternal employment starting in infancy (accompanied by increasingly stringent work requirements associated with welfare reform) will continue to place large demands on the non-pre-k, non-Head Start segment of the early care and education market, namely community-based profit and nonprofit child-care centers and home-based programs, as well as informal child-care arrangements. In stark contrast to the discussion around education for 4-year-olds and the federal Head Start program, efforts to improve the quality of child care remain largely under the radar screen of policy discussion and thus sporadic and poorly or inconsistently funded.

This uneven attention to the developmental environments of early care and education settings flies in the face of evidence that the trajectory of early learning begins well before the fourth year of life and that the vast majority of children spend this vitally important developmental period in child care, as distinct from pre-k and Head Start or Early Head Start, settings.[1] Large-scale studies over the last two decades have shown that most community-based child care is of mediocre quality and that these programs compare unfavorably to pre-k and Head Start settings.[2] Moreover, research has highlighted a perverse juxtaposition of circumstances regarding low-income children. Specifically, while low-income children benefit more than their advantaged peers from high-quality early childhood programs,[3] they are less likely to attend high-quality early care and education arrangements. This has been found repeatedly for home-based arrangements, whether licensed or not. With regard to center-based arrangements, there is some evidence that very low-income children can receive higher quality center-based care than children with modestly higher incomes when they have access to programs, such as Head Start, with strict income eligibility requirements.[4] Thus, the poorest of the poor may actually receive some of the best and some of the worst center-based care this country has to offer, whereas, in home-based settings, they tend to receive poor quality care.[5]

This study was designed to examine the full range of early care and education services available in one community—Alameda County, California—to families with different levels of income and/or access to public subsidies: licensed center-based care, licensed family child-care homes, and license-exempt home-based care.[6] The findings presented here focus on the first two sectors. They provide an in-depth look at the quality of services offered in child-care programs receiving public subsidies, and in programs not receiving subsidies. Nonsubsidized programs were divided into two groups: those located in low-income neighborhoods and those located in middle-income neighborhoods. As such, this research informs pressing questions about the extent to which existing early care and education programs that serve children from different socioeconomic groups, including those receiving subsidized care, provide them with the high-quality experiences, resources, and interactions that will prepare them for formal schooling.

METHODS

The sample for these findings reported in this paper consists of licensed, center- and home-based child care programs operating in low- and middle-income neighborhoods and serving subsidized and nonsubsidized children in Alameda County, California. This site was selected because it has a diverse local child-care market and population of families using care. It also represents a relatively "high end" site with regard to having a strong record of developing initiatives to improve the quality of early care and education and to offer child-care workers incentives to pursue professional development. In addition, it is important to note that California, unlike many states, uses both contracts and vouchers to support care for low-income children in centers. As noted below, the contract mechanism is accompanied by added requirements for the centers regarding quality of care. Thus, the findings in this report are most appropriately approached as a good case scenario of the quality of care experienced by low-income children.

The final sample consisted of 102 programs, 42 centers, and 60 licensed family child-care homes. All participating programs had been in operation for at least 9 months prior to being observed and we sought the participation of programs that provided care not only for preschoolers, but also for infants and toddlers. The centers consisted of 20 programs receiving state contracts to serve low-income children (all considered low-income subsidized and including part-day State Preschools [$n = 4$] or Head Start programs [$n = 5$] and full-school-day programs funded by the State Department of Education [$n = 2$]), 5 additional centers serving 25 percent subsidized children through vouchers (and thus added to the contracted programs to create 25 low-income, subsidized centers), 8 centers in low-income neighborhoods that served fewer than 25 percent subsidized children (the low-income, nonsubsidized subgroup), and 9 centers in middle-income neighborhoods that served fewer than 25 percent subsidized children (the middle-income, nonsubsidized subgroup). The homes were similarly characterized by the neighborhood in which they resided and whether they enrolled 25 percent or more subsidized children. The final sample consisted of 23 low-income, subsidized homes, 19 low-income, nonsubsidized homes, and 18 middle-income, nonsubsidized homes.

All programs were visited by observers trained to reliability between February and August 2001. The observers assessed the quality of the child-care environments using the Early Childhood Environment Rating Scale-Revised Edition (ECERS-R)[7] for preschool rooms in center-based settings, and the Infant and Toddler Environment Rating Scale (ITERS)[8] for infant and toddler rooms. The Family Day Care Environment Rating Scale (FDCRS)[9] was used for licensed home-based settings. These instruments cover a wide range of characteristics of the child-care environment, ranging from learning activities to personal care routines. Scores range from 1 to 7, with 1 indicating care that is inadequate and 7 indicating excellent care. An observational measure of ratios and group size was obtained in conjunction with the ECERS-R, ITERS, or FDCRS observations.

In addition, a more detailed measure of caregiver–child interactions was obtained using a modified version of the Observational Record of the Caregiving Environment (ORCE) used in the NICHD Study of Early Child Care.[10] This instrument, named the Child-Caregiver Observation system (C-COS), captured the one-on-one interactions between caregivers and the children in their care. Specific behaviors coded include verbal interaction, stimulation of age-appropriate learning, and the sensitivity of the interactions. Finally, the Caregiver Interaction Scale[11] was used to capture more global ratings of the providers' harshness, sensitivity, and detachment toward the children in their care; it captures more emotional-affective qualities of caregiving. Observer reliabilities were obtained as part of preobservation training and assessed periodically during data collection. Reliabilities were .93 for the Caregiver Interaction Scale, .79 for the C-COS, .91 for the ECERS-R/ITERS, and .87 for the FDCRS.

Adult literacy was assessed using the Documents scale of the Tests of Applied Literacy Skills (TALS), developed by the Educational Testing Service to assess performance on English literacy tasks that adults typically encounter at home, at work, and in day-to-day activities. The Documents scale specifically assesses the knowledge and skills required to locate and use information contained in various formats, including job applications, payroll forms, transportation schedules, tables, and so forth.[12] These skills are relevant to being familiar with child-care regulations and safety procedures, participating in training, finding information in a phone book or through written materials (e.g., written emergency procedures), and completing forms such as Individual Education Plans for children with special needs. Scores on TALS scales range from 0 to 500, with scores below 275 representing limited literacy proficiency and scores between 276 and 325 considered the minimum literacy needed for success in today's labor market. The mean score on the document scale for a large, nationally representative sample of U.S. adults is 267.[13]

FINDINGS

Where Are the Children?

The demographics of center- and home-based arrangements tell different stories about the distribution of low-income children across programs serving different populations of families. Over 80 percent of the centers (83%), but only 48 percent of the licensed family child-care homes in our sample served at least one subsidized child. Many of the centers that did serve this population enrolled very few subsidized children. For example, 10 of the 35 centers with subsidized children—5 in low-income and 5 in middle-income neighborhoods—had fewer than 8 percent subsidized children. At the same time, 13 centers, all in low-income neighborhoods, served 75 percent or more subsidized children. It thus appears that low-income children were dispersed across subsidized (25% subsidized children) and nonsubsidized centers and across centers in low- and middle-income neighborhoods, perhaps as a result of children using vouchers to purchase center care in programs without large numbers of subsidized children. At the same time, centers with large concentrations of subsidized children were located in low-income neighborhoods. It is important to note that these patterns may be specific to our sample which, by design, over-represented centers with state contracts relative to those accepting children with vouchers.

Because licensed family child-care providers were asked to estimate the family income level of the children in their care, we were able to examine the distribution

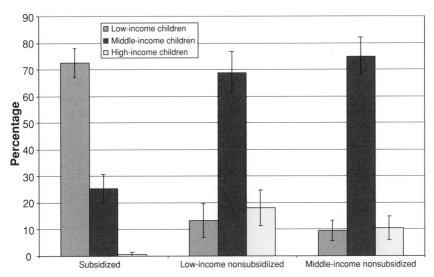

Figure 1.1
Family Income of Children in Licensed Family Child Care, by Income Subsidy Groups
Note: **Bars indicate standard errors of the means. Bars that do not overlap indicate statistically significant differences. For example, low-come children are significantly more likely to be in subsidized programs than are middle- or high-income children.**

of children, by family income, across groups of providers defined by neighborhood income and receipt of subsidies. As shown in Figure 1.1, in contrast to center care, low-income children appeared to be more concentrated within some segments of the home-based market. Specifically, subsidized providers in low-income neighborhoods had the largest percentage of children from low-income families (73%) ($F(2, 55) = 44.97$, $p < .001$). Providers in middle-income neighborhoods enrolled mainly children of middle- and high-income families (86%). Interestingly, nonsubsidized providers in low-income neighborhoods also enrolled primarily children of middle- and high-income families (87%), perhaps driven by economic necessity given the difficulty that low-income families have in covering the full cost of care when they do not receive subsidies.

In sum, many more centers than homes provided care for subsidized, low-income children and these children were somewhat dispersed across contracted and non-contracted centers in low- and middle-income neighborhoods. Within the family child-care sector, in contrast, low-income children were over-represented in homes in low-income neighborhoods and in which at least 25 percent of the children received subsidies to defray the cost of care.

Because we did not collect data on the income or subsidy status of individual children in the centers, as we did in the homes, we are not able to provide data on the overall distribution of low-income or subsidized children across centers and homes in our sample. However, a study conducted by the state of California in 2000 revealed that about 55 percent of children receiving subsidies were in center-based care. About 17 percent were in licensed family child care. The remainder were in license-exempt care. Among children attending subsidized licensed care, 63 percent were in the contracted programs with higher standards. It appears, therefore, that within the regulated sector of child care, children receiving subsidies are disproportionately enrolled in center-based programs, as compared to licensed homes. Large numbers of these children, however, are in care that operates beyond the regulatory system altogether.

What Quality of Care Are Low-Income Children Receiving?

Associations between quality of care and the income of the enrolled children varied by type of care. Among center-based programs, those serving at least 25 percent subsidized children and those serving fewer subsidized children provided comparable levels of care and education, as did centers in low- and middle-income neighborhoods. There were only two exceptions to this conclusion. First, as shown in Figure 1.2, subsidized centers in low-income neighborhoods had better ratios of teachers to preschool-age children (but not to infants) than did other centers ($t(65) = 2.09$, $p < .05$). Second, nonsubsidized centers in low-income neighborhoods ($M = 3.81$) were observed to provide significantly poorer quality in the area of personal care routines (e.g., diapering and feeding) than other centers (subsidized $M = 4.8$,

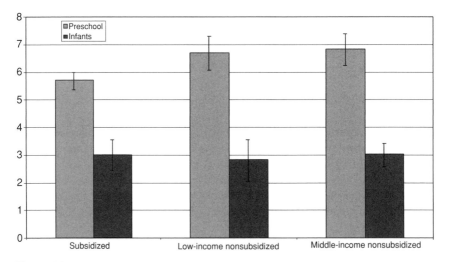

Figure 1.2
Child:Teacher Ratios, by Income and Subsidy Status of Center
Note: **Bars indicate standard errors of the means. Bars that do not overlap indicate statistically significant differences. For example, there is no significant difference in child to adult ratios for infants across income and subsidy groups, but subsidized centers have significantly better preschool child to adult ratios than nonsubsidized centers.**

middle-income, nonsubsidized $M = 5.0$, $F(2, 66) = 3.15$, $p < .05$). Thus, in low-income neighborhoods, subsidized centers had a slight edge over nonsubsidized centers on these basic indicators of safe and appropriate care.

In licensed family child-care homes, both the income level of the neighborhood and the subsidy status of the home predicted dimensions of child care quality that are strongly associated with developmental outcomes. Specifically, homes in middle-income neighborhoods offered more sensitive caregiving ($M = 3.30$) than did those in low-income neighborhoods ($M = 2.96$, $t(57) = 2.06$, $p < .05$). Homes in middle-income neighborhoods also offered greater opportunities for social development ($M = 4.9$) than did homes in low-income neighborhoods ($M = 4.1$, $t(46) = 2.04$, $p < .05$). Observed learning activities, based on the Family Day Care Environment Rating Scale, were of significantly higher quality in nonsubsidized homes in both low-income ($M = 3.96$) and middle-income neighborhoods ($M = 3.90$) than in subsidized homes in low-income neighborhoods ($M = 2.99$, $F(2, 57) = 4.47$, $p < .02$) (see Figure 1.3). This pattern of findings is of concern in light of the high concentration of children from low-income families in subsidized family child-care homes.

Children's access to providers and teachers with higher levels of adult literacy was also inequitably distributed by income.[14] Specifically, middle-income, nonsubsidized providers had significantly higher scores on the TALS than did low-income, nonsubsidized and low-income, subsidized providers (332, 299, and 275, respectively; $F(2, 95) = 11.3$, $p < .001$). When examined by type of care, this finding was driven

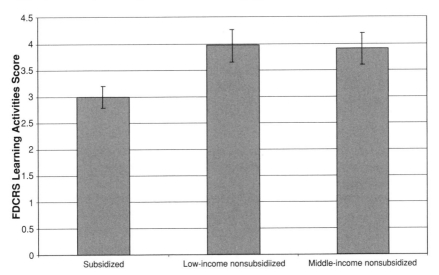

Figure 1.3
Mean Learning Activity Scores, by Income and Subsidy, for Licensed Family Child Care
Note: **Bars indicate standard errors of the means. Bars that do not overlap indicate statistically significant differences. For example, Subsidized providers have significantly lower FDCRS learning activities scores than either nonsubsidized group.**

Table 1.1
Literacy Scores by Income-Subsidy Group and Type of Care

	N	TALS Mean (SD)	PPVT-III Mean (SD)
Home Licensed			
Subsidized	6	263 (84)	90 (7)
Low-income nonsubsidized	15	313 (49)	92 (22)
Middle-income nonsubsidized	12	329* (31)	98 (11)
Centers			
Subsidized	41	277 (47)	90 (11)
Low-income nonsubsidized	12	282 (54)	98 (33)
Middle-income nonsubsidized	12	335* (33)	100 (11)

*Starred groups are significantly different than Subsidized Centers (Games-Howell post-hoc test).

largely by centers. Teachers in subsidized centers had significantly lower TALS document scores ($M = 277$, $SD = 47$) than did teachers in middle-income centers ($M = 335$, $SD = 33$) and than providers in nonsubsidized middle-income homes ($M = 329$, $SD = 31$, respectively). Nevertheless, the lowest TALS scores were found among subsidized home providers in low-income neighborhoods ($M = 263$, $SD = 84$) and, as can be seen in Table 1.1, the trend among home-based providers was the same as among center-based teachers, with the lowest averages in subsidized care and the highest in middle-income nonsubsidized care. The sample size of home-based providers may have been insufficient to obtain statistically significant differences.

In sum, we found large inequities in the quality of care that low-income, subsidized children received within the licensed child-care market based on whether they attended a center- or home-based program. Within the center market, low-income children were much more likely to receive care of comparable quality regardless of the neighborhood location of the center or its status as a subsidized (i.e., contracted or having 25% subsidized children) center, than was the case in the home-based sector. In fact, subsidized centers in low-income neighborhoods were characterized by higher ratios and better personal care routines than other centers. In contrast, homes serving 25 percent subsidized children and in low-income neighborhoods provided significantly poorer quality care than other homes, notably in the critical areas of sensitive caregiving, support for social development, and learning activities. This pattern of results mimics prior evidence that in center-based care the odds that children from a low-income family will receive quality care may not deviate greatly from the odds for children from higher-income families, but that low-income children typically receive poorer quality care than their higher-income peers in home-based care settings.

DISCUSSION

These findings highlight the fact that public child-care subsidies are not buying equitable care across sectors of the system for low-income children and that public dollars are frequently purchasing substandard care. This appears to be especially true in family child care homes where low-income children are highly concentrated in homes based in low-income neighborhoods that provide care for subsidized children. This evidence suggests that, as a growing share of public child care dollars are shifted away from contracted arrangements with centers (that often involve more stringent quality standards), it is essential to examine not only differences in quality of early care and education for children receiving and not receiving subsidies, but also for low-income children receiving care in different kinds of settings given the vastly different experiences they appear to receive.

In California there are two sets of state policies that place our findings in context. The first has to do with the stringency of regulations that apply to different sectors of the child-care market. To access subsidies in home-based care, providers are not required to meet any more stringent requirements than those set forth by the state licensing agency. Those requirements are minimal, focused mostly on CPR and other safety issues, but with little focus on child development. Though providers are encouraged to participate in professional development, and many do, there is nothing that mandates that they must do so. With regard to centers, the situation is more complex. Centers receiving vouchers are not required to meet standards for teacher education or ratios beyond those set by licensing, but centers contracted with the state must employ more teachers per children and teachers, for example, must complete 24 units of early childhood plus 16 units of general education at the college level in contrast to the 12 units required by licensing.

The second issue relates to the incentive structures to serve subsidized children that are built into the varying generosity of reimbursement rates, particularly as they relate to per child expenditures. Contracted programs predate the voucher system and the spending levels are set through a complicated reimbursement system that has failed to grant adequate cost of living increases for many years. In contrast, rates paid to centers and homes accepting vouchers are based on periodic market rate surveys. As a result, many contracted centers actually receive lower reimbursement rates per child than voucher centers even though they must meet higher standards. Subsidies for home-based providers who accept vouchers are generally considered more ample, if still falling short, than those in center care. In practice, then, there is a stronger incentive to provide home-based care to subsidized children supported with vouchers than to provide contracted center-based care for these children. Given the higher quality of care that these children receive in centers (perhaps especially in contracted centers with their higher standards, although our sample did not permit a direct comparison of contracted and voucher-based centers), from a developmental perspective this is perverse financial incentive system.

Within the world of K-12 education, inequities among and within school-districts have been deemed unacceptable, leading to court challenges and other policy inter-ventions. While disparities continue to exist, there is a prevailing belief that they should be remedied. This sensibility is less prevalent in the world of early care and education, in large part because concern focuses on access to care, rather than on ensuring that all children attend developmentally supportive programs. To the extent that policy debate focuses on low-income children, its emphasis is on the many children who qualify for subsidies but cannot access them due to limited supply.

The evidence reported here paints a stark picture of inequities in access to quality care and education among children from low-income families that are likely to perpetuate inequities in school readiness not only between low- and higher-income children, but within the most disadvantaged group of children in our society. Today, multiple voices are arguing that the earliest postnatal years are essential to future success and, accordingly, that efforts to address the hard realities of unequal life chances among children before rather than after they enter school are the most cost-efficient target for gaining greater socioeconomic opportunity throughout the life course. To these arguments, we add a strong recommendation that the time has come to apply the same expectations and goals to the early care and education field that we currently apply to K-12 education and, increasingly, to preschool programs. A broad, inclusive reassessment of the kinds of opportunities for young children that public dollars are purchasing is long overdue.

NOTES

* This research was made possible by the generous support of the Administration for Children and Families, U.S. Department of Health and Human Services; the Foundation for Child Development; and the A.L. Mailman Foundation.

1. U.S. Census Bureau (October 2005). *Who's minding the kids? Child care arrangements: Winter 2002.* Current Population Reports, P70–101. Washington, DC. U.S. Department of Commerce.

2. J.I. Layzer, B.D. Goodson, and M. Moss (1993). *Life in preschool: Final report, Volume I.* Cambridge, MA: Abt Associates; J.M. Love, R.C. Cohen, H.H. Raikes, E.E. Kisker, and M.M. Klute (2006). *What makes a difference? Early Head Start, Head Start, and more: The cumulative effects of program participation, birth to 5, on children and families living in poverty.* Symposium presented at the National Head Start Research Conference, Washington, DC, June 27, 2006.

3. D. Phillips, K. McCartney, and A. Sussman (2006). Child care and early development. In K. McCartney and D. Phillips (Eds.), *The Handbook of Early Child Development* (pp. 471–489). New York: Blackwell Publishers.

4. NICHD Early Child Care Research Network (1997). Poverty and patterns of child care. In J. Brooks-Gunn and G. Duncan (Eds.), *Consequences of growing up poor* (pp. 100–131). New York: Russell-Sage.

5. D. Phillips, M. Voran, E. Kisker, C. Howes, and M. Whitebook (1994). Child care for children in poverty: Opportunity or inequity. *Child Development*, 65: 472–492.

6. M. Whitebook, D. Phillips, D. Bellm, N. Crowell, M. Almaraz, and J. Yong Jo (2004). *Two years in early care and education: A community portrait of quality and workforce stability.* Berkeley, CA: Center for the Study of Child Care Employment, University of California at Berkeley.

7. T. Harms, R. M. Clifford, and D. Cryer (1988). *Early Childhood Environment Rating Scale*, revised edition. New York: Teachers College Press.

8. T. Harms. D. Cryer, and R. Clifford (1990). *Infant-Toddler Environment Rating Scale.* New York: Teachers College Press.

9. T. Harms, and R.M. Clifford (1989). *Family Day Care Rating Scale*. New York: Teachers College Press.

10. NICHD Early Child Care Research Network (1996). Characteristics of infant child care: Factors contributing to positive caregiving. *Early Childhood Research Quarterly*, 11(3): 269–280.

11. J. Arnett (1989). Caregivers in day-care centers: Does training matter? *Journal of Applied Developmental Psychology*, 10, 541–552.

12. I.S. Kirsch, A. Jungeblut, and A. Campbell (undated). *The ETS Tests of applied literacy skills: Administration and scoring manual*. Princeton, MJ: Educational Testing Service.

13. A. Sum, I. Kirsch, and R. Taggart (2002). *The twin challenges of mediocrity and inequality: Literacy in the U.S. from an international perspective*. Princeton, NJ: Educational Testing Service.

14. N.A. Crowell, D.A. Phillips, and M. Whitebook (2006). *Adult literacy of early care and education providers*. Unpublished manuscript, Georgetown University, Washington, DC.

CHAPTER 2

WHICH SCHOOLS HAVE THE MOST SEGREGATED CLASSROOMS? A LOOK INSIDE NEW YORK CITY SCHOOLS

Dylan Conger

Relative to research on the racial segregation of students across neighborhoods and schools, far less is known about patterns in racial segregation across classrooms within schools. Most of the research on classroom segregation consists of now-dated studies that narrowly focus on the effect of tracking programs on segregation between white and black students in relatively small samples of high schools.[1] There are two notable exceptions that use recent, large sample, datasets to ask and answer broader questions about patterns in within-school segregation, including which racial groups are most segregated, how severe within-school segregation is relative to across-school segregation, and how within-school segregation varies across grade levels, substate and subcity districts, and over time.[2] These two studies, one relying on the census of North Carolina public school students and the other on the census of New York City (NYC) public-elementary and middle-school students, reveal that in addition to experiencing high rates of segregation across schools, students of all races are further isolated within their schools. Yet relative, and partially due to the extremely high rates of across-school segregation in both areas, within-school segregation is quite low. It also varies across racial groups: In NYC, Hispanics and blacks are more segregated within their schools than are Asians and whites, a result that differs from across-school segregation patterns where white students tend to be a highly segregated group.

This chapter aims to build on these two studies by focusing on the variation in classroom segregation across schools where classroom assignment decisions are made. Using data on NYC public elementary schools, the chapter answers the following two questions: (1) What is the variation in within-school segregation across schools? and (2) What distinguishes schools with highly segregated classrooms from those with more integrated classrooms? To answer question one, a measure of classroom segregation is computed for each racial group in each school for two elementary school grades (first and fifth) in two school years (1996–1997 and 2000–2001) and the resulting distributions are observed. As noted above, within-school segregation in general, and the variation across schools in particular, is an under-explored topic, primarily due to the lack of large sample studies with data at the classroom level and to the shortcomings of segregation indexes when applied to contexts where the subunit sizes (classrooms) are small and the number of subunits and the minority shares vary widely across larger units (schools). One contribution of this paper is to compute a measure of segregation for each school that corrects this inadequacy of standard segregation measures and allows for comparisons across schools with different numbers of classrooms and minority shares.

To answer question two, I compare the student characteristics and resources of schools at the top and bottom of the distribution in within-school segregation. To be clear, the purpose of this exercise is purely descriptive. I do not offer a behavioral model of within-school segregation, one that determines the underlying motivations behind principals' classroom assignment decisions. Yet, by examining the differences between the most and least segregated schools, this chapter lays the foundation for further investigation of why some schools are more segregated than others. Unlike school assignments, which are largely driven by family residential choices and central administrative decisions, classroom assignments are determined by school-level administrators, with some input from parents, district-level administrators, and other school personnel.[3]

As with racial segregation across schools and neighborhoods, segregation across classrooms could result from race-related preferences or discrimination. For instance, parents may want their children placed with co-race peers, independent of the educational attributes of those peers. Yet, principals are likely motivated by more pedagogical choices, such as whether to separate students according to their prior academic ability, English language proficiency, and special needs. Given racial differences along these characteristics, a school that employs such sorting practices is likely to have higher rates of racial segregation across classrooms than one that does not.[4] Decisions about whether to segregate students by educational characteristics or by race may, in turn, be influenced by the resources of the schools, including the experience and education of the teachers, the size of the school, and the funding available. At the very least, if classroom racial segregation is driven by the composition of the students and the resources available, highly segregated and highly integrated schools should differ along these characteristics. The goal of this chapter is to uncover such differences. While a considerable amount of research has explored the possible correlates of racial segregation across neighborhoods, and to a lesser extent schools, very little work has taken an empirical look inside schools.[5]

This analysis raises two important questions. First, why study within-school segregation when so little progress is being made to integrate schools? Indeed, recent national trends in school segregation show a growth in black/white segregation in Southern schools during the late 1980s and 1990s, reversing gains made during the previous decade.[6] In addition, NYC has among the highest levels of white and black school segregation in the nation.[7] Yet when the implicit definition of integration, that between black and white students, is broadened to consider other racial groups, mixed race schools are fairly common in the city. Almost 63 percent of the elementary and middle schools in NYC served at least 20 percent of two racial groups in school year 2000–2001. Most commonly, these duo-racial schools were comprised of Hispanic and black or Hispanic and white students. One-third of the schools in 2000–2001 contained at least 10 percent of three different racial groups, the typical combination being Asian, Hispanic, and white. What is more, the city experienced modest declines in school segregation for all racial groups except Asians between school years 1995–1996 and 2000–2001.[8] Thus, though school integration is far from complete, there are certainly enough mixed-race schools in the city to warrant concerns about the potential for within-school segregation.

Second, if schools become integrated, why should educators be concerned about segregation within schools? Two reasons, which correspond with the two goals of racial integration, stand out. The primary purposes of integration are to equalize educational resources across racial groups (including the educational preparation of the peers students are exposed to) and to increase interracial contact, which in turn is expected to foster positive inter-racial relations. Through complete school desegregation, students will be exposed to other racial groups in their schools and to the same school-wide resources and peer groups. Yet a multiracial school, with perfectly segregated classrooms, could significantly erode these goals of school desegregation. To the extent that teacher and peer quality varies within a school, racial segregation across classrooms could contribute to significant disparities. Moreover, inter-racial contact may be quite limited in multiracial schools since students have been found to self-segregate across the lunch tables, playgrounds, and extra curricular activities of the same school.[9] In fact, the classroom could be the only environment during or outside of school hours that students from different ethnic groups are truly required to socialize.

MEASURING WITHIN-SCHOOL SEGREGATION

To describe patterns in within-school segregation, I use the same unevenness measure that is used in the earlier studies of within-school segregation: the gap-based segregation index (S). Though the S is not as popular an unevenness index as the Dissimilarity index for example, it is easy to interpret and has the advantageous feature of being decomposable into within- and across-schools components.[10]

To compute the S, one begins by calculating the exposure index (E), an index that captures the probability of contact between two dichotomous groups in a given context, such as a classroom, school, or neighborhood. For illustration, I will discuss the exposure rate of Hispanic to non-Hispanic students. The classroom exposure rate of Hispanics to non-Hispanics (E_c) is the percentage non-Hispanic in the average Hispanic student's classroom, simply the weighted average of classroom percentage non-Hispanic where the weight is the number of Hispanics in each classroom. An equivalent exposure rate can be calculated at the school level (E_s), providing the likelihood that a Hispanic student will come into contact with a non-Hispanic student in school.

The degree of exposure between groups is determined both by the share of the groups in the population and the extent to which they are segregated across classrooms and schools. If Hispanics are evenly distributed across classrooms and schools, then the classroom and school exposure rate of Hispanics to non-Hispanics should equal the school district share of non-Hispanics. Deviations from perfect integration can be measured with the S, which normalizes the exposure rate to its theoretical maximum, the share of non-Hispanics in the larger unit. The formula for classroom segregation in a school district is written as: $S_d = (P_d - E_c)/P_d$, where P_d is the percentage non-Hispanic in the district. The S ranges from 0 (perfect integration) to 100 percent (perfect segregation) and measures the percentage gap between the exposure of two groups to one another in a smaller unit (e.g., classroom, school) and the maximum exposure possible in the larger unit (e.g., school, school district).

The S can also be computed for an individual school (S_c) where instead of using the school district share of non-Hispanics as the maximum exposure possible, we substitute the school share of non-Hispanics as follows: $S_c = (P_s - E_c)/P_s$, where P_s is the percentage non-Hispanic in the school. Correspondingly, the S for an individual school measures the percentage gap between the exposure of two groups to one another in their classrooms and the maximum exposure possible at the school.

While the theoretical boundaries of the S are 0 and 100, the minimum and maximum values for a given school depend upon the number and size of the classrooms along with the minority share. The reason for this variation is that the number of students in one group is rarely perfectly divisible into the number of classrooms, consequently preventing a school from achieving a perfectly even or uneven distribution. Consider a school with two classrooms of 20 students each and five Hispanic students. If the administrators in this school sought to segregate all the Hispanic students, they would have to create a classroom of five Hispanic and 35 non-Hispanic students. While possible, such a classroom configuration would likely raise eyebrows and result in large inefficiencies. Instead, this segregation-maximizing school would place the five students in a classroom of 20, resulting in a Hispanic to non-Hispanic classroom exposure rate of 75 percent and a segregation level of 14.3 percent, nowhere near the 100 percent value that would indicate complete segregation of Hispanics.[11] Given practical class sizes, schools with small minority shares and small numbers of classrooms are less able to achieve high segregation values on the S and other unevenness indexes than other types of schools. The minimum segregation possible for a given school is less sensitive to these constraints. This index inadequacy, which all unevenness indexes are subject to, prevents trustworthy comparisons of schools with varying minority shares and classrooms.

To address these issues, I compute two levels of segregation for each school in addition to the implicit boundaries of 0 and 100. The first is computed after assigning students to their classrooms in an effort to minimize segregation (Min S) and the second is computed after assigning students to their classrooms in an effort to maximize segregation (Max S). Both assignment mechanisms assume existing numbers and sizes of classes so as to represent the upper and lower bounds a principal could obtain given practical classroom configurations. Using the minimum and maximum boundaries, I

Table 2.1
Student and School Characteristics by Race, 5th Grade, 2000–2001

	All	**Hispanic**	**Black**	**White**	**Asian**
Number of students	77,654	29,524	26,601	12,023	9,228
% of all students	100.0	38.0	34.3	15.5	11.9
% of students who are:					
Poor/Near poor	85.2	93.9	92.0	50.6	81.3
Limited English Proficient (LEP)	8.0	14.5	1.6	3.4	11.7
Part-time special education (PTSE)	8.4	9.6	8.1	9.0	4.1
Average test scores					
Math	0.00	−0.18	−0.26	0.09	0.72
Reading	0.00	−0.17	−0.19	0.55	0.45
Average school characteristics					
Enrollment	816	897	773	694	842
% teachers 5+ years experience	53.8	52.0	50.9	60.3	59.7
% teachers with masters degrees	75.3	73.1	71.4	83.6	82.8
Expenditures (in thousands)	$10.4	$10.4	$10.7	$10.1	$9.6

Note: (i) average school characteristics are measured as the weighted mean of school level variables where the weights are the number of students in total or in each racial group in the school. (ii) The sample of 5th graders includes students from 665 schools.

then create a standardized version of the segregation index (S^*) which normalizes the observed segregation level to these alternative benchmarks as follows: $S^* = (S - \text{Min } S)/(\text{Max } S - \text{Min } S)$. S^* has no intuitive interpretation but it allows for comparisons of within-school segregation across schools while taking into account variation in the capability of each school to reach the theoretical boundaries of the index. This index correction does not address the additional concern that the segregation of students across classrooms may fall within the realm of a random allocation, a possibility I am currently exploring elsewhere.[12]

DATA AND SAMPLE

Data on students and their schools were obtained from the NYC Department of Education. For each first through fifth grade student in school years 1996–1997 through 2000–2001, the dataset includes sociodemographic (e.g., race, eligibility for free or reduced price lunch) and educational variables (e.g., test scores, performance on English language test) as well as indicators of the schools and classrooms to which students are assigned. Using these school and classroom codes, I calculate the racial composition of students' classrooms and schools. This study also uses information on expenditures and teacher characteristics from two NYC school-level databases: the Annual School Reports and the Student Based Expenditure Reports.

For most of the analyses reported in this chapter, I rely on the fifth grade in 2000–2001, which consists of almost 78,000 students in almost 600 schools. Differences in other grades and years, where observed, are noted in the text. As shown in Table 2.1,

NYC's students are incredibly diverse: while most students are Hispanic (38%) or black (34%), there are also sizeable shares of white (16%) and Asian (12%) students.[13] Most students (85.2%) qualify for the federally subsidized lunch program and are considered poor (up to 130% of federal poverty level) or near poor (between 130% and 185% of poverty level). Approximately 8 percent of students score below the 40th percentile on the Language Assessment Battery, designating them as Limited English Proficient (LEP) and eligible for bilingual education or English as a Second Language services. An equivalent percentage of students receive part-time special education (PTSE) services for relatively mild disabilities, such as speech impediments and dyslexia. Reading and math tests scores are standardized to a mean of 0 (as shown in the table) and a standard deviation of one.

Students in this fifth grade cross section attended 655 schools. The average student attended a school where approximately 54 percent of teachers have taught for at least 5 years, and over three-quarters have obtained master's degrees. The average level of per pupil spending across the 655 schools is approximately $10,400.

The additional columns in the table show the extent to which these measured student and school characteristics vary by racial group. Notably, white students are the least poor among all racial groups at a rate of only 50.6 percent. Hispanic and Asian students have the highest LEP rates and Asians have the lowest rates of participation in special education programs. Consistent with national trends, black and Hispanic students score lower on standardized tests than Asian and white students. Students from each racial group also attend different types of schools: white and Asian students attend schools with slightly more experienced and educated teachers on average, yet they also attend schools with lower overall spending. Interestingly, black and white students attend smaller schools than Hispanic and Asian students.

RESULTS

A necessary first step in exploring variation in segregation across schools is to examine the overall levels of within-school segregation in the entire school district. Table 2.2 provides these levels of within-school segregation and the levels of across-school segregation for comparison. The table indicates that for every racial group, an additional amount of segregation occurs within schools leading to higher levels of total classroom segregation. For instance, Hispanic fifth graders are 5.2 percent less exposed to non-Hispanics in their classrooms than in their schools and 33 percent less exposed to non-Hispanics in their schools than in the district. In total, Hispanics are 37.9 percent less exposed to non-Hispanics in their classrooms than in the school district and within-school sorting processes accounts for almost 14 percent (5.2/37.9) of this total classroom segregation.

Though within-school segregation is generally trumped by across-school segregation, the relative severity varies by race. The maximum within-school segregation across all racial groups is among Hispanics at 5.2 percent (accounting for 14% of total segregation). In contrast, within-school segregation of whites is 2.8 percent (accounting for only 6% of total segregation). The amount of within-school segregation is similar for Asian and black students (approximately 4%), but the portion of total

Table 2.2
Within- and Across-School Segregation (S), 5th Grade, 2000–2001

	Within-School	Across-School	Total
Hispanic			
Component	5.2	32.7	37.9
% of total	13.7	86.3	100.0
Black			
Component	4.0	45.7	49.7
% of total	8.0	92.0	100.0
White			
Component	2.8	41.9	44.7
% of total	6.3	93.7	100.0
Asian			
Component	3.6	28.0	31.6
% of total	11.4	88.6	100.0

Table reads: Hispanic 5th graders are 5.2% less exposed to non-Hispanic 5th graders in their classrooms than in their schools and 32.7% less exposed in their schools than in the school district. The total classroom segregation between these two groups is 37.9%, 13.7% (5.2/37.9) of which can be attributed to within-school segregation.

classroom segregation accounted for by within-school segregation is much higher for Asians than for blacks, 11 percent and 8 percent respectively. Though not shown in the table, cross-racial classroom exposure rates indicate where integration across schools and classrooms occurs; it disproportionately occurs between black and Hispanic students on the one hand and between white and Asian students on the other, though Asian students tend to be fairly integrated with all three other racial groups. Overall, black and white students are highly segregated from one another across schools and classrooms.[14]

Variation in Within-School Segregation Across Schools

The previous analysis indicates that most of the segregation between racial groups occurs across schools and that once students reach the same school, within-school segregation is quite rare. Yet the experience of the average student in the district could mask variation experienced by students in different schools, where assignment decisions are made. Table 2.3 shows the variation in observed within-school segregation (S) across schools in 2000–2001, along with the distributions in the minimum (Min S), maximum (Max S), and standardized segregation (S^*).

The average segregation levels are very similar to those reported at the district level yet schools vary in the extent to which they segregate their classrooms. For instance, while the average level of within-school Hispanic segregation from non-Hispanics is 6.1 percent, it ranges from one school with 0 percent segregation to another school with 86.7 percent segregation. Despite this wide range, as indicated by the median

Table 2.3
Observed, Minimum, Maximum, and Standardized Within-School
Segregation Across Schools, 5th Grade, 2000–2001

	Mean	Median	75th %tile	Min	Max
Observed Segregation (S)					
Hispanic	6.1	3.6	7.4	0.0	86.7
Black	5.6	3.4	6.8	0.0	81.0
White	4.6	3.2	5.8	0.0	36.4
Asian	4.2	3.1	5.6	0.0	32.5
Minimum (Min S)					
Hispanic	0.2	0.1	0.2	0.0	2.8
Black	0.3	0.1	0.2	0.0	3.3
White	0.4	0.1	0.2	0.0	3.8
Asian	0.3	0.1	0.2	0.0	3.4
Maximum (Max S)					
Hispanic	67.5	80.1	94.2	3.5	100.0
Black	59.1	65.5	93.2	1.6	100.0
White	63.0	75.5	91.9	2.5	100.0
Asian	56.9	62.9	89.1	1.6	100.0
Standardized Segregation (S*)					
Hispanic	9.7	5.7	11.6	0.0	100.0
Black	11.7	6.6	13.3	0.0	100.0
White	9.5	5.5	11.7	0.0	100.0
Asian	10.6	6.1	12.0	0.0	100.0

Note: (i) Schools with fewer than two students of the racial group in question were not examined, which resulted in different numbers of schools used for each type of racial segregation. (ii) Standardized segregation is calculated as follows: $S^* = (S - \text{Min } S)/(\text{Max } S - \text{Min } S)$.

of 3.6 percent and the 75th percentile of 7.4 percent, the overwhelming majority of schools have relatively low levels of within-school segregation. For each racial group, three-quarters of the schools have a segregation level below 7.4 percent. On a scale that ranges from 0 to 100, these averages and 75th percentiles are remarkably modest.

As described in the measurement section above, the minimum (Min S) and particularly the maximum segregation (Max S) possible for a given school are substantially influenced by the minority share as well as the number and size of the classrooms in the school. Though most schools are able to reach a minimum quite close to 0 as shown in Table 2.3, the same is not true for maximum obtainable values. In fact, the average maximum obtainable value does not exceed 67.5 percent and, as indicated by the minimum values on the maximum obtainable segregation, some schools are unable to exceed 3.5 percent segregation of Hispanics, 2.5 percent segregation of whites, and 1.6 percent segregation of Asians and blacks.

Given these constraints, the standardized segregation (S^*) provides a more accurate assessment of the variation in within-school segregation across schools. Once practical minimum and maximum obtainable values are taken into consideration, the average segregation levels double in most cases and the minimum and maximums have the natural reference points of 0 and 100 percent. Yet still, as indicated by the 75th percentiles, most of the schools do not exceed 13.3 percent segregation. On a true scale that ranges from 0 to 100, the overall level of within school segregation is not exceedingly high for most schools. In addition, once more practical boundaries on the segregation index are employed, the relative segregation of the racial groups changes: black and Asian students show higher rates of within-school segregation than Hispanic and white students on all moments of the distributions.

Results for the first grade and for both the first and fifth grades in an earlier school-year (1996–1997) show similar distributions on observed, minimum, maximum, and standardized within-school segregation. Some differences are worth noting. For instance, the standardized segregation averages for each racial group were higher in the earlier year and, in both school years, the averages were higher for younger elementary school students.

Differences Between Highly Segregated and Highly Integrated Schools

Despite the relatively low levels of within-school segregation for most schools, some schools have markedly high levels of segregation. Ultimately, we are interested in understanding why some schools are more segregated than others. As a first step toward this goal, Table 2.4 considers the characteristics of the most and least segregated schools for each racial group. Specifically, the characteristics of schools in the top quartile (at or above 75th percentile) and the bottom quartile (at or below 25th percentile) of each distribution in standardized within-school segregation (S^*) are provided. Along with the average characteristics of each group, the table provides the results of a two-sample hypothesis test of these averages. For instance, schools in the bottom 25 percent of the Hispanic segregation distribution average 30.7 percent Hispanic students and schools in the top 25 percent of the distribution average 38.9 percent Hispanic, a difference that is statistically significant at the 1 percent level.

The results indicate that the racial composition of the students in the school cor-relates with classroom segregation, though the correlations are not always statistically significant and not always in the same direction. Overall, the presence of Hispanic and black students tends to associate with higher levels of classroom segregation for all racial groups, while the presence of white and Asian students tends to associate with lower levels of segregation. There are some exceptions, for instance, the racial composition of the school seems to have no relationship to black segregation. In fact, the black share is lower in schools with high levels of black segregation than it is in schools with low levels of black segregation, a difference that is, nevertheless, statistically insignificant.

In addition to the racial composition of the students, other student attributes distinguish high from low segregating schools. The more segregated schools tend to have higher shares of students who are poor or near poor, though the differences

Table 2.4
Characteristics of Schools at Top and Bottom Quartile of Within-School Standardized Segregation (S^*) Distribution, 5th grade, 2000–2001

	Hispanic		Black		White		Asian	
	0%–25%	75%–100%	0%–25%	75%–100%	0%–25%	75%–100%	0%–25%	75%–100%
% of 5th graders who are:								
Hispanic	30.7	38.9[a]	31.5	36.5	28.0	38.3[a]	31.0	38.9[b]
Black	38.3	38.5	43.0	37.9	15.0	31.6[a]	17.3	27.9[a]
White	17.2	13.6	14.3	16.5	36.1	16.9[a]	27.9	24.2
Asian	13.4	8.7[b]	10.8	9.0	20.6	12.8[a]	23.3	8.8[a]
Poor/near poor	79.1	83.6[c]	82.7	83.0	67.8	79.2[a]	72.8	76.0
LEP	4.4	10.0[a]	4.4	9.3[a]	5.1	7.0[b]	6.7	6.4
PTSE	9.6	8.0[a]	8.7	8.5	9.6	8.7	8.8	8.8
Average test scores								
Math	0.08	−0.06[b]	0.02	−0.04	0.34	0.15[a]	0.31	0.12[a]
Reading	0.07	−0.07[b]	0.02	−0.05	0.30	0.15[a]	0.25	0.15
Average school characteristics								
Enrollment	600	760[a]	621	725[a]	644	817[a]	625	800[a]
% teachers 5+ years experience	55.3	52.5[c]	54.1	54.5	61.7	55.7[a]	59.2	56.4
% teachers masters degrees	75.5	73.2	74.0	74.3	83.3	78.4a	79.3	79.2
Expenditures (in thousands)	$11.3	$10.7[b]	$10.9	$10.9	$10.2	$10.4	$10.5	$10.4

Note: (i) LEP = Limited English Proficient, PTSE = Part-time special education. (ii) Tests of significance refer to a test of the difference between schools in the bottom and top quartiles of the distribution ($a = p < .01$; $b = p < .05$; $c = p < .10$). (iii) Schools with fewer than two students of the racial group in question were not examined, which resulted in different numbers of schools used for each type of racial segregation. The total number of schools used for each analysis is as follows: Hispanic (143 schools in each quartile); black (133 schools in each quartile); white (78 schools in each quartile); Asian (83 schools in each quartile).

are only statistically significant in segregation of Asians and whites. The presence of LEP students also associates with higher rates of segregation for all but Asians. The more segregated schools also tend to have far lower average reading and math test scores than the less segregated schools; however, not all the differences are statistically significant. Special education rates are slightly lower in the more segregated schools for Asians but not for any other group.

Overall, schools with the most segregated classrooms tend to be larger. Yet the most and least segregated schools appear to differ little in measured resources: while schools with more Hispanic and white segregation have relatively less experienced and less educated teachers and schools with more Hispanic segregation have relatively lower expenditures, no statistically significant differences exist among the other types of segregation.

Similar analyses were conducted using the first grade and using the earlier school year, 1996–1997. The differences observed in Table 2.4 for the fifth grade in 2000–2001 were in the same direction but generally more pronounced, more likely to be statistically significant, and more consistent across the racial groups in the earlier year and in the younger grade. For instance, schools with higher levels of black segregation across classrooms also tended to have fewer whites and more qualified teachers in the other cross sections. The share of students in part-time special education programs also tended to be higher in schools that were less segregated than in schools that were more segregated, though the difference was not always significant at conventional levels.

CONCLUSIONS

This chapter adds to a relatively limited literature exploring patterns in within-school segregation. Answers to the two questions posed in the introduction move us in the direction of better understanding the severity, consequences, and causes of classroom segregation.

Previous studies have focused almost exclusively on measuring within-school segregation at the district or subdistrict level, to the neglect of measurement at the school-level where classroom assignment decisions are made. One reason is that the segregation level obtainable for an individual school is substantially influenced by the minority share and classroom configurations, preventing reliable comparisons of classroom segregation across schools. This study creates a segregation measure for each school using more realistic boundaries than the theoretical boundaries of 0 and 100 percent. Even after these constraints are taken into account, most schools appear not to be segregating at very high levels. In fact, three-quarters of all schools do not exceed a segregation of 14 percent on the standardized segregation index, which has boundaries of 0 and 100 percent. In addition, within-school segregation has declined in recent years and tends to decrease as students reach the end of elementary school. In short, the average levels of within-school segregation at the elementary school level are not extreme, the variation across schools is not extensive, and there is no evidence of a growing problem.

There are, however, a handful of schools with highly segregated classrooms. In order to determine what might be different about these schools, I compared them to very integrated schools on the composition of the students and the resources of the schools. Though some of the comparisons are not statistically significant at conventional levels in the fifth grade 2000–2001 cross section, across both the first and fifth grade cross sections in 2 years, schools with more segregated classrooms tend to have more Hispanic, black, poor, LEP, and low-achieving students, all relatively disadvantaged groups. In somewhat of a departure from this trend, the more segregated schools also have lower shares of students receiving part-time special education services. Highly segregated schools are also typically larger and have less qualified and experienced teachers. Thus, the less endowed schools that already serve disadvantaged populations appear also to be the most segregated. To the extent that racial segregation prevents positive interethnic relations and inhibits academic achievement, this is an unfortunate reality.

Whether segregation in these schools is a byproduct of these school characteristics or whether these characteristics are themselves driven by the existing levels of segregation has not been determined here. Yet, the distinct differences in high- and low-segregated schools suggests that classroom sorting practices on nonracial characteristics, such as into bilingual education, ability grouping, and compensatory education programs, may contribute to racial segregation across classrooms. They also suggest that schools with greater resources, including higher teacher-to-pupil ratios and more experienced teachers, may be less likely to segregate students along racial or educational characteristics. In order to sufficiently isolate the sources of classroom segregation, a causal model that incorporates underlying preferences and motivations, and that provides conditional expectations would be necessary. In the meantime, the observations in this chapter suggest many possibilities worth exploring further.

It is important to keep in mind that this study highlights the experience of a somewhat unique public school system. NYC is the largest school district in the country and home to markedly high levels of school segregation and a rare diversity of students. Research that explores classroom segregation in less urban, less multiracial, and less segregated school systems, such as that conducted in North Carolina, is important for understanding within-school segregation in all environments and all types of students.

Additionally, the emphasis here on students' first five years of school is important given the impact of early education on later experiences. However, the isolation of students in junior and high schools has been found to be much higher.[15] And although most of the existing research on tracking and segregation already focuses on high schools, further work is required to identify the existence, persistence, and consequences on a large scale.

Finally, this study uses a popular segregation index, which like other indexes has its limitations. While useful when units and minority members are numerous, such indexes limit reliable comparisons of within-school segregation across school districts and schools. Further research devoted to modifying these indexes or exploring alternative sensitivity analyses as was done in this study would help tremendously in further analysis of segregation in units smaller than neighborhoods and large schools districts.

NOTES

1. Linda Darling-Hammond, *Equality and Excellence: The Educational Status of Black Americans.* (New York: College Entrance Examination Board, 1985); Kenneth J. Meier, Joseph Stewart Jr., and Robert E. England, *Race, Class, and Education: The Politics of Second-Generation Discrimination* (Madison, WI: The University of Wisconsin Press, 1989); Jeannie Oakes, *Multiplying Inequalities: The Effects of Race, Social Class, and Tracking on Opportunities to Learn Mathematics and Science* (Santa Monica, CA: The RAND Corporation, 1990); Roslyn Arlin Mickelson, "Subverting Swann: First- and Second-generation Segregation in the Charlotte-Mecklenburg Schools," *American Educational Research Journal* 38.2 (2001): 215–252.

2. Charles T. Clotfelter, Helen F. Ladd, and Jacob L. Vigdor, "Segregation and Resegregation in North Carolina's Public School Classrooms," *North Carolina Law Review* 81.4 (2003): 1463–1511; Dylan Conger, "Within-School Segregation in an Urban School District," *Educational Evaluation and Policy Analysis* 27.3 (2005): 225–244.

3. There is very little research on how classroom assignment decisions are made. Personal correspondence by the author with several principals and teachers as well as at least one study of principals in a small sample of schools suggests that while principals often decide how to group students, their decisions are sometimes influenced by school district personnel, teachers, parents, and students. See David H. Monk, "Assigning Elementary Pupils to Their Teachers," *The Elementary School Journal* 88.2 (1987): 167–187.

4. For research on the possible effects of educational sorting practices (including ability grouping, compensatory education, bilingual/ESL instruction, and special education) on racial segregation see Janet Eyler, Valerie J. Cook, and Leslie E. Ward, "Resegregation: Segregation Within Desegregated Schools." In Christine H. Rossell and Willis D. Hawley (Eds.), *The Consequences of School Desegregation* (Philadelphia, PA: Temple University Press, 1983); Meier, Stewart Jr., and England, 1989; Kevin G. Welner, *Legal Rights, Local Wrongs: When Community Control Collides With Educational Equity* (New York: State University of New York Press, 2001); Tamela McNulty Eitle, "Special Education or Racial Segregation: Understanding Variation in the Representation of Black Students in Educable Mentally Handicapped Programs," *Sociological Quarterly,* 43.4 (2002): 575–605.

5. For research on school segregation see Gary Orfield and John T. Yun, *Resegregation in American Schools* (Cambridge, MA: The Civil Rights Project, Harvard University 1999); Sean F. Reardon, John T. Yun, and Tamela M. Eitle, "The Changing Structure of School Segregation: Measurement and Evidence of Multiracial Metropolitan-area School Segregation, 1989–1995," *Demography,* 37.3 (2000): 351–364; Hamilton Lankford and James Wyckoff, "Why are Schools Racially Segregated? Implications for School Choice Policies." In Janelle T. Scott (Ed.), *School Choice and Diversity: What the Evidence Says* (New York: Teachers College Press, 2005).

6. Orfield and Yun, *Resegregation in American Schools.*

7. Erica Frankenberg and Chungmei Lee, *Race in American Public Schools: Rapidly Resegregating School Districts* (Cambridge, MA: The Civil Rights Project, Harvard University, 2002); John R. Logan and Deirdre Oakley, *The Continuing Legacy of the Brown Decision: Court Action*

and School Segregation, 1960–2000, (Albany, NY: Lewis Mumford Center for Comparative Urban and Regional Research University of Albany).

8. Conger, "Within-School Segregation in an Urban School District."

9. Janet W. Schofield and H. Andrew Sagar, "Peer Interaction Patterns in an Integrated Middle School," *Sociometry* 40.2 (1977): 130–138; Charles T. Clotfelter, "Interracial Contact in High School Extracurricular Activities," *Urban Review* 34 (March 2002): 25–46.

10. For other applications of the *S*, see Barbara S. Zoloth, "Alternative Measures of School Segregation," *Land Economics* 52.3 (1976): 278–291; Charles Clotfelter, "Public School Segregation in Metropolitan Areas," *Land Economics* 75(1999): 487–504.

11. Exposure rate (E_c) is calculated as $[(5*0.75) + (0*1)]/5$ and segregation (Ss) is calculated as $(0.88-0.75)/0.88$.

12. For a discussion of indexes that use the random allocation of students as a lower bound, see William J. Carrington and Kenneth R. Trokse, "On Measuring Segregation in Samples with Small Units," *Journal of Business and Economic Statistics* 15.4 (1997): 402–409 and Christopher Winship, "A Reevaluation of Indexes of Residential Segregation," *Social Forces* 55.4 (1977): 1058–1066.

13. The Department of Education identifies five categories of race: white, black, Hispanic, Asian, and Native American. Although these categories combine race, ethnicity, and linguistic origin, the term "race" is used for simplicity.

14. For instance, the average black fifth grader shares a classroom with 67% black, 24% Hispanic, 5% white, and 4% Asian students. The average white fifth grader shares a classroom with 53% white, 16% Asian, 20% Hispanic, and 10% black students.

15. Clotfelter, Ladd, and Vigdor, "Segregation and Resegregation in North Carolina's Public School Classrooms."

CHAPTER 3

FAMILY POVERTY, CLASSROOM INSTRUCTION, AND MATHEMATICS ACHIEVEMENT IN KINDERGARTEN

Annie Georges

Current education policies view quality instruction, student testing, and holding schools and students accountable as the levers for improving learning of mathematics, reading, and increasingly science. To that end, state and federal policies require instruction to de-emphasize lectures, encourage understanding of concepts, and develop skills in problem solving and reasoning skills.[1] These kinds of instructional practices are assumed to be effective in improving students' academic achievement and to moderate the risks of school failure. This emphasis on instruction often overshadows policies that could minimize the social inequalities that contribute to unequal educational outcomes among children. The children that are targeted are not only in low performing schools, they are more likely to face adverse family and community disadvantages such as poverty, high unemployment among adult family members, inadequate nourishment, overcrowded and unsafe environments, and violence.[2] Research has shown that there are negative educational consequences if, for example, a parent is not employed, or if the child is growing up in poverty.[3]

Scholars, educators, and policymakers have long been interested in understanding how schools can be structured to minimize unequal educational outcomes for students of varying social backgrounds. Much attention is paid to how schools can minimize the achievement gaps for students from economically disadvantaged families, students with disabilities, students with limited English proficiencies, and minority groups. However, the national emphasis to change instructional practices, a decision which has traditionally been made by school districts and individual teachers, as the lever by which schools can be structured to minimize unequal educational outcomes is a relatively recent phenomenon in education policy discourse. Yet, the amount of research on whether instructional practices can moderate the economic inequalities that contribute to low academic achievement is relatively thin. Using data from the

Early Childhood Longitudinal Study (ECLS-K), a nationally representative sample of the 1998–1999 kindergarten class, this chapter examines whether instruction moderates the adverse effects of family poverty on mathematics achievement during kindergarten.

The present study advances our understanding of young children's mathematics achievement in important ways. First, previous research that examines the association between mathematics instruction and mathematics achievement has relied on small and targeted populations. Targeted and small samples do not provide a broad and sweeping view of heterogeneous classes of students. In contrast, analyses that use nationally representative samples are well suited to inform policies that are designed to move whole classes of students toward specified academic goals. Second, the concurrent effects of different kinds of instructional practices on mathematics achievement have not been analyzed. It is important to understand whether a single approach to mathematics instruction works best, or whether multiple approaches that are used in concert will work best in the classroom. The data that are used for the analysis in this chapter, the Early Childhood Longitudinal Study (ECLS-K), permit a full exploration of the independent effects of a range of mathematics instructional practices that could affect mathematics achievement.

BACKGROUND

Children in low-income families enter kindergarten below the level of academic achievement that children in high-income families exhibit, which suggests that family income, even prior to the start of school, may be positively associated with academic achievement.[4] As early as 36 months of age children below poverty whose families experienced an increase in their income of at least one standard deviation above the mean had similar cognitive outcomes as children in families who were not below poverty.[5] In contrast, similar increases in income had little effect for children in families who were not below poverty.[6] After children begin school their rate of academic progress continues to differ. For example, during kindergarten children in low-income families make greater strides in their basic mathematics skills such as being able to count beyond ten, whereas children in high-income families make greater stride in solving basic addition/subtraction problems.[7]

Policies that increase family income can improve students' academic achievement. In a random assignment to assess the impact of the New Hope Project, an antipoverty program in Wisconsin that offered wage supplements sufficient to raise income above the poverty threshold, children whose families received earnings supplement had higher academic achievement compared to a similar group of children whose families did not receive earnings supplement.[8] However, the effects of earnings supplement on academic achievement were significant for boys, but not for girls. Also, a comprehensive synthesis of several large-scale experimental programs that offered earnings supplement for families living in poverty found that programs which increased employment and income had positive effects on academic achievement.[9]

Even though these experimental studies show that family income is a powerful predictor of academic achievement and that income policies could improve academic achievement, other factors such as choice of child-care arrangements, participation in structured activities, parenting, social processes in the home, as well as the community's resources are major forces that could also affect students' academic achievement. For example, Richard Rothstein[10] conducted a comprehensive review of the social, economic, and education literature to understand how to close the black-white achievement gap. Rothstein's analysis illustrated a strong association between family background and academic achievement. He concluded that even with the existence of high-quality teaching, schools might not be equipped to simultaneously address long-term social differences such as access to books and other literacy experiences, parenting practices, child-care experiences as well as the lack of community resources which existed before as well as during the time that children are in school.

The effects of instruction on mathematics achievement have been primarily examined with small samples of elementary school students, and these studies have not examined whether instruction may be a moderator of the adverse effects associated with family poverty during childhood. The lessons from this literature are that emphasizing critical thinking, individualizing instruction, and using collaborative teaching techniques improves mathematics achievement.[11] In addition, if the instructional practice relies on children's own thinking rather than imposes knowledge, and if the instructional practice requires children to be actively engaged then there are positive effects on mathematics achievement.[12] The positive association between these kinds of instructional practices and mathematics achievement are illustrated in a collection of studies, which employed data from a random assignment of first grade teachers. This collection of studies showed children were more likely to recall number facts, and to exceed in problem solving abilities when their teachers emphasized application of concepts, provided examples of concepts, used collaborative techniques that promoted interaction in small group and de-emphasized strategies that evolved from the teacher.[13]

An experimental study of low-achieving and low-income elementary school students evaluated the effects of problem solving and peer collaboration practices on mathematics achievement. The students were assigned to a problem-solving instructional group, a peer collaboration instructional group, and a control group. This experimental study, which was conducted by Marika Ginsburg-Block and John Fantuzzo,[14] concluded that problem solving and collaborative teaching strategies resulted in higher mathematics achievement when compared to similar students who were not exposed to either of these strategies. However, since their analysis was based on a small cross-sectional sample, the results cannot be generalized to all low-income elementary school students.

An observational study of second grade classrooms found that collaborative instructional practices had positive effects on mathematics achievement. Specifically, classrooms in which there was an emphasis on practicing prescribed computation procedures from the textbook had lower scores than classrooms where students collaboratively engaged with each other to develop solution strategies.[15] However, an observational study of similar classroom activities concluded that encouraging children to work collaboratively were not beneficial for girls' mathematics achievement.[16]

In contrast to the small experimental and observational studies just discussed, statistical analyses that relied on larger samples and on older cohorts of elementary school students have not produced a consistent set of findings of the effects of instruction on mathematics achievement. The first set of findings suggests instruction is not associated with mathematics achievement. For example, Stephen Klein and Brian Stecher[17] used a stratified random sample of elementary and middle-school students from 11 schools in six cities. After controlling for student characteristics, the authors found a positive but not a statistically significant association between instruction and mathematics achievement. In their analysis mathematics instruction was defined as the sum of 22 teacher-reported items covering questions about the teacher's use of cooperative learning groups, inquiry-based activities and open-ended assessment techniques. Klein and Stecher also found that lecture, practice, memorization, and short answer assessment techniques were unrelated to mathematics achievement. Another analysis of elementary school students in high-poverty school districts in San Antonio, Texas, reinforced the finding that collaborative learning strategies as well as lecture, use of worksheets, practice, or drill were not significantly related to mathematics achievement.[18] In another study with data on eighth graders from the National Assessment of Educational Progress (NAEP), Harold Wenglinsky[19] also found that drill and practice were not effective teaching strategies.

The second set of findings suggests mathematics instruction is significantly associated with mathematics achievement. Using a sample of elementary schools in California, David Cohen and Heather Hill[20] found that mathematics achievement improved when teachers emphasized different methods to solve a problem, had students work in small groups, work on individual projects and on mathematics questions with more than one solution. However, they measured student achievement at the school level whereby schools with higher achievement scores were interpreted as having a more proficient student body. Another study of students in high-poverty schools suggested that implementing instructional reforms which involved more student-initiated activities and collaborative activities among students had positive effects on mathematics achievement, whereas activities that were more teacher-initiated activities were negatively associated with mathematics achievement gains.[21] In analyses with data from the National Assessment Educational Progress, mathematics instruction involving higher-order thinking skills such as developing skills in problem solving and reasoning skills, and mathematics instruction which encouraged understanding of concepts rather than memorizing facts were positively associated with mathematics achievement.[22]

The literature suggests that mathematics instruction matters. Studies with larger samples of students show that instructional practices such as lecture, use of worksheets, practice, or drill are more likely to repress mathematics achievement. The literature also suggests that actively engaging children and incorporating their thinking into the instructional activities have positive effects on mathematics achievement. On the other hand, in some studies collaborative learning activities have been found to have positive but not statistically significant effects on mathematics achievement. Although instruction matters, it is also the case that social class plays an important role in understanding differences in mathematics achievement. Children from middle-class families enter school with more basic knowledge of mathematics than children from lower-class families. The effects of social class and family poverty which are present even before school begins could be due to differences in access to quality child care and preschool, access to books and literacy activities, differences in parenting practices as well as other long-term social differences which schools might not be equipped to address.

PERSPECTIVES AND HYPOTHESES

An in-depth research synthesis by the National Research Council[23] concluded that the school environment should emphasize learning through understanding rather than the acquisition of disconnected sets of facts and skills. Instructional practices that de-emphasize lectures, encourage understanding of concepts, and develop skills in problem solving and reasoning skills are more likely to promote an effective learning environment than rote drill and practice of mathematical facts and skills.[24] If these kinds of instructional practices are adopted then the school will have instituted an effective learning environment, and student achievement will improve.[25]

The National Research Council's research synthesis, though it recognized the significance of quality classroom instruction, also emphasized that the family remained the child's primary source of support for learning. If the family's income is low, parental investments in educational resources might, often time, be inadequate to improve children's school readiness, or to help sustain the academic skills children acquire during school.

Given the importance of the family in understanding the differences in students' academic skills, it cannot be ignored that the effects of poverty and other family disadvantages will continue to affect children's educational potentials even after the school's influences begin to weigh in. Undoubtedly school influences do matter, but it is unclear whether school influences outweigh the disadvantages that are associated with family poverty. There is strong evidence that students have tremendous growth in their mathematics and reading skills, especially during kindergarten[26] as well as during elementary school.[27] Moreover, research has suggested that, at least in the early grades, schools are more effective at improving children's proficiencies in mathematics than they are at improving children's proficiencies in reading.[28] Given that schools contribute to young children's learning outcomes, it is important to understand how the classroom environment operates to enhance students' learning. If the classroom environment plays a significant role in improving mathematics achievement and in minimizing the achievement gaps for different groups of children, it seems worthwhile to identify and to expand our knowledge about the specific classroom practices which might improve mathematics achievement and could moderate the effects of social disadvantages such as family poverty.

Based on the literature, it is expected that engaging children in activities in problem solving and reasoning skills will have positive effects on mathematics achievement. It is also expected that children below poverty will benefit the most from these instructional practices in terms of higher mathematics scores.

THE DATA AND SAMPLE

The analysis draws data from the Early Childhood Longitudinal Study, Kindergarten cohort (ECLS-K), sponsored by the U.S. Department of Education, National Center for Education Statistics (NCES). The ECLS-K followed a nationally representative sample of the 1998–1999 kindergarten cohort who were in public and private kindergarten programs. Data were collected from the child, the parents or guardians, schools and teachers. Children used pointing devises or gave verbal responses while participating in various activities during an untimed one-on-one assessment. Each time the child was assessed their parents or guardians provided information about themselves and the child's family. Also, this is the first nationally representative sample where child, family, and classroom characteristics can be modeled simultaneously. Each sampled child is linked to his or her school as well as their teacher. Teachers provided information about their teaching practices, educational background, teaching experience and the classroom setting for the sampled children in their classroom.

The ECLS-K used a multistage probability sample design to select a nationally representative sample of kindergartners. The primary sampling units are geographic areas consisting of counties or groups of counties. In the second stage schools within the sampled primary geographic areas were selected. In the final stage students within each of the sampled schools were selected.

The analysis includes students who were assessed in fall and spring of the kindergarten year, and who attended a public or a private kindergarten program. The final sample includes 13,054 students who did not change teacher or school during the year. The sample is distributed among 1,558 teachers in 608 public kindergarten programs and 214 private kindergarten programs.[29]

Measuring Mathematics Achievement

The Early Childhood Longitudinal Study (ECLS-K) used a two-stage format for the mathematics assessment. The first stage is a routing performance that determined the second stage to be administered based on the child's level of ability. The mathematics domain includes recognizing numbers, counting, comparing and ordering numbers, solving word problems, recognizing and solving problems involving graphs and geometric relationships. The mathematics scores are calculated from an Item Response Theory (IRT) model, which are estimates of the number of items students would have answered correctly if they had taken all the questions in the mathematics assessment. The assessment also allows for estimates of the child's score within a narrow range of defined mathematics subskills taught in kindergarten. The five mathematics subskills, which are derived from the K-4 curriculum standards of the National Council of Teachers of Mathematics, are:

(1) Counting, which is the ability to identify one-digit numbers, recognize geometric shapes, and one-to-one counting up to ten objects;

(2) Relative Size, which is the ability to read all one-digit numbers, count beyond ten, recognize a sequence of patterns, and use nonstandard units of length to compare objects;

(3) Skills in ordinality/sequence are the ability to read two-digit numbers, recognize the next number in a sequence, identify the ordinal position of an object, and solve a simple word problem;

(4) Addition/Subtraction is the ability to solve simple addition and subtraction problems; and

(5) Multiplication/Division is the ability to solve simple multiplication and division problems and to recognize more complex number patterns.

Each of the five specific mathematics subskills is measured as the probability of a correct response, which is also calculated from an IRT model. The score for each of these five specific mathematics subskills takes on values between zero and one. The IRT scoring makes longitudinal measurement of achievement gains possible because the common items in the routing test and in the overlapping second-stage forms allow the scores to be placed on the same scale. The IRT scores are already computed with the ECLS-K data.

Family Poverty and Classroom Instruction

Six dichotomous variables represent the child's poverty status.[30] The first variable represents children below 50 percent the poverty threshold. The second variable represents children between 50 and 100 percent the poverty threshold. The third and fourth variables capture children who are marginally above poverty, which include children between 100 and 150 percent the poverty threshold and children between 150 and 200 percent the poverty threshold. The last two variables capture children in more economically advantaged families; their family income is between 200 and 300 percent the poverty threshold, or above 300 percent the poverty threshold.

Seven percent of the children are below 50 percent poverty, and 11 percent are between 50 and 100 percent poverty. The majority of the children, 43 percent, are above 300 percent poverty. About 8 percent of the children are in families where English is not the primary language that is spoken at home, 7 percent of the children have parents who do not have a high school diploma, and 21 percent of the children live in a single-parent family. Forty-nine percent of the sample are girls, 15 percent are blacks, 14 percent are Latinos, and 65 percent are whites.

Teacher-reported answers are relied upon to derive quantitative indicators of mathematics instruction. In the ECLS-K teachers are asked two sets of questions about their teaching practices. One set of questions asked teachers to answer on a scale from one (never) to six (daily) how often children in their class engaged in various mathematics activities. The available responses were: never, once a month or less, two or three times a month, once or two times a week, three or four times a week, and daily. The second set of questions asked teachers to answer on a scale from one (skill is not taught in kindergarten) to seven (daily) how often each of various mathematics skills is taught in their class. The available responses were: skill is not taught in kindergarten, should already know, once a month or less, two or three times a month, once or two times a week, three or four times a week, and daily. The items were combined into five classroom instruction scales. The scales were determined based on results from two factor analysis models. Each of the instruction scales is adjusted for the number of items with valid data. At least two-thirds of the items must have valid data, otherwise the composite scale is set to missing.

Four of the instruction scales are based on the first set of questions which asked about mathematics activities teachers engaged in. One scale is a sum composite score of the items that capture activities with "worksheets, textbooks, and chalkboard." These activities are usually thought of as rote drill and practice. The second scale, "manipulative, measurement and rulers," includes playing mathematics related games, working with manipulative (e.g., solid blocks), using rulers, using measuring cups, using spoons or other measuring instruments. The third scale, "collaborative learning activities," includes activities such as explaining how a mathematics problem is solved, solving problems in small groups or with a partner, working on problems that reflect real-life situations, working in mixed achievement groups and peer tutoring. The fourth scale, "aesthetic activities," includes activities with music, using creative movement or drama to understand mathematics concepts.

The fifth instruction scale, "data analysis, statistics and probabilities," is based on the second set of questions which asked about the mathematics skills that teachers used. This scale includes items such as reading simple graphs, performing simple data collection and graphing, fractions, using measuring instruments accurately, estimating probabilities, estimating quantities and writing mathematics equations to solve word problems. These skills are more likely to incorporate the child's own thinking, to engage the child to think critically about solving problems in mathematics, and to help the child build reasoning skills.

The data show that kindergarteners spend most of their instructional time in activities with geometric manipulatives to learn basic operations, work with rulers, use measuring cups, spoons or other measuring instruments, and play math related games. Kindergarteners also spend a substantial amount of time in collaborative learning activities, such as solving math problems in small groups or with a partner, and working in mixed achievement groups on math activities.

HOW KINDERGARTNERS FARE IN MATHEMATICS

Figure 3.1 shows mathematics score is negatively associated with family poverty. That is, the average mathematics score decreases as poverty increases. However, during kindergarten the average gain in mathematics score is similar irrespective of the family's

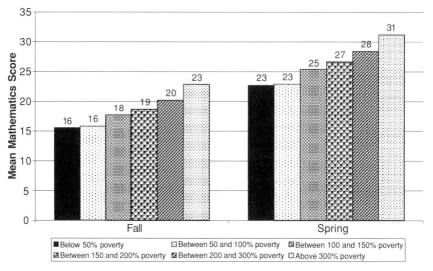

Figure 3.1
Mean Mathematics Scores by Family Poverty during Fall and Spring Kindergarten

poverty status. Children below poverty gain about 7 points, and children above poverty gain about 8 points (Figure 3.1). Since the average number of points children gain is similar whether they are below or above poverty, the poverty achievement gap, which is evident at the beginning of kindergarten, persists as children leave kindergarten.

Figure 3.2 shows the association between mathematics score and family socioeconomic status (SES), a composite score that includes parents' level of education, family income, and parental employment. Mathematics score is positively associated with family SES. That is, as family SES increases mathematics score increases. The average number of points gain is similar to the number of points gain when scores are examined by family poverty. For example, as shown in Figure 3.2, children in low- and middle-SES families gain about 8 points and children in high-SES families gain about 9 points.

Because education is one of the most important facets of income, poverty, and social class the differences in mathematics score and the number of points gained are also examined by parent education. Figure 3.3 shows children whose parents have at least a college degree enter kindergarten with more skills in mathematics than children whose parents have a high school diploma or whose parents have not graduated high school. However, once enrolled in school even children whose parents did not complete high school make large and significant gains in their mathematics skills. As shown in Figure 3.3, children whose parent did not complete high school gain about 8 points in their mathematics scores, which is similar to the number of points gained when the data are examined by family poverty and family SES.

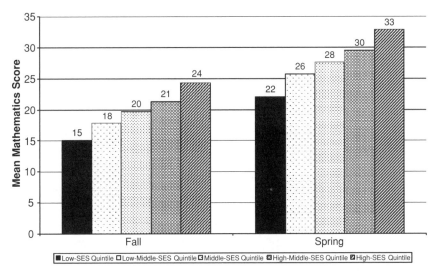

Figure 3.2
Mean Mathematics Scores by Family SES during Fall and Spring Kindergarten

A persistent achievement gap in mathematics is also evident by gender, race/ethnicity, living in a single-parent family, whether English is spoken in the home, and whether the child is in a public or a private school. For example, at the beginning of kindergarten, the average mathematics score is 18 points for children in single parent families, and 21 points for children in two-parent families. At the end of

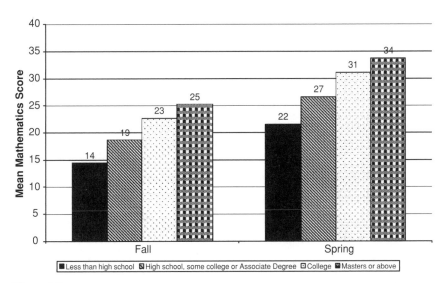

Figure 3.3
Mean Mathematics Scores by Parent Education during Fall and Spring Kindergarten

kindergarten, the average mathematics score is 25 points for children in single-parent families, an increase of 7 points; and the average score for children in two-parent families increases from 8 points to 29 points. The difference in score between the two groups remains since both groups improve on their mathematics skills. Similarly, children whose primary home language is not English have lower mathematics score than their counterparts. The average mathematics score for children whose primary home language is not English increases to 24 points from 17 points; and for children whose primary language is English the gain in their average mathematics score is 8 points, an increase to 28 points from 20 points.

Black and Latino children have lower mathematics score than white children. The average mathematics score for blacks and Latinos is 4 points lower than the average mathematics score for white children. The data also show that Asian children have higher mathematics score than white children. However, the higher mathematics score for Asian children are likely due to differences in social class. Asian children who could not pass the English assessment test were not given the mathematics assessment. Thus, the sample of Asian children who took the mathematics assessment and received a score is more likely to be fluent in English, and they are in more affluent families. In contrast, the sample of white children is more heterogeneous in terms of family characteristics such as parent education, income, and social class. The data also show that boys have higher mathematics score than girls; however, the difference is not statistically significant.

The average number of points gained in total mathematics score ranges from 7 to 9 points; however, the gains differ in specific mathematics subskills—counting up to ten, recognizing the sequence of basic patterns (relative size), comparing the relative size of objects (ordinality/sequence), solving basic problems in addition/subtraction, and multiplication/division. Specifically, children below poverty make gains in basic mathematics skills (counting up to ten, recognizing the sequence of basic patterns), whereas children above poverty make gains in more complex mathematics skills (solving problems in addition/subtraction and multiplication/division).

Figure 3.4 shows how students score in solving basic mathematics problems—counting up to ten, recognizing the sequence of basic patterns (relative size) and comparing the relative size of objects (ordinality/sequence)—and family poverty at the beginning of kindergarten.

Figure 3.5 shows the same information as Figure 3.4 at the end of kindergarten.

A comparison of Figures 3.4 and 3.5 reveals that, at the end of kindergarten, children below poverty have closed the gap in counting up to ten. However, as shown in Figure 3.5, at the end of kindergarten there still remain large differences in students' ability to recognize the sequence of patterns and comparing the relative size of objects. The average score in knowledge of recognizing the sequence of basic patterns (relative size) and in comparing the relative size of objects (ordinality/sequence) for children below poverty more than doubled. Since all children improved in recognizing the sequence of patterns (relative size) and in comparing the relative size of objects (ordinality/sequence), the average score for children below poverty did not increase by a large enough amount to eliminate the gap (Figures 3.4 and 3.5).

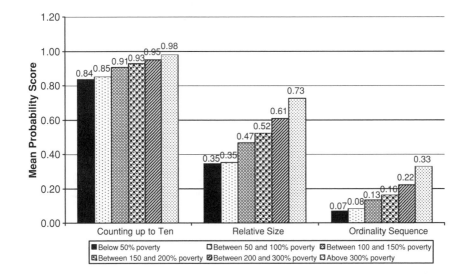

Figure 3.4
Mean Probability Score in Basic Mathematics Subskills during Fall Kindergarten

Figure 3.6 shows that, at the beginning of kindergarten, the mean score in solving addition/subtraction and multiplication/division problems was low. In particular, few children were able to correctly solve any basic problems in multiplication/division, irrespective of their poverty status. Over the course of the kindergarten year, children above poverty made significant stride in solving problems in addition/subtraction

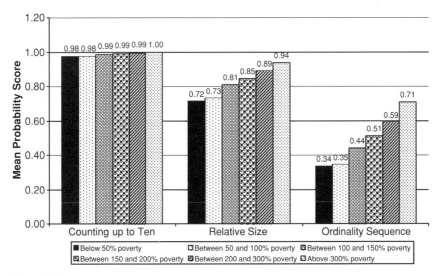

Figure 3.5
Mean Probability Score in Basic Mathematics Subskills during Spring Kindergarten

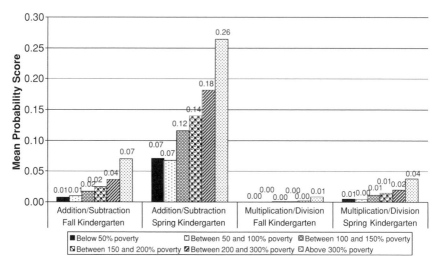

Figure 3.6
Mean Probability Score in Addition/Subtraction, Multiplication/Division during Fall and Spring Kindergarten

compared to children below poverty. Even though the average score in multiplication/division remained relatively low during kindergarten, Figure 3.6 shows that children above poverty did make substantially more progress than children below poverty in solving these kinds of mathematics problems. In fact, as shown in Figure 3.6, the poverty achievement gap in addition/subtraction and in multiplication/division actually grew during kindergarten. A widening achievement gap in children's ability to solve basic addition/subtraction and multiplication/division problems, also exists by family SES, parent education, and race/ethnicity.

The data were examined for differences in kindergartners' problem-solving ability in all five mathematics subskills by gender, parent education, and race/ethnicity. An examination of academic performance in each of the five mathematics subskills reveals mixed evidence that boys are ahead academically. Girls are slightly ahead in counting up to ten and in recognizing the sequence of basic patterns (relative size). However, by the end of kindergarten girls lost their slight advantage in being able to compare the relative size of objects (ordinality/sequence). Boys, on the other hand, started kindergarten with a slight advantage in being able to perform basic addition, subtraction, multiplication, and division problems, and they continue to build on those skills during kindergarten.

Children with a college-educated parent are more likely to accurately compare the relative size of objects; they are also more likely to correctly solve basic problems in addition/subtraction, and multiplication/division than children whose parents have a high school diploma.

Black and Latino children enter kindergarten with lower mathematics skills than white children. During the kindergarten year, black and Latino children make substantial progress in basic mathematics skills (e.g., counting up to ten, recognizing the sequence of patterns). Black and Latino children make significantly less progress than white children in comparing the relative size of objects, solving problems in addition/subtraction, and in multiplication/division. Consequently, a race/ethnic achievement gap in solving problems in multiplication/division, which did not exist at the beginning of kindergarten, has grown significantly by the end of the kindergarten year.

Children who attend private schools are able to answer more questions correctly in all five mathematics subskills compared to children in public schools. This, however, probably reflects differences in family poverty, SES or parent education between children who attend private schools and those who attend public schools.

MATHEMATICS INSTRUCTION AND ACHIEVEMENT GAINS

To examine the effects of mathematics instruction and the extent to which instruction might account for the lower achievement gains for children in poverty, a classroom fixed model—a two-level hierarchical linear model where students are nested within classrooms—is estimated. The results, shown in Table 3.1, are consistent with the descriptive results presented above. Mathematics scores are negatively associated with family poverty. That is, children who are below poverty have the lowest achievement gains, and children who are marginally above poverty (between 100 and 150 percent of poverty) have slightly higher achievement gains than children below poverty. For example, the estimates presented in Model 1 in Table 3.1, show that the average gains in mathematics for children below poverty is 0.44 point lower than the average gains for children above 300 percent poverty, and the average gains for children who are marginally above poverty is 0.35 point lower than the average gains for children above 300 percent of poverty. There is no statistical difference among children above 150 percent poverty after controlling for initial mathematics score, demographic variables, and other confounding variables.

The effects of parent education on achievement gains are very robust. Children with a parent without a high school diploma have significantly lower gains than children with a parent with a high school diploma, as well as lower gains than children with a college-educated parent. The model was estimated to account for the interaction between poverty and having a parent with a college degree. The interaction term is positive, indicating that children below poverty with a parent with a college degree performed better than children below poverty with a parent without a college degree.

The effects of instruction are not as robust as the effects of family poverty or parent education. Certain kinds of instructional practices do have significant positive effects on achievement gains. Instructional activities with worksheets as well as instructional activities using graphs, estimating probabilities and quantities, and writing mathematics equations to solve word problems—activities which engage the child, and which employ the child's own thinking and reasoning skills—have positive and significant effects on achievement gains (Table 3.1). The average gain is 0.26 point as the amount of time devoted to activities with worksheets increases, while the average

Table 3.1
Estimates of Models to Explain the Effects of Mathematics Instruction and Poverty on Achievement Gains during Kindergarten

	Model 1		Model 2	
	Estimated Coefficients	Significance Level	Estimated Coefficients	Significance Level
Achievement at the beginning of kindergarten	0.90	***	0.90	***
Family Poverty				
Below 100% poverty	−0.44	**	−0.45	**
Between 100 and 150% poverty	−0.35	*	−0.36	*
Between 150 and 200% poverty	−0.14		−0.16	
Between 200 and 300% poverty	−0.08		−0.08	
Parent Education				
Less than high school	−0.42	*	−0.42	*
College	0.35	**	0.35	**
Masters or above	0.57	***	0.57	***
Gender and Ethnicity				
Child is female	−0.31	***	−0.30	***
Latino (a)	−0.52	**	−0.53	***
Black	−1.22	***	−1.21	***
Asian	0.31		0.32	
Other ethnicity	−0.32		−0.32	
Mathematics Instruction				
Worksheets, textbooks, chalkboard	0.26	***	−	
Collaborative activities	0.10		−	
Aesthetic activities	−0.05		−	
Geometry manipulative, measurements, rulers	−0.29	**	−	
Data analysis, statistics, probabilities (Reasoning Skills)	0.21	***	−	
Variance between classrooms	2.62		2.80	
Variance among students within classrooms	21.28		21.29	
Percent of total variance between classrooms	11%		12%	

See note 33.

gain is 0.21 point as the amount of time devoted to activities with graphs, estimating quantities, and writing math equations to solve word problems increases. The results confirm the effectiveness of critical thinking and actively engaging students in problem solving skills. On the other hand, the finding of a significant positive effect from using activities with worksheets is unexpected. Other studies have shown either no effect or a negative effect on mathematics score from using rote drill and practice. However, since the present analysis uses a much younger cohort of students than the samples from prior studies, the results suggest that it is effective to frequently allow kindergarteners to practice basic computational skills.

As family income increases, the amount of time spent on activities with worksheets, using collaborative groups as well as activities with music or creative movement or drama (e.g., aesthetic activities) decreases significantly. This indicates that children below poverty spend significantly more time exposed to these instructional practices than other children. As previously discussed children below poverty lag behind in basic mathematics skills at the beginning of kindergarten, and they do have higher rate of gains in basic mathematics skills such as counting up to ten and recognizing the sequence of basic patterns (relative size). The positive coefficient for instructional activities with worksheets most likely suggests that such activities are beneficial in helping young children practice basic computational skills.

The amount of time spent on activities with graphs, estimating quantities, and writing math equations to solve word problems—those activities which incorporate children's own thinking, engage children to think about mathematics and help them build reasoning skills—increases with family income. In essence children below poverty have the least exposure to these kinds of practices, which is contrary to the desire to increase low-income children's exposure to the practices that will help them develop skills in problem solving and reasoning skills.

Working with manipulatives such as using solid blocks, rulers, and other instruments like cups and spoons for measuring is the most frequently used practices during mathematics lessons in kindergarten. Yet, as the results in Table 3.1 show, achievement gains are lower by about 0.29 point as the amount of time in those activities increases. Using collaborative learning activities such as solving problems in small groups or with a partner, working in mixed achievement groups and peer tutoring, are not significantly associated with achievement gains. These findings of negative effect from using manipulatives, and of no significant effect from using collaborative learning activities could indicate ineffective use of the time spent in those activities. Although the model controls for the amount of time spent in mathematics lessons on a typical school day, the data cannot differentiate the quality of time that is devoted to any particular instructional practice. Since teachers rely on a multitude of practices during their mathematics lessons, any advantages associated with the most effective instructional practices—using worksheets, and using skills to engage the child to think critically about solving problems in mathematics, and to help the child build reasoning skills—are trumped by the negative effects associated with activities with manipulative, and the use of drama and music to teach mathematics.

The results indicate that 12 percent of the variance in mathematics achievement gains occurs between classrooms, and 89 percent of the variance occurs among students within classrooms. Adding the mathematics instruction variables to the model accounts for 6 percent of the variance between classrooms, but does not account for any of the variance among students within classrooms.

An assessment of the extent to which mathematics instruction might explain the poverty achievement gap is made by comparing the change in the coefficients for family poverty before and after the instruction variables are introduced in the model. Model 1 in Table 3.1 shows the results with mathematics instruction, and Model 2 shows the results without mathematics instruction. The magnitude of the coefficients for family poverty decreases by negligible amounts after controlling for the fact that children of different social backgrounds might have less exposure to the instruction practices. Similarly, the coefficients for parent education, and race/ethnicity decrease by negligible amounts after mathematics instruction is added to the model. Thus, mathematics instruction, though significantly associated with achievement gains, does not explain much of the poverty achievement gap, or the gap associated with parent education and race/ethnicity. In fact, the poverty achievement gap is reduced substantially only after initial achievement in mathematics is taken into account. After controlling for achievement at the beginning of kindergarten, the reduction in the coefficient is 74 percent for children below 100 percent poverty, and 66 percent for children between 100 and 150 percent poverty. This suggests that children in the poorest families are less well positioned in their knowledge of mathematics when they begin kindergarten than other children, and it could very well be the most important contributor in perpetuating unequal educational outcomes.

SUMMARY AND IMPLICATIONS

Current education policies view quality instruction, student testing and holding schools and students accountable as the levers for improving student learning of mathematics, reading, and increasingly science. The emphasis on instruction often overshadows policies that could minimize the social inequalities contributing to un-equal educational outcomes among children. Research consistently shows that grow-ing up in poverty has long-term effects on students' academic achievement. Emerging research reveals that there are negative effects associated with family poverty even before school begins. Consequently, children in poverty begin school less prepared academically. Family circumstances that undercut cognitive skills such as poverty, high unemployment among adult family members, inadequate nourishment, overcrowded and unsafe environments, and violence continue to be present throughout school. These family circumstances are important contributors to the persistent achievement gaps. The disparity in the basic mathematics skills students possess even before they begin kindergarten contributes to the achievement gap that persists in later grades. The results presented in this chapter suggest policies should seek to minimize the disadvantages that undermine the academic potentials of children in poverty before they begin school.

During the kindergarten year, children below poverty make gains in different set of mathematics skills than children above poverty. For example, by the end of kindergarten children below poverty do catch up and do close the achievement gap in basic mathematics such as counting up to ten, and recognizing the sequence of patterns (relative size). On the other hand, children above poverty have already begun to make significant gains in solving problems in addition/subtraction and multiplication/division. The fact that children above poverty are able to make these kinds of gains during their first year of school is likely due to their advantages in basic mathematics skills at the start of kindergarten.

The effects of instruction on mathematic scores are not as large as anticipated, and the effects of instruction are not always consistent with the assumptions behind educational policies. Children below poverty benefit more from formal classroom instruction than children who are not in poverty. It was expected that activities with worksheets, often viewed as a mode of rote drill and practice, would have negative effects or at least would have no effects on mathematics score. The analysis showed this was not the case. It is possible that practicing with worksheets is beneficial when children are learning the most basic computational skills that are taught in kindergarten. It is also possible that the reliance on this kind of instruction could lose its potency in later grades when the mathematics curriculum requires greater student engagement to reason and solve problems rather than simple computational skills.

The findings presented in this chapter suggest that exposing students to instructional practices that emphasize learning through understanding, and minimizing emphasis on the acquisition of disconnected set of facts and skills is a sound approach to improve mathematics skills. The analysis also shows, however, that the benefits associated with increasing the amount of time engaging the child to think critically are potentially muted because children below poverty formally begin school with fewer mathematics skills than children above poverty. The social disadvantages, including the effects of family poverty, which restrict the most disadvantaged groups of children from attaining their full cognitive potentials before they enter school should also be addressed.

A possible explanation why the direct effects of instruction are not larger than the effects of family poverty is that kindergarten teachers may lack the specialized knowledge to effectively employ the kinds of instructional practices that promote learning of mathematical skills in the way intended by the policies. The policies governing the training and content knowledge that kindergarten and elementary school teachers are required to possess are modest.[31] For example, states rarely require the educational training of elementary teachers to include mathematics courses or mathematics teaching methods courses. Moreover, teacher licensure tests do not include substantive questions to test teachers' content knowledge in mathematics.[32] This suggests that elementary school teachers might be inadequately equipped from their teacher preparation program to effectively employ the practices that will have much larger effects on young children's mathematics knowledge and skills. Yet, another possibility is that there is insufficient amount of time devoted to mathematics instruction. In kindergarten, literacy activities tend to absorb much of the total instructional time. Given that some instructional effects exist, school districts and schools should seek to find ways to set in place the policies and practices that will prepare elementary teachers to deliver more quality mathematics instruction that is consistent with the goals of engaging all children and allow them to acquire higher mathematical thinking skills early and consistently throughout school.

NOTES

1. Council of Chief State School Officers, *State Indicators of Science and Mathematics Education* (Washington, DC: 2003).

2. Gary Natriello, Edward L. McDill, and Aaron M. Pallas, *Schooling Disadvantaged Children: Racing Against Catastrophe* (New York: Teachers College Press, 1990); National Science and Technology Council, Committees on Fundamental Science, and Health, Safety, and Food, *Investing in Our Future: A National Research Initiative for America's Children for the 21st Century* (Washington, DC: 1997) (http://www.ostp.gov/children[June 10, 2002]).

3. Lawrence J. Aber, "Poverty, Violence and Child Development: Untangling Family- and Community-Level Effects," in *Threats to Optimal Development: Integrating Biological, Psychological and Social Risk Factors The Minnesota Symposium on Child Psychology*, edited by Chris Nelson (Hillsdale, NJ: Lawrence Erlbaum Associates, 1994); Lawrence J. Aber, Neil G. Bennett, D. C. Conley, and J. Li. "The Effects of Poverty on Child Health and Development," *Annual Review of Public Health* 18(1997): 463–483; Jeanne Brooks-Gunn, and Greg J. Duncan, "The Effects of Poverty on Children," *The Future of Children* 7 (1997): 55–71; Margie K. Shields and Richard E. Behrman, "Children and Computer Technology: Analysis and Recommendations," *The Future of Children* 10(2000): 4–30; Richard Rothstein, *Class and Schools: Using Social, Economic, and Educational Reform to Close the Black-White Achievement Gap* (Washington, DC: Economic Policy Institute and New York: Teachers College Columbia University, 2004); Judith R. Smith, Jeanne Brooks-Gunn, and Pamela K. Klebanov, "Consequences of Living in Poverty for Young Children's Cognitive and Verbal Ability and Early School Achievement," in *Consequences of Growing Up Poor*, edited by Greg J. Duncan and Jeanne Brooks-Gunn (New York: Russell Sage Foundation, 1997), pp. 132–191.

4. Eric Dearing, Kathleen McCartney, and Beck A. Taylor, "Change in Family Income-to-Needs Matters More for Children with Less," *Child Development* 72(2001): 1779–1793; Roland G. Fryer and Steven D. Levitt, "Understanding the Black-White Test Score Gap in the First Two Years of School," *The Review of Economics and Statistics* 86(2004): 447–464; Valerie E. Lee and David T. Burkam, *Inequality at the Starting Gate: Social Background Difference in Achievement as Children Begin School* (Washington, DC: Economic Policy Institute 2002); David Kaplan, "Methodological Advances in the Analysis of Individual Growth with Relevance to Education Policy," *Peabody Journal of Education* 77(2002): 189–215; Jerry West, Kristin Denton, and Germino Hausken, *America's Kindergartners: Findings from the Early Childhood Longitudinal Study, Kindergarten Class of 1998–99, Fall 1998,* NCES 2000-070 (Department of Education, National Center for Education Statistics, 2000); Jerry West, Kristin Denton, and Lizabeth Reaney, *The Kindergarten Year: Findings from the Early Childhood Longitudinal Study, Kindergarten Class of 1998–99,* NCES 2001-023 (Department of Education, National Center for Education Statistics, 2000).

5. Eric Dearing, Kathleen McCartney, and Beck A. Taylor, "Change in Family Income-to-Needs Matters More for Children with Less," (See note 4).

6. Ibid.

7. Jerry West, Kristin Denton, and Lizabeth Reaney, *The Kindergarten Year* (See note 4).

8. Aletha C. Huston, Greg J. Duncan, Robert Granger, Johannes Bos, Vonnie McLoyd, Rashmita Mistry, Danielle Crosby, Christina Gibson, Katherine Magnuson, Jennifer Romich and Ana Ventura, "Work-Based Antipoverty Programs for Parents can Enhance the School Performance and Social Behavior of Children," *Child Development* 72(2001): 318–336.

9. Pamela A. Morris, Aletha C. Huston, Greg J. Duncan, Danielle A. Crosby, and Johannes M. Bos, *How Welfare and Work Policies Affect Children: A Synthesis of Research* (New York: Manpower Demonstration Research Corporation, 2001).

10. Richard Rothstein, *Class and Schools* (See note 3).

11. National Research Council, *How People Learn: Brain, Mind, Experience, and School. Committee on Developments in the Science of Learning*, edited by John D. Bransford, Ann L. Brown and Rodney R. Cocking, Division of Behavioral and Social Sciences and Education. (Washington, DC: The National Academy Press, 1999); National Research Council, *How Students Learn: History, Mathematics and Science in the Classroom. Committee on How People Learn. A Targeted Report for Teachers*, edited by M. Suzanne Donovan and John D. Bransford (Washington, DC: The National Academies Press, Division of Behavioral and Social Sciences and Education, 2005).

12. Arthur J. Baroody and Herbert P. Ginsburg, "Children's Mathematical Learning: A Cognitive View," in *Constructivist Views of the Teaching and Learning of Mathematics*, edited by R.B. Davis, C.A. Maher, and N. Noddings (*Journal for Research in Mathematics Education Monograph* 44, 1990), pp. 51–64. National Council for the Teaching of Mathematics.

13. Thomas P. Carpenter and Elizabeth Fennema, "Cognitively Guided Instruction: Building on the Knowledge of Students and Teachers," *International Journal of Educational Research* 17(1992): 457–470; Thomas P. Carpenter, Elizabeth Fennema, and Megan L. Franke, "Cognitively Guided Instruction: A Knowledge Base for Reform in Primary Mathematics Instruction," *Elementary School Journal* 97(1996): 3–20; Thomas P. Carpenter, Elizabeth Fennema, Penelope Peterson, C. Chiang, and M. Loef, "Using knowledge of children's mathematics thinking in classroom teaching: An experimental study," *American Educational Research Journal* 26(1989): 499–531.

14. Marika D. Ginsburg-Block and John W. Fantuzzo, "An Evaluation of the Relative Effectiveness of NCTM Standards-Based Interventions for Low-Achieving Urban Elementary Students," *Journal of Educational Psychology* 90(1998): 560–569.

15. James Hiebert and Diana Wearne, "Instructional Tasks, Classroom Discourse, and Students' learning in Second-Grade Arithmetic," *American Educational Research Journal* 30(1993): 393–425.

16. Penelope Peterson and Elizabeth Fennema, "Effective Teaching, Student Engagement in Classroom Activities, and Sex-Related Differences in Learning Mathematics," *American Educational Research Journal* 22(1985): 309–335.

17. Stephen Klein and Brian Stecher, *Mosaic Evaluation of Systemic Reform Initiatives* (Santa Monica, California: RAND, 2000).

18. Mark Berends, JoAn Chun, Gina Schuyler, Sue Stockly, and R. J. Briggs, *Challenges of Conflicting School Reforms: Effects of New American Schools in a High Poverty District* (Santa Monica, California: RAND, 2002).

19. Harold Wenglinsky, *How Teaching Matters: Bringing the Classroom Back Into Discussions of Teacher Quality* (Princeton, NJ: Milken Family Foundation and Educational Testing Service Policy Information Center, 2000).

20. David K. Cohen and Heather C. Hill, "Instructional Policy and Classroom Performance: The Mathematics Reform in California," *Teachers College Record* 102(2000): 294–343.

21. U.S. Department of Education, Office of Deputy Secretary, Planning and Evaluation Service, *The Longitudinal Evaluation of School Change and Performance in Title I Schools, Volume I: Executive Summary* (Washington, DC: 2001).

22. Harold Wenglinsky, "Closing the Racial Achievement Gap: The Role of Reforming Instructional Practices," *Education Policy Analysis Archives* 12(2004): 1–24 (http://epaa.asu.edu/epaa/v12n64/[December 14, 2004]).

23. National Research Council, *How People Learn* (See note 11).

24. Ibid.; National Research Council, *How Students Learn* (See note 11).

25. Ibid.

26. Jerry West, Kristin Denton, and Lizabeth Reaney, *The Kindergarten Year* (See note 4).

27. Doris R. Entwisle and Karl L. Alexander, "Summer Setback: Race, Poverty, School Composition, and Mathematics Achievement in the First Two Years of School," *American Sociological Review* 57(1992): 72–84; Karl L. Alexander, Doris R. Entwisle, and Linda S. Olson, "Schools, Achievement, and Inequality: A Seasonal Perspective," *Educational Evaluation and Policy Analysis* 23(2001): 171–191; Douglas B. Downey, Paul T. von Hippel and Beckett A. Broh "Are Schools the Great Equalizer? Cognitive Inequality during the Summer Months and the School Year," *American Sociological Review* 69(2004): 613–635.

28. Karl L. Alexander, Doris R. Entwisle, and Linda S. Olson, "Schools, Achievement, and Inequality" (See note 27).

29. The sample excludes children who changed school or teacher because retaining students who moved to another school or changed teacher makes it difficult to disentangle the separate effects of family and school factors that contribute to learning since those students are members of multiple schools and classrooms during the year. Retaining only the students that progress normally without interruptions yields estimates that can be said to generalize to those students only. During the kindergarten year 1,255 students changed school, and an additional 628 students had a different teacher in the same school in the spring of the kindergarten year. It could not be ascertained whether 1,497 students had a different teacher during the school year because teachers for 225 students were interviewed in fall only, and teachers for 1,272 students were interviewed in the spring only. Those cases are excluded because of the ambiguity whether it is the same teacher in both fall and spring.

An additional 695 children were excluded because they did not have a baseline mathematics score. Some of the reasons that children are not assessed are: absenteeism on the days the assessment was scheduled for their school, or children whose home language is not English and who did not pass the English assessment test. Children whose home language is Spanish are given a Spanish version of the mathematics assessment. The children who are not assessed are disproportionately from low-income families; they are more likely to be Asian, Latino, and Black.

30. The poverty thresholds are the total money income, which the federal government estimates, a family should have to meet its basic needs. The poverty thresholds take into account the number of individuals in the family and children under the age of 18. The thresholds are adjusted annually for cost of living using the consumer price index. In 2004 the poverty threshold for a family of four persons was $19,223. Families whose income is below their thresholds are considered poor; and families whose income is above their thresholds are considered not poor.

31. Annie Georges, Borman Kathryn, and Reginald Lee, *Variations in Policy Adoption and Implementation: Case of Mathematics Education in Elementary Education*, paper presented at the American Educational Research Association, held at San Francisco, 2006.

32. Ibid.

33. *** significant at 0.001 level; ** significant at 0.01 level; * significant at 0.05 level;— indicates the variable is not included in the models in Table 3.1. The following variables are not shown: whether parent is employed full time, whether parent is not employed, age of child at the start of kindergarten, number of months that elapsed between fall and spring child assessment, child's weight at birth, whether the child is enrolled in a part-time kindergarten program; the child's primary mode of care arrangements prior to kindergarten: care by relative, care by a nonrelative, Head Start Program, center care, parental care, all other care arrangement including multiple arrangements; the child's participation in structured activities: parent play activities with child (sum composite of the following items: tell stories, sing songs, help child with arts and crafts, involve child with household chores, play games or do puzzles, talk about nature or do science projects, build or play construction toys with child, play a sport or exercise together), child reading activities (dichotomous variable: if the child reads at least three to six times per week: parents read books to child, child looks at picture books outside of school, child reads or pretends to read), performance and creative activities (dichotomous variable: if the child engages in at least one of those activities: dance lessons, organized clubs, organized performing arts), music, drama and language activities (dichotomous variable: if the child engages in at least one of those activities: music lessons, drama classes, non-English instruction), sports and athletic activities (dichotomous variable: if the child engages in both of these activities: organized athletic activities, athletic or sporting events), arts and craft activities (dichotomous variable: if the child engages in at least one of those activities: art classes, craft classes), educational trips (dichotomous variable: if the child engages in at least two of those activities: visited library, gone to play, concert or other live shows, gallery, museum or historical site, zoo, aquarium or petting farm), number of children's books and media (sum composite: how many children books in the home, how many children's records); whether it is a single parent family, number of siblings in the household, whether English is the language spoken at home, number of places the child lived since birth; how class time is structured: teacher-directed whole class activities, teacher-directed small group activities, child selected activities; how much class time is used for math lessons; whether it is a private kindergarten program; whether the school is located in central city or a small town and rural; proportion of students in the school who are minority; average SES in the classroom.

CHAPTER 4

ARE CHILDREN IN POVERTY CLOSING THE LEARNING GAP? EDUCATION REFORM AND ELEMENTARY SCHOOL PERFORMANCE IN KENTUCKY

Edward B. Reeves

The effects of family socioeconomic status on student achievement have been reported in thousands of studies over the past 40 years: The higher the socioeconomic status of the family, the higher the achievement of students will be. This finding has been substantiated for a wide variety of measures of socioeconomic status (SES), including family income, parents' educational level, and parents' occupation. Student SES is related to grades, achievement test scores, curriculum placement, dropout, college plans, years of schooling completed, high school graduation, and postsecondary enrollment and degree completion. Student's family background has also been shown to correlate with occupational success. Furthermore, these patterns are not restricted to the United States, but are found in virtually every industrialized society.[1]

Recently, this "iron law" linking student SES and education outcomes has been questioned by education reform in the United States. The issue hangs on evidence that has been compiled only in the last decade by a few researchers. These sparse studies suggest that student SES has a negligible effect on *change* in academic achievement compared with the large effect it has on academic achievement measured at *a single point in time*.[2] This new perspective has come about with the sea change in education policy that has washed across the country during the past two decades. Since the mid-1980s, various state governments have been making schools accountable for what students learn and insisting that steady improvements in learning must be demonstrated by achievement test results that are given on a recurring basis.[3] Kentucky was in the vanguard of states that undertook sweeping educational reform.

With the passing into law of the Kentucky Educational Reform Act of 1990, the Kentucky Department of Education began requiring that public schools make annual assessments of academic progress at various grade levels. Originally, Kentucky lawmakers gave little thought to how student poverty could influence the state-mandated assessment results,[4] but this has changed. In 2002, the federal No Child Left Behind Act mandated the closing of the learning gap between low-income children and more advantaged children. Now, all states are expected to conduct annual testing in their public schools to assess the learning gap, although each state is permitted to devise its own system for accomplishing this objective.[5]

It still remains to be discovered if the states are going to be successful in closing the learning gap for children in poverty, and if so how quickly can this be done. The mandate is to achieve the goal of general educational proficiency by the year 2014. No one knows if this goal is attainable, although as annual data on school performance continues to be collected reasonable projections can be made.[6] The present study documents the effects of low-income children on public elementary school performance and improvement in Kentucky during a 7-year period, from 1999 to 2005. It will be shown that poverty causes some schools to lag well behind other schools that serve advantaged student populations. Furthermore, the evidence that the gap in learning could be shrinking is not supported when the achievement data are correctly analyzed and interpreted. Kentucky elementary schools—even when they have a preponderance of poor students—are making progress if the state assessment tests are to be believed, but the learning gap between affluent and poor remains as wide currently as in previous years. One feature of Kentucky public schools that provides some basis for optimism, however, is the state's high proportion of rural schools. These schools, which also serve lower-income students, are showing a rate of improvement that exceeds nonrural schools.

EDUCATION AND CHILDREN IN POVERTY

The United States is a society where individual achievement through dedication and effort has long been celebrated. Americans embrace rags-to-riches stories and the life histories of persons who overcome adversity to rise to pinnacles of success. American society and culture offer numerous avenues for the expression of individual achievement. These deeply held values extolling individual freedom and success, born no doubt in the history of immigration and pioneer settlement of the nation, make it difficult for many Americans to understand how debilitating poverty can be for children. Oddly enough, in education where the welfare of children is taken very seriously, poverty is too often ignored—as if this were a form of adversity that ought to be overcome—or is recognized but then dealt with ineffectively. A recent speech at a major conference attended by educational researchers made these points in dramatic fashion.

At the 2005 annual meeting of the American Educational Research Association, the featured speaker was the well-known educational psychologist David Berliner. Professor Berliner's topic was education and children in poverty.[7] He captured the attention of his large audience with two striking images. First, he called poverty the "600-pound gorilla in the school house" that Americans don't want to confront or talk about. The second image that Berliner presented concerned the story of a drunken man who was searching for his lost keys under a street lamp. When asked by a passerby what he was looking for, the drunk replied that he had dropped his keys in the dark across the street and was now looking for them. The passerby asked why he was looking for his keys under the lamp if he dropped them elsewhere. To this the drunk replied, "The light is better over here." Berliner noted that No Child Left Behind policy is like the drunk, looking for solutions to low achievement in the most convenient spot (in schools) and failing to look where the fundamental causes of low achievement are to be discovered (in impoverished homes and economically disadvantaged neighborhoods). "I believe we need to worry whether the more important keys to school reform are up the block, in the shadows, where the light is not bright," is how Berliner put it.[8]

The research linking low educational achievement and poverty is voluminous, as I have stated. But, despite the myriad studies, we are only beginning to grasp the huge scope of this problem. A review of the research literature will suggest what I mean.

A good place to start is the *Equality of Educational Opportunity* report that was published in 1966 following a 2-year study of more than 650,000 students in 4,000 schools nationwide.[9] Often referred to by the name of the study's lead author, James Coleman, the "Coleman Report" was intended to make a comprehensive study of the equality of educational opportunity in American public schools. The education policymakers who commissioned the study as well as Coleman himself were fairly sure of what the study would find. Vast differences between schools in the academic achievement of their respective students would be found and these differences would be directly related to gross inequalities in the distribution of resources among the nation's schools. In other words, Coleman and others expected that differences between schools with regard to their financial capacity, physical plant and facilities, the quality of their teaching staff and so on would go a long way toward explaining the great differences in achievement. What they found was something very different.

The core finding of the Coleman Report was this: there is much greater variation in achievement test scores within schools than between schools. This finding carried a momentous implication. Whatever characteristics cause schools to be different in their resources and quality, they account for only 10 to 20 percent of the variation in student achievement. Schools do not have a large influence on student achievement. But if schools play such a small role in determining student achievement, what determines the rest of the variation? The answer proposed by the Coleman Report was that the characteristics of students' families and neighborhoods were responsible for the largest share of the variation in student achievement. This finding was met with shock and consternation—not the least from educators who saw that their importance to the education process might be far less than anyone had suspected. Since the publication of *Equality of Educational Opportunity*, numerous efforts have been made to refute its conclusions, but the evidence supporting it has been overwhelming.

Christopher Jencks and colleagues at Harvard University reinforced the Coleman Report's finding by demonstrating that family background characteristics explained 50 percent of the individual differences in educational achievement.[10] These background characteristics constitute advantages or disadvantages that children bring with them to school, and schools are not successful in altering their influence. Another study, by Coleman and Hoffer, compared student achievement in public and private high schools.[11] This study was a milestone because it began to systematically define the multidimensional resources that families possess in large or small measure which foster their children's success in school.

The material resources of the family constituted one dimension influencing student achievement, according to Coleman and Hoffer. Material resources include family income as well as household amenities, such as separate bedrooms for children, a place to study where the child will not be interrupted, reading material kept in the home, and so forth. Another dimension of family resources consists of the parent's own educational level and experiences. Well-educated parents are role models for their children's success. A third dimension of family resources consists of parents' relations with their children: whether they discuss their children's experiences at school, supervise their homework, and similar supportive activities at home. Parents' effort to foster their children's success at school was discovered to be further improved if the family structure was characterized by the presence in the home of the biological mother and father and a limited number of siblings. Single-parent families, blended families, and families with large numbers of children were noted to have difficulty providing needed supervision and support for children. Coleman and Hoffer also concluded that religiously oriented private high schools were more successful educating minority and low-income students because the "functional community" of these schools overcame many of the deficiencies at home.

Later research, extending the earlier work of Coleman and Hoffer, showed that many types of family resources are correlated with income.[12] And more evidence of family resources was uncovered. Parental involvement in the school—such as PTO participation and volunteering to help at the school—had a positive influence on achievement test scores and grade point average; and parent involvement in the school was related to the family's socioeconomic status.[13] Other research showed that the nature of the community or neighborhood in which families lived could significantly affect children's learning. Strong communities and neighborhoods where parents know one another and can compare notes on how their children are progressing in school are localities where achievement is nourished.[14] Some research pointed out that rural communities were more likely to have these qualities than metropolitan areas.[15]

Other studies have shown that upper-middle-class parents are more effective negotiating with school officials to obtain desired benefits for their children than are working-class or unemployed parents.[16] Middle- and upper-income parents see to it that their children take advantage of enriching out-of-school activities, such as private music lessons, visits to museums, attendance at concerts, and similar cultural activities.[17] When school is not in session, families with greater incomes can assure rewarding experiences for their children that translate into greater academic achievement. Especially during the summer break, children of middle- and upper-income parents may take vacations to interesting locations and the children may benefit from well-supervised camp experiences and summer courses that enhance the child's educational skills in foreign languages, computers, art, and so forth.[18] Extracurricular activities provided by the school are another area where greater participation by middle class and affluent students is associated with academic success.[19]

A recent study found that social class background is associated with significant differences in vocabulary knowledge as early as 36 months of age. The vocabulary gap does not narrow as a result of schooling.[20] In addition, David Berliner has catalogued a variety of illnesses and health conditions that often go untreated for children in poverty and that have clear implications for poor performance in school. Among the health conditions that he discusses are ear infections, vision problems, asthma, nutritional deficiencies, lead and mercury poisoning, and complications from low birth weight. Moreover, he catalogues childhood traumas that are social in their origin. These traumas can also afflict the children of more affluent families, but they are more likely to escape detection and assistance when they occur within poor families because of the social disorganization within impoverished neighborhoods. These are the traumas that result from alcoholism, drug addiction, abusive treatment in the home, violence at school, violence going from school to home, and criminal activity generally.[21] Thus, it appears that the evidence for an association between child poverty and low performance in school is strong, multistranded, and one of the best-documented relationships in all of social science.

KENTUCKY: A CASE STUDY

An Impoverished State with Disadvantaged Children

In 1990, Kentucky ranked 46th among the States with a poverty rate of 19.0 percent. The national average in that year was 13.1 percent of the population in poverty. A decade later, Kentucky was tied with Arkansas in the 44th position with a poverty rate of 15.8, a reduction of 3.2 percentage points from the previous decade. Meanwhile, the national average had declined at a much slower rate (–0.7) to 12.4 percent in poverty. These trends suggest that poverty, overall, declined in Kentucky during the 1990s. Nevertheless, Kentucky remains one of the most impoverished states. Only Alabama, Louisiana, Mississippi, New Mexico, and West Virginia have greater proportions of their residents below the poverty level.[22]

The picture doesn't improve when we turn to the indicators of child welfare in Kentucky. For 2005, The Annie Casey Foundation gave Kentucky an overall rank of 42nd among the 50 states for the welfare of its children.[23] Table 4.1 details the information on which this low ranking is based. The median income of Kentucky families with children is well below the national average. Moreover, Kentucky has larger percentages of children in low-income families, of children in poverty, and of children in extreme poverty than does the nation at large. The percentage of Kentucky children in households where the household head has a work disability is greater than twice the national percentage, while the percentage of Kentucky children in low-income households where no adult has worked in the past 12 months exceeds the national average by 3 percentage points. Even more sobering is the evidence of the poor health status and higher mortality of children in Kentucky. The percentage of

Table 4.1
Kentucky and National Indicators of Child Welfare

	Kentucky	National
Median income of families with children	$40,000	$50,000
Children in low-income families (income below 200% of poverty level)	46%	39%
Children in poverty (income below 100% of poverty level)	24%	18%
Children in extreme poverty (income below 50% of poverty level)	11%	8%
Children in households where the household head has a work disability	9%	5%
Children in low-income households where no adult has worked in the past 12 months	8%	5%
Low-birth-weight babies	8.6%	7.8%
Infant mortality rate (deaths per 1000 live births)	7.2	7.0
Child death rate (deaths per 100,000 children ages 1–14)	25	21

Note: All data are 2002–2003 estimates.
Source: The Annie Casey Foundation, KIDS COUNT State Level Data Online; retrieved on February 11, 2006 from www.kidscount.org.

low-birth-weight babies, the infant mortality rate, and the child death rate are higher in Kentucky than across the nation.

Not all comparisons between Kentucky and the nation are this invidious. For example, Kentucky approximates the national average in the percentages of children who have health insurance, 2-year-olds who are immunized, and children in single-parent households.[24] But these few areas in which Kentucky is on par with the rest of the country do not erase the hard evidence of child welfare deficiency.

It is surprising, therefore, to turn to the evidence for the educational performance of Kentucky's children. When compared with the national averages Kentucky's performance gets a mixed review, but it is better than one could have expected. Recent results from the National Assessment of Educational Progress (NAEP) show that Kentucky fourth and eighth graders exceed the national averages in the percentages scoring at or above proficient in reading and science. However, Kentucky lags well behind the national average in mathematics proficiency at both the fourth and eighth grade levels.[25] According to a recent report by SchoolMatters,[26] Kentucky is one of a handful of states where fourth- and eighth-grade reading performance exceeds expectations after controlling for the percentage of economically disadvantaged students. And what is perhaps even more impressive, the report noted that Kentucky's fourth-grade proficiency in mathematics is within the performing-as-expected zone when student poverty is controlled. However, Kentucky eighth graders still perform at less than the expected level, even after the adjustment for poverty has been made. With some reservations, then, this report provides evidence that Kentucky does well by its children educationally, despite the many handicaps that the state's children face.

Kentucky Education Reform

Kentucky public schools have elevated educational achievement across the state since the passage of the Kentucky Educational Reform Act of 1990. This progress has been measured by the state's own testing system as well as by the National Assessment of Educational Progress (NAEP) testing program. Below, we will be concerned with determining if the learning gap seen in elementary schools serving economically disadvantaged students is closing. To lay the groundwork for this, it will be useful to briefly describe education reform in the state and the testing system that has been implemented to assess progress in the schools.

Kentucky was among the first states to implement a comprehensive educational reform in 1990.[27] The reform legislation mandated annual testing of selected grade levels in all Kentucky public schools. From the beginning, the testing protocol was innovative, calling for open-ended (essay) questions and writing portfolios. Student achievement was assessed in a variety of academic subject areas, most importantly in the areas of reading, mathematics, and science. More recently, norm-referenced (NAEP-like) questions have been added. A major revision of the test protocol occurred in the late 1990s. One cannot easily examine testing trends across this change in testing methods. Nevertheless, there is currently 7 years of test data available using the revised protocol, encompassing the years 1999 through 1995. These are the data that will be used in the analysis presented in the next section.

It is probably not inappropriate to credit Kentucky's positive educational performance relative to the national average to the success of the state's educational reform initiative. The NAEP achievement *gains* in reading and mathematics of Kentucky schools have outstripped the national gains, and Kentucky's gains are comparable to those achieved by Texas and Minnesota, where educational reform was implemented a few years earlier, in the 1980s.[28] But what are the implications of these gains for poor students closing the learning gap in Kentucky schools? The gains in test scores do not automatically signal that economically disadvantaged students are posting higher gains than more advantaged students. Conceivably, Kentucky's gains could be achieved by strong growth in economically advantaged schools and lesser or equal performance gains in disadvantaged schools. Or it could be achieved with exceptional gains in schools with disadvantaged students. To find out which scenario is correct, we need to examine the evidence. Moreover, as we will see below, performance gains have occurred in rural schools where many of the most economically disadvantaged students in the state are served. Kentucky has a large number of rural schools and relatively few schools that exclusively serve inner-city disadvantaged students. Thus, there may be evidence for a closing of the learning gap specifically in rural schools.

Are Poor Students Closing the Learning Gap?

Before we turn to the question of poor students closing the learning gap, it will be helpful to visualize how Kentucky elementary schools have been performing on the state-mandated tests. Figure 4.1 plots the mean of each year's test scores for

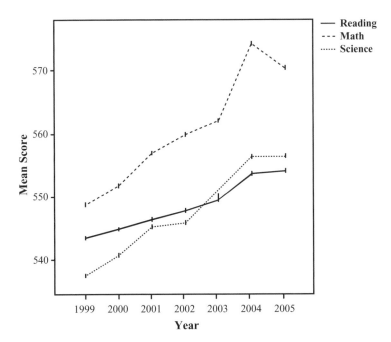

Figure 4.1
Trends in Reading, Mathematics, and Science Scores for Kentucky Elementary Schools, 1999–2005

the subject areas of reading, mathematics, and science. As the graph shows, the test scores usually moved upward between 1999 and 2005. The slope of the gain may be slightly steeper for mathematics and science than for reading. Another conclusion that can be drawn from these plotted trends is that they are not smooth and linear, but exhibit kinks and plateaus. The statewide mathematics score even moved downward in 2005! Such anomalies are not uncommon with school performance scores, and they are related to the problem of measurement error that I will discuss below. One conclusion that should not be drawn from the trends shown in Figure 4.1 is that students are performing better in mathematics than in either reading or science. The scale scores that measure school performance are designed for consistency across years and within subject area; they are not designed for making comparisons between two or more subject areas.

We can gain an understanding of whether poor students are closing the learning gap in Kentucky by correlating elementary school test scores with the percent of economically disadvantaged students[29] in the school. Thus, in this section, we will correlate low-income students with test results in reading, mathematics, and science. Table 4.2 shows the coefficients[30] when percent student poverty is correlated with test scores in reading, mathematics, and science across the 7-year period for which there is data. The coefficients shown in the table represent the average correlations

Table 4.2
Correlations of Elementary School Test Scores
with Percent Student Poverty, 1999–2005

Academic Area Tested	*N*	Correlation Coefficient	Sig.
Reading	5,350	−0.47	0.00
Math	5,289	−0.46	0.00
Science	5,350	−0.36	0.00

Note: The correlation coefficients are averaged across 7 years.

across the 7 years. The three correlation coefficients indicate substantial negative associations between student poverty and test scores. All of the coefficients are statistically significant. This is certainly the result we should expect given the vast literature linking poverty with lower educational achievement. In Kentucky, as in the nation at large and in many international contexts, the presence of economically disadvantaged students means lowered test scores.

The analysis in Table 4.2 is static, however. It only compares academic achievement with student poverty in a year-by-year fashion. This approach indicates that, from year to year, academic achievement and student poverty are negatively correlated. It does not tell us if the learning gap between poor and advantaged students is closing. To determine that, the *change in test scores* (from 1999 to 2005) must be correlated with percent student poverty. It turns out that this seemingly simple operation is fraught with difficulties! The measurement of change is always problematic. The reasons for this are not hard to understand, and their ramifications are serious. Failure to consider these issues can lead to erroneous conclusions about what is happening to the learning gap.

First of all, it is important to recognize that measurement is never free of error. Whenever we take measurements of members of a population, or of a sample drawn from the population, there will be error in our measurements. For example, I note this every time I step on the scales to determine my weight. My bathroom scales are digital and measure weight in 0.5 pound units. When I step on the scale more than once I usually get slightly different results. Therefore, if I want a more accurate estimate of my weight, I sometimes step on the scales three times in quick succession and take an average of the three measurements. An analogous method of dealing with measurement error can be adopted to estimate test scores and changes in scores.

Generally speaking, we attempt to minimize the error inherent in any act of measurement by taking greater care with our measurements, by using more discriminating instruments for measuring, or by averaging repeated measurements. With respect to measuring educational performance, the first two approaches concern improvements to test administration and design. The third approach—which involves averaging repeated test results—is particularly useful for suppressing the error that results from measuring school performance with tests that have been administered annually. Single-year test results are notoriously subject to cohort error. Cohort error means that test scores are sensitive to the unique qualities of the cohort of students who took the tests that particular year—qualities that may be quite different for the cohort taking the tests in another year. Because of the error that can be attributed to cohort differences, a plot of school performance across a period of years often moves erratically. Averaging scores across adjacent years is a widely used technique for dampening this source of error.

Second, if we take two measurements at different points in time, both sets of measurements will contain error. Now, if we try to relate the two sets of measurements, subtracting the measurement taken earlier in time from the later measurement in order to estimate the change that has occurred, we will find that this measure of change contains even greater error than either of the measurements that were used for its calculation. It is important to realize that this will always be true: the measurement of change will always have greater error than the measurements that were used to calculate change. So now we have a serious problem. How do we deal with it?

Again, averaging provides the solution. We make the original measurements on which our calculation of change is to be based more accurate—that is, less prone to error. Repeated measurements are averaged to obtain a more accurate estimate of the baseline, or initial score. Likewise, an average is taken of the repeated measurements of the final score. Now, when the average initial score is subtracted from the average final score, the resulting measure of change will contain less error. Averaging scores in this manner is a common way to reduce (but not eliminate) the error that is intrinsic to the measurement of change.

Unfortunately, our problems are not yet behind us. There is another potential source of error when analyzing change. It is referred to by various terms, such as: "regression to the mean," "reversion to the mean," or, more simply, "mean reversion." For convenience, I will employ the latter term. "Mean reversion" refers to the curious fact that the measure of change—call it the "gain score"—and the initial score, which was also used to calculate the gain score, will be negatively correlated.[31] Figure 4.2 shows an example of this. The graph plots the association of the reading gain score from 1999 to 2005[32] in Kentucky elementary schools with the initial reading score in 1999. Notice that the plot shows a remarkable tendency: the lower the 1999 reading score, the greater the gain score, and the opposite is also true. Note that when the 1999 reading score is high, the gain score may well be less than zero. In other words a high initial score may be associated with a negative gain. In contrast, schools that initially score the lowest usually achieve not just a positive gain; their gain scores are the largest of all! The diagonal line running through the scatter plot shows the negative association between the reading score in 1999 and the gain score. This downward sloping line illustrates the effect of mean reversion.[33]

Mean reversion is not something that we can wish away or ignore, any more than we can wish away or ignore measurement error, but it does not always pose a serious problem for the study of change. Mainly, it is a problem when we confuse the effect of mean reversion with the effect on the gain score of some other variable—percent student poverty, for example. Let me be clear about this. Mean reversion is a negative

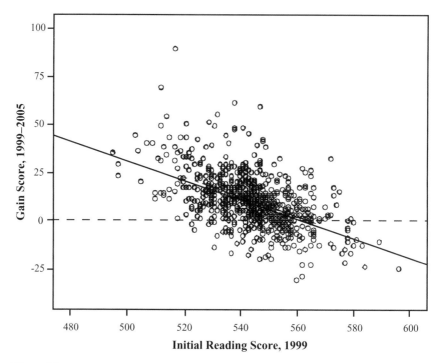

Figure 4.2
The Gain Score is Negatively Correlated with the Initial Score: An Illustration of Mean Reversion
Note: **Each dot is an elementary school;** $N = 726$ **schools.**

relationship between the initial score and the gain score. If another variable, such as student poverty, is associated with the gain score and also negatively associated with the initial score, then the possibility exists that the apparent association between student poverty and achievement gain is spurious. That is to say, the apparent association is confounded by mean reversion, and may not be real at all! In the present example, student poverty is negatively correlated with the 1999 reading, mathematics, and science scores, and the correlation coefficients are rather large: -0.6, -0.6, and -0.5, respectively. If the correlations between the gain scores in these subject areas and student poverty turn out to be significantly positive, there is ample reason to suspect that the relationships are confounded by mean reversion.

Table 4.3 shows the results of correlation analyses in which we obtain the results, first, by not suppressing measurement error with averaging and, second, by using averaged measurements. Secondly, the table compares the results from simple correlations with the results from partial correlations that adjust for mean reversion. These various methods of achieving correlation are not academic exercises; they are of utmost importance if we are to obtain an accurate assessment of whether or not poor students are closing the learning gap.

Table 4.3
Correlations of Elementary School Gain Scores with Percent Student Poverty

Academic Area Tested	N	Simple Correlation		Adjusted for Mean Reversion	
		Correlation Coefficient	Sig.	Correlation Coefficient	Sig.
A. 7-Year Gain Score					
Reading	726	0.24	0.00	−0.11	0.00
Math	699	0.25	0.00	−0.14	0.00
Science	726	0.26	0.00	−0.06	0.12
B. 5-Year Gain Score (averaged for measurement error)					
Reading	721	0.24	0.00	−0.03	0.40
Math	695	0.25	0.00	0.01	0.88
Science	721	0.25	0.00	0.02	0.52

Table 4.3A presents results based upon the gain score from 1999 to 2005 without averaging for greater measurement accuracy. This table presents two sets of results for comparison, simple correlation and partial correlation adjusted for mean reversion. The simple correlations between the gain scores in reading, mathematics, and science and the 7-year average of percent student poverty[34] range from 0.24 to 0.26. These moderate positive correlations also have high statistical significance. The effects on the correlation coefficients of adjusting for mean reversion are dramatic. The correlation of reading and mathematics gain scores, after the adjustment, are −0.11 and −0.14 respectively, with strong statistical significance for both of these coefficients. By adjusting for mean reversion, we have achieved an "about face" in the results. Instead of the moderate positive correlations obtained without adjusting for mean reversion, we now find the correlations to be negative. And although these negative correlations are not strong, their statistical significance is great. The correlation of the science gain score with student poverty is also negative but roughly half as strong as the other two, and it is, not surprisingly, insignificant. That is, we might as well say that the correlation between the science gain score and student poverty is equal to zero.

The results displayed in Table 4.3A tell a clear story. We would be incorrect to rely upon the simple correlations that show positive relationships between student poverty and the elementary school gain scores in any of the three subject areas. Any policymaker, educator, or citizen who saw these results and took comfort from them would be seriously mistaken. The real relationships between the 7-year gain scores and student poverty are either weakly negative, as in the case of reading and mathematics, or near zero, as in the case of science. However, we do not want to conclude our analysis here. We want to know what the results are when we use the more conservative 3-year averaging method of measuring the initial score and the final score.

By using the 3-year averaging method, we gain greater accuracy in our estimate of the gain score but at the cost of constricting the range of the scores from 7 to 5 years. The simple correlations shown in Table 4.3B are of moderate size and their statistical significance is strong. To this point, averaging the measurements produces correlations little different from what was found in Table 4.3A. The difference comes when we examine the results of adjusting for mean reversion. In Table 4.3B, adjusting for mean reversion renders correlation coefficients that are not significantly different from zero for any of the academic areas tested. Thus, these calculations suggest that schools with greater percentages of economically disadvantaged students are not closing the learning gap in reading, mathematics, and science, but neither are they falling behind. It appears from these findings that Kentucky elementary schools are reproducing about the same learning gap in each new cohort of students. Meanwhile, all schools are improving regardless of the prevalence of poverty among their students.

Rural Elementary Schools Are Closing the Gap

There is more to this story, and it concerns the progress being made in Kentucky's rural schools. This is relevant to the topic because the student populations of rural elementary schools have lower family incomes than their peers in nonrural elementary schools. In Kentucky, 45 percent of the elementary schools are rural. Rural elementary schools are located in nonmetropolitan counties and are associated with communities where the population is less than 2,500 inhabitants. The percentage of low-income students in rural and nonrural elementary schools is significantly different. In rural elementary schools, the mean percent student poverty is 61.0, whereas in nonrural elementary schools it is 48.5—a 12.5 percentage-point difference. These statistics are important because rural elementary schools are closing the learning gap despite their greater numbers of low-income students.

This can be demonstrated using the same methods employed previously. Table 4.4 presents the results of correlating elementary school gain scores with rural location of the school. The simple correlations in Table 4.4A show positive, relatively weak, yet very significant associations between the gain scores and rural school. After adjusting for mean reversion, the correlations for reading and mathematics gain scores are substantially reduced, while the adjusted correlation for science is little affected. These adjusted correlation coefficients remain positive and significant for reading and science, but the adjusted correlation for mathematics has been reduced nearly to zero.

Table 4.4B uses the more conservative, 3-year averaging method. In this table we find that the simple correlations are also weak, positive, and statistically significant. After adjusting the correlations for mean reversion in Table 4.4B, the results are similar to what was presented in Table 4.4A: Rural schools are gaining on their nonrural counterparts in the academic areas of reading and science (but not mathematics), despite their greater percentages of economically disadvantaged students.[35] Both methods of calculating the adjusted correlations support this conclusion. The effects of rural location on elementary school gains in reading and science are very small, as indicated by the fact that the adjusted correlation coefficients do not exceed 0.10.

Table 4.4
Correlations of Elementary School Gain Scores with Rural School

Academic Area Tested	N	Simple Correlation		Adjusted for Mean Reversion	
		Coefficient Coefficient	Sig.	Coefficient Coefficient	Sig.
A. 7-Year Gain Score					
Reading	724	0.16	0.00	0.09	0.01
Math	708	0.12	0.00	0.02	0.70
Science	724	0.11	0.00	0.10	0.01
B. 5-Year Gain Score (averaged for measurement error)					
Reading	718	0.13	0.00	0.08	0.03
Math	704	0.11	0.00	0.05	0.20
Science	721	0.09	0.02	0.08	0.03

Still, slow progress closing the learning gap is being made in rural schools in reading and science.

What accounts for the success of rural schools? In a more comprehensive analysis than I have presented here, Reeves and Bylund[36] concluded that in Kentucky,

. . . rural schools may be advantaged by a readiness for improvement under the stimulus of educational reform. What we mean by "readiness for improvement" is this: prior to educational reform, rural schools languished in a climate of low expectations; after reform raised expectations, rural schools have responded dramatically.[37]

But whatever the reason for the progress of rural schools in Kentucky, low-income students in these schools are the beneficiaries. Of course, a corollary of this is that in metropolitan areas low-income students are not benefiting.[38]

CONCLUSIONS

After taking proper precautions for analyzing the effects of poverty on change scores, we have discovered that public elementary schools with economically disadvantaged student bodies are not closing the learning gap in reading, mathematics, or science, but neither are they falling farther behind. For each new cohort of students, schools reproduce the same inequality of learning as for previous cohorts. Kentucky has, at this point, not addressed closing the learning gap in a comprehensive or effective manner. Indeed, until recently, state educational officials were content to note that some schools with high percentages of economically disadvantaged students are listed each year among the top gainers. This is taken to be evidence that disadvantaged schools are capable of substantial progress. No attention was given to mean reversion as an explanation for such anomalies.

Slow progress is being made in rural elementary schools, however, in the areas of reading and science, although not in mathematics. This is significant because the student populations of rural schools are at a greater economic disadvantage than their nonrural counterparts. Although the reasons for this pattern are not completely clear, it appears likely that rural communities and rural schools are more closely interrelated than occurs in metropolitan areas. This creates a form of "social capital"[39] that sustains the improvement of student performance in rural schools. By changing the expectations of teachers as well as parents in rural areas, Kentucky education reform may have provided the catalyst that activated rural social capital and resulted in the slight but statistically significant gains in achievement that were identified.

Issues of poverty and educational improvement are extremely complex. We know this from a voluminous record of research, some of which was reviewed above. "One size fits all" solutions are unlikely to achieve uniform results. Kentucky, a state characterized by a large percentage of rural schools with economically disadvantaged students, does not fit the same profile as a state like Illinois, which has a huge multi-ethnic, economically deprived urban school population in Chicago.[40] In Kentucky, the best hope for closing the learning gap lies in building on the strength of rural communities. In Chicago, this task is made far more difficult, but not impossible, by the socioeconomic disparities and ethnic diversity that characterize urban schools and neighborhoods. If "trust in schools" is a core resource for school improvement, as Anthony Bryk and Barbara Schneider[41] suggest, then perhaps Kentucky's poor children are in a somewhat better position to close the learning gap than are poor children in America's large cities.

NOTES

1. Cornelius Riordan, *Equality and Achievement*, 2nd edition (Upper Saddle River, NJ: Pearson Prentice Hall, 2004), chap. 3; Samuel Bowles and Herbert Gintis, "*Schooling in Capitalist America* Revisited," *Sociology of Education* 75 (2002): 1–18; Samuel Bowles, Herbert Gintis, and Melissa Osborne Groves (Editors), *Unequal Chances: Family Background and Economic Success* (Princeton, NJ: Princeton University Press, 2005); Alan C. Kerckhoff, "Education and Social Stratification Processes in Comparative Perspective," *Sociology of Education* (Extra Issue) 2001: 3–18; Adam Gamoran, "American Schooling and Educational Inequality: A Forecast for the 21st Century," *Sociology of Education* (Extra Issue) 2001: 135–153.

2. Stephen W. Raudenbush, *Schooling, Statistics, and Poverty: Can We Measure School Improvement?* The ninth annual William H. Angoff Memorial Lecture presented at The Educational Testing Service, Princeton, New Jersey (April 1, 2004). See also, William L. Sanders and Sandra P. Horn, "The Tennessee Value-Added Assessment System (TVAAS): Mixed-Model Methodology in Educational Assessment," *Journal of Personnel Evaluation in Education* 8 (1994): 299–311; L. Sanders and Sandra P. Horn, "Research Findings from the Tennessee Value-Added Assessment (TVAAS) Database: Implications for Educational Evaluation and Research," *Journal of Personnel Evaluation in Education* 12(1998): 247–256.

3. Helen F. Ladd (Editor), *Holding Schools Accountable: Performance-Based Reform in Education*, (Washington, DC: The Brookings Institution, 1996); Adam Gamoran, "High Standards: A Strategy for Equalizing Opportunities to Learn?" *A Notion At Risk: Preserving*

Public Education as an Engine for Social Mobility, edited by Richard D. Kahlenberg (New York: The Century Foundation Press, 2000), 93–126.

4. Edward B. Reeves, "High-Stakes Accountability and Contextual Effects: An Empirical Study of the Fairness Issue," *Research in the Schools* 7: 49–58.

5. For a critical assessment of this policy, see Robert L. Linn, E. L. Baker, and D. W. Betebenner, "Accountability Systems: Implications of the Requirements of the No Child Left Behind Act of 2001," *Educational Researcher* 31 (2002): 3–16.

6. For Kentucky public schools, see Edward B. Reeves, "Disentangling the Effects of Nonmetro Location and Student Poverty on School Performance/Improvement," *Journal of Research in Rural Education* 18 (2003): 17–30.

7. For the text of the speech, see David C. Berliner, "Our Impoverished View of Educational Reform," *Teachers College Record* (August 2, 2005). Retrieved on February 10, 2006 from www.tcrecord.org.

8. Op. cit., 2.

9. James S. Coleman, Ernest Q. Campbell, Carol J. Hobson, James McPartland, Alexander M. Mood, Frederic D. Weinfeld, and Robert L. York, *Equality of Educational Opportunity* (U.S. Office of Education, U.S. Government Printing Office, 1966).

10. Christopher Jencks, Marshall Smith, Henry Acland, Mary Jo Bane, David Cohen, Herbert Gintis, Barbara Heynes, and Stephan Michaelson. *Inequality: A Reassessment of the Effect of Family and Schooling in America* (New York: Harper and Row, 1972).

11. James S. Coleman and Thomas Hoffer, *Public and Private High Schools* (New York: Basic Books, 1987).

12. Barbara Schneider and James S. Coleman (Editors), *Parents, Their Children, and Schools*. (Boulder, CO: Westview Press, 1993); Karl L. Alexander, Doris R. Entwisle, and Carrie S. Horsey, "From First Grade Forward: Early Foundations of High School Dropout," *Sociology of Education* 70 (1997): 87–107.

13. Chandra Muller, "Parent Involvement and Academic Achievement: An Analysis of Family Resources Available to the Child," in Schneider and Coleman, op. cit., 77–113.

14. James S. Coleman, "Schools and the Communities They Serve," *Equality and Achievement in Education* (Boulder, CO: Westview Press, 1990), 315–324.

15. N. K. Khattri, K. W. Riley, and M. B. Kane. "Students At Risk in Poor, Rural Areas: A Review of the Research," *Journal of Research in Rural Education* 13 (1997): 79–100; see also, Glenn D. Israel, Lionel J. Beaulieu, and G. Hartless, "The Influence of Family and Community Social Capital on Educational Achievement," *Rural Sociology* 66 (2001): 43–68.

16. Annette Lareau, *Home Advantage: Social Class and Parental Intervention in Elementary Education* (New York: Falmer Press, 1989); Ellen Brantlinger, *Dividing Classes: How the Middle Class Negotiates and Rationalizes School Advantage* (New York: RoutledgeFalmer, 2003).

17. Muller, op. cit.; Karen Aschaffenburg and Ineke Maas, "Cultural and Educational Careers: The Dynamics of Social Reproduction," *American Sociological Review* 62 (1997): 573–587.

18. The classic study of the effects of family resources on summer activities and student learning is Barbara Heynes, *Summer Learning and the Effects of Schooling* (San Diego, CA: Academic Press, 1978). A more recent study along the same line is Douglas B. Downey, Paul T. von Hippel, and Becket Broh, "Are Schools the Great Equalizer? Cognitive Inequality During the Summer Months and the School Year," *American Sociological Review* 69 (2004): 613–635.

19. L. B. Otto, "Extracurricular Activities," *Improving Educational Standards and Productivity*, edited by Herbert J. Walberg (McCutchan, 1982); Beckett A. Broh, "Linking

Extracurricular Programming to Academic Achievement: Who Benefits and Why?" *Sociology of Education* 75 (2002): 69–91.

20. George Farkas and Kurt Beron, "The Detailed Age Trajectory of Oral Vocabulary Knowledge: Differences by Class and Race," *Social Science Research* 33 (2004): 64–97.

21. David Berliner, op. cit.

22. These figures are based upon data presented in John Iceland, *Poverty in America: A Handbook* (Berkeley, CA: University of California Press, 2003), 53–54.

23. The Annie Casey Foundation, 2005 KIDS COUNT. Retrieved on February 11, 2006 from www.kidscount.org.

24. The Annie Casey Foundation, op. cit.

25. National Center for Educational Statistics, The Nation's Report Card: National Assessment of Educational Progress, State Profiles: Kentucky. Retrieved on February 10, 2006 from nces.ed.gov/nationsreportcard/ states/profile.asp.

26. Standard and Poor's, "Leveling the Playing Field 2005: Identifying Outperforming and Underperforming States on the NAEP in Demographic Context" (SchoolMatters, December 2005). Retrieved on February 11, 2006 from www.schoolmatters.com.

27. Gamoran, op. cit.; Thomas R. Guskey, *High Stakes Performance Assessment: Perspectives on Kentucky's Educational Reform* (Thousand Oak, CA: Corwin Press, 1994).

28. Gamoran, op. cit.

29. I use the common measure of economic disadvantage: the percentage of students in the school eligible for participation in the free or reduced-price lunch program. Participation in this program is restricted to children in low-income and poverty-level families.

30. The correlation coefficient is an estimate of the association between two variables. A correlation coefficient that is near the maximum value of −1.0 indicates a strong positive association. When the coefficient is near the minimum value of –1.0, this indicates a strong negative association. A correlation of 0.0 (or thereabouts) means that no association between the two variables exists. Correlation coefficients can also be subjected to significance testing.

31. The phenomenon of mean reversion was first noted in the 19th century. Measurements to compare the height of parents and their adult children showed that, when other influences on height were controlled, parents of less than average height tended to have children taller than themselves while parents of greater than average height tended to have shorter children.

32. The gain score was calculated by subtracting the 1999 reading score from the 2005 reading score.

33. Donald T. Campbell and David A. Kenney, *A Primer on Regression Artifacts* (New York: Guilford Press, 1999) is a basic reference on mean reversion. For a more technical presentation, see Kenneth Y. Chay, Patrick J. McEwan, and Miguel Urquiola, "The Central Role of Noise in Evaluating Interventions That Use Test Scores to Rank Schools," *The American Economic Review* 95 (2005): 1237–1258.

34. This extremely conservative, and accurate, measurement of percent student poverty is also used for the results shown in panel B of Table 4.3.

35. Here is an instance where mean reversion does not have a profound influence on the results.

36. Edward B. Reeves and Robert A. Bylund, "Are Rural Schools Inferior to Urban Schools? A Multilevel Analysis of School Accountability Trends in Kentucky," *Rural Sociology* 70 (2005): 360–386.

37. Op. cit., 384.

38. Op. cit.

39. See James S. Coleman, "Social Capital in the Creation of Human Capital," *American Journal of Sociology* 94 (1988): S95–S120.

40. Frank D. Beck and Grant W. Shoffstall, "How Do Rural Schools Fare Under a High Stakes Testing Regime?" *Journal of Research in Rural Education* 20 (2005): 2–12.

41. Anthony S. Bryk and Barbara Schneider, *Trust in Schools: A Core Resource for Improvement* (New York: Russell Sage Foundation, 2002).

CHAPTER 5

THE ACCUMULATION OF DISADVANTAGE: THE ROLE OF EDUCATIONAL TESTING IN THE SCHOOL CAREER OF MINORITY CHILDREN*

Sandra Mathison

This chapter discusses the ways standardized testing puts children of color and children living in poverty at a disadvantage. This disadvantage begins early in the school career of a child and repeats itself again and again. Education, when driven by standardized testing, is not the great equalizer it is so often portrayed to be in the mythical world where merit counts most.

TESTING IN K-12

Testing starts early and it occurs often in the life of an average student, even more often if a student is at either end of the achievement spectrum, that is, gifted or learning disabled. In a recent analysis of the U.S. Department of Education's Early Childhood Longitudinal Study, Kindergarten Cohort (ECLS-K), Lee and Burkam conclude: "There are substantial differences by race and ethnicity in children's test scores as they begin kindergarten. Before even entering kindergarten, the average cognitive score of children in the highest SES group are 60 percent above the scores of the lowest SES group. Moreover, average math achievement is 21 percent lower for blacks than for whites, and 19 percent lower for Hispanics."[1] Setting aside the unjustified confidence in the meaningfulness of standardized test scores for young children,[2] this report illustrates just the beginning of a lifetime of characterizations and decisions that will be made and indeed institutionalized for children of color and those living in poverty.

Beginning in kindergarten, test results are used to sort, track, and monitor the abilities, achievements, and potentials of students. The danger is that standardized test results will be weighed more heavily than they ought to be, that decisions once made cannot or will not be reversed, and that other compelling information may be ignored.

The uses of standardized testing are more far ranging than most people realize. While there is considerable variation from one district to the next, children will be administered at least one but typically many more standardized tests within a single year. Except for Iowa and Nebraska, every other state administers English and mathematics state-mandated tests from grades 3 to 8, and of those 48 states, 31 administer state-mandated tests in at least two of grades 9–12.[3]

Table 5.1 illustrates the testing experience of a child from kindergarten through high school in an upstate New York school district.

The Case of High Stakes Tests

What are high stakes tests? They are tests that have serious consequences attached to the results—these consequences may be for students, teachers, principals, schools, and even states. For students, these consequences include whether they will graduate from high school, whether they will be promoted to the next grade or retained, whether they will spend their summer in school, or whether they will be required to participate in tutoring that extends their time in school substantially. Although high stakes tests can confer rewards as well as sanctions, more often there are punishments. These punishments can be direct (such as taking over or closing school, replacing administrators or teachers, or withdrawing accreditation) or indirect (such as publishing test scores in the local newspaper, shaming, or job reassignment).

High stakes testing is disproportionately found in states with higher percentages of people of color and living in poverty. A recent analysis of the National Educational Longitudinal Survey (NELS) shows that 35 percent of African American and 27 percent of Hispanic eighth graders will take a high stakes test, compared to 16 percent of whites.[4] Looked at along class lines, 25 percent of low-SES eighth graders will take a high stakes test compared to 14 percent of high-SES eighth graders.

The *Quality Counts* report indicates that of the 23 states that require passing a standardized test to graduate, about half are in the south, that is, states with substantial minority populations.[5] Another two states (Maryland and Washington) and the District of Columbia are either piloting a graduation test or phasing one in the next couple of years. States that do NOT have a graduation test include West Virginia, Oklahoma, Kentucky, Illinois, Hawaii, Delaware, Colorado, Michigan, Vermont, Wisconsin, Pennsylvania, S. Dakota, N. Dakota, Connecticut, Arkansas, Oregon, Rhode Island, Maine, Kansas, New Hampshire, Missouri, Nebraska, Wyoming, Montana, and Iowa.

Students of color are more likely to take high stakes tests and they also score lower than white students. From the Web sites of a sample of any state department of education (for illustrative purposes Massachusetts, New York, and Kentucky are described here) one can demonstrate this conclusion. In 2003 in Boston, 43 percent of white students and 85 percent of Hispanic students failed the tenth grade math

Table 5.1
An Illustration of the Testing in the Life of a Student

Grade	Test
Kindergarten	Boehm Test of Basic Concepts
1st	Gates MacGinitie Reading Test[a]
2nd	Gates MacGinitie Reading Test[a]
	Stanford Diagnostic Math Test[a]
	Terra Nova (reading and math)
3rd	Gates-MacGinitie Reading Testing[a]
	Stanford Diagnostic Math Test[a]
	Terra Nova (reading and math)
	School and College Ability Test (SCAT)[b]
	Cognitive Abilities Test (CogAT)
4th	Gates MacGinitie Reading Test[a]
	Stanford Diagnostic Math Test[a]
	School and College Ability Test (SCAT)[b]
	NYS English Language Arts Test
	NYS Math Test
	NYS Science Test
5th	Gates MacGinitie Reading Test[a]
	Stanford Diagnostic Math Test[a]
	Terra Nova (reading and math)
	School and College Ability Test (SCAT)[b]
	NYS Social Studies Test
6th	Terra Nova (reading and math)
	School and College Ability Test (SCAT)[b]
7th	Terra Nova (reading and math)
	Cognitive Abilities Test (CogAT)
8th	NYS English Language Arts Test
	NYS Math Test
	NYS Science Test
	NYS Social Studies Test
	NYS Foreign Language Test
	NYS Technology Test
9th	Regents Exams:
10th	English Language Arts
11th	Mathematics
12th	Global History and Geography
	U.S. History and Government
	Science
	Language other than English
	PSAT
	SAT

[a]For remedial students only.
[b]Johns Hopkins Talent Search test for gifted program.

test. In Schenectady, New York, 62 percent of children of color and 41 percent of white students failed the fourth grade ELA. In a neighboring Albany school district, 68 percent of children of color failed this test, compared to 33 percent of whites. In Kentucky's Jefferson County Public Schools, scores on reading tests demonstrate the same relationship: 63 percent of white fourth graders were proficient, compared to 34 percent of African American children; 54 percent of white seventh grade students were proficient, compared to 27 percent of African Americans; and in eleventh grade 37 percent of whites were proficient compared to 13 percent of African American students.

The remainder of this discussion will focus on three outcomes of high stakes testing, and the ways in which minority children are particularly disadvantaged:

- The disproportionate impact of state testing on drop out rates for minorities.
- The bizarre effect of monetary rewards for students.
- The diminishment in the quality of education as a consequence of testing, for all, but especially for minority students when differential performance on tests is translated into the "achievement gap."

The Impact of Testing on Drop Out Rates for Minorities

Both graduation tests and tests given earlier in a students' career are having a substantial impact on the numbers of students who drop out of school. The increased drop out rates are based on two factors, the graduation tests themselves and the impact of increased rates of retention in grade, especially in eighth and ninth grades.

Graduation Tests

The number of states requiring graduation tests is on the rise and by 2008 more than half of the states plan to have such a test in place. (See Figure 5.1.) This represents a dramatic increase in a less than 30-year period. In 1983 when *A Nation at Risk*, the flash point for the standards-based and test-driven educational reform movement, was published, three states had minimum competency testing in place (Florida, North Carolina, and Nevada) that amounted to a graduation or exit test. *A Nation at Risk* called for rigorous tests to assess exiting high school students. Dorn points out that concerns about a decrease in high school graduation rates is particularly pointed given that most teenagers graduate.[6] The proportion of all students who obtain a high school diploma has steadily increased in the last 50 years with more dramatic increases for minorities. It is this context that suggests backsliding in national educational aspirations with the advent of high stakes graduation tests.

Amrein and Berliner report actual or estimated percentages of students who take and fail high school graduation tests in 18 high stakes testing states (Figure 5.2).[7] They find a considerable variability across states: a low of 0.5 percent in Virginia where the basic skills graduation test is administered in sixth grade to a high of 10 percent in New York and 12 percent in Georgia. Looking at pass rates on graduation

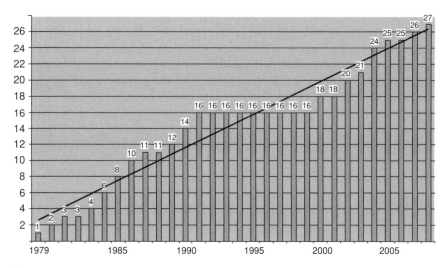

Figure 5.1
Number of States with High School Graduation Tests 1979–2008
Source: **Amrein & Berliner (2001)**

tests for subgroups of students, in 10 states the percentage of black and Hispanic students passing the test on the first try is consistently lower than the percentage of white students.[8] Usually the difference is quite dramatic (for example, in Florida 32 percent of black, 45 percent of Hispanic, and 73 percent of white students pass the reading exit examination on the first try) and even when it is not, the pass rates for all students in the state are high (for example, in Georgia, New Mexico, and South

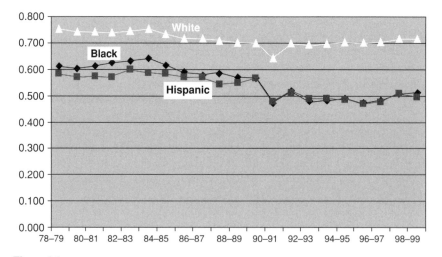

Figure 5.2
Illustration of Differential School Graduation
Source: **Haney (2000)**

Carolina.) "These gaps are worrisome because if a failure to pass an exit exam on the first try does encourage students to drop out of school, then minority students and other subgroups with lower initial pass rates will be much more negatively affected by exit exams."[9]

Although the relationship is a complex one, the presence of an exit exam is related to students either dropping out or taking the GED. An examination of data from the National Center for Education Statistics illustrates that since 1985 there has been a more than 20 percent increase in the number of GED test takers nationwide, mostly for people 19 years of age or younger.

In addition, "states requiring graduation exams had lower graduation rates and lower SAT scores. Individually, students from states requiring a graduation exam performed more poorly on the SAT than did students from states not requiring an exam."[10] So, while failing the graduation tests may keep a substantial number of students from receiving a high school diploma, these tests also reverberate through schools in many other ways. It is likely that graduation tests affect what is taught and that this may create a mismatch with college entrance exams and thus work against even those students who succeed on the state-mandated tests.

Retention in Grade

There are two grade levels at which retention is most common: first grade when under-age boys are retained to permit them time to "mature," and again in eighth and ninth grade when students are on the cusp of entering high school. Currently, Louisiana, Florida, Georgia, Delaware, North Carolina, Wisconsin, Texas, and Missouri have state policies that permit the retention of students based on state-mandated tests.[11] The extent to which state test scores may be used informally or at the local district level for retention decisions is not known.

Students of color are retained at high rates and there is an unhealthy interaction between grade retention and the presence of high stakes testing. Analyses of the NELS data indicate the mere presence of a high stakes test is a strong predictor of higher drop out rates.[12] Thirty years ago only about 4 percent of students were expected to repeat grade nine but that percentage has grown to about 12 percent, and as high as 20 percent in states with high stakes tests such as Florida, South Carolina, and New York.

Haney found, "Only 50 percent of minority students in Texas have been progressing from grade nine to high school graduation since the initiation of the TAAS testing program. Since about 1982, the rates at which black and Hispanic students are required to repeat grade nine have climbed steadily, such that by the late 1990s, nearly 30 percent of black and Hispanic students were "failing" grade nine (Figure 5.3). Cumulative rates of grade retention in Texas are almost twice as high for black and Hispanic students as for white students."[13] One conclusion from this study is that retaining students in ninth grade boosts the tenth grade TAAS scores (because the potential low scorers are excluded) *and in effect* keeps many of these students from ever taking the test as the likelihood they will drop out of school increases dramatically. New York City's retention of third grades is another example of testing in a grade

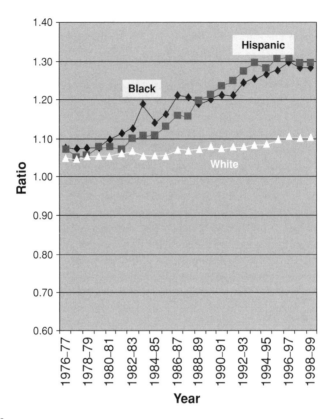

Figure 5.3
Illustration of Differential Retention in Grade Effects
Source: **Haney (2000)**

prior to the state-mandated tests—this strategy potentially culls out students who would do less well on the test and who, if promoted to fourth grade with their age cohort, might potentially lower the overall school and district scores.

In Massachusetts, with the implementation of a tenth grade high stakes test the overall retention rates for ninth graders jumped from 6.3 percent in 1995 to 8.4 percent in 2001. In 2001, 12 districts held back 20 percent of ninth graders. The districts with the highest ninth grade retention rates, between 27 and 38 percent, enroll a majority of nonwhite students.

In parallel to these changes in retention rates, we see increases in the number of students dropping out of school. Being retained in grade, especially in middle and high school, at least triples a student's likelihood of dropping out of school.

If students persist and take a high school graduation test, those who do poorly on the test are more likely to drop out of school *and* this poor test performance disproportionately affects students with high grades. In other words, students who have by other indicators done reasonably well in school are disproportionately influenced by poor test scores to drop out of school. It appears that high stakes testing contributes substantially to grade retention in middle and high school and to the failure of students to graduate from high school.

The Bizarre Effect of Monetary Rewards for Students

Six states give scholarships to students for high performance on state-mandated tests—California, Delaware, Massachusetts, Michigan, Missouri, Nevada, and Ohio.[14] These scholarships provide neither incentives nor opportunities for minority students to go to college, in spite of the rhetoric to that effect. Scholarship money goes to students who would have attended college anyway—they maintain the status quo with regard to access to a college education.

Michigan's Merit Scholarship Program, administered by the Treasury Department, is a good example of this scenario. Using money from a settlement with cigarette companies, Michigan awards scholarships based on performance on the Michigan Education Accountability Program, or MEAP. In Michigan, one in three white, one in five Native American, one in five Hispanic, and one in fourteen African American test takers receive scholarships. In the Detroit area, 80 percent of students in affluent suburban districts, which are white, compared to 6 percent of students in the Detroit city schools received scholarships. Not only does the Michigan scholarship program reward those already college bound, but does so by diverting money that should have gone to Michigan's poor and indigent who are suffering from tobacco-related diseases. Michigan is currently being sued by the ACLU, MALDEF, and the NAACP for these and other corrupting effects of high stakes testing in that state.

The Diminishing Quality of Education for All Children, and Especially for Minority Students As Manifest in the "Achievement Gap" Rhetoric

Many researchers are concluding that high stakes testing not only does not improve education, but indeed diminishes its quality. High stakes testing is contributing to the,

- deprofessionalization of teachers,
- narrowing of the curriculum,
- adoption of curriculum driven by tests that under-represent the purposes of schooling,
- only teaching what is tested,
- elimination of project-based student work, field trips, recess,
- creation of unproductive stress.[15]

High stakes testing has these negative consequences for all children, but it is especially so for children of color, because they are disproportionately exposed to and punished by the effects of high stakes tests. In addition, because the use and impact of tests is ubiquitous we are diverted from thinking about causes, from thinking about the basic technical shortcomings of the tests as well as the scoring, standard setting, and interpretation, and from the interests served by these test-based accountability schemes. An obvious manifestation of this diversion is the rhetoric of the "achievement gap."

Is there really an achievement gap? The rhetoric of the achievement gap adopts a deficit model of those scoring lower on tests, often seeking explanations based on differences in natural abilities, a harkening back to early eugenics of standardized testing. Or at least to the identification of cultural deficiencies among those doing less well on the tests. This rhetoric leads to a search for solutions in those children and families deemed deficient. Solutions advocated tend to be more of the same strategies that aren't working now—tutoring, grade retention, extended school days/years, and the adoption of pedagogies that deskill both teachers and students, like direct instruction techniques and phonics-only curriculum. These strategies might lead to short-term gains in test scores, but do not result in meaningful learning.

The rhetoric of the achievement gap looks for solutions that alter children and families of color and those living poverty, but not for solutions that alter teachers competencies, curriculum, pedagogy, school organization or school finance. Alternatives to the search for how to remedy poor and minority children and families might be,

- fundamental restructuring of schools (e.g. alternatives to top down management);
- improvement of school climate (e.g., sufficient paper, books kids can take home and even keep, toilet paper in the bathrooms, air conditioning, adequate space, classrooms instead of trailers, quiet places for one-on-one interactions with students— "Books, supplies, and lower class size!");
- curricular alternatives (e.g., Afro-centric or Latino-centric curriculum, bilingual education);
- efforts to decrease class size or create small schools;
- reform of school financing (e.g., elimination of local property taxation for school financing);
- the racial profiling inherent in discipline policies and practices;
- the Courts' role in resegregating schools, creating what the Harvard Civil Rights Project calls apartheid schools;
- much greater caution about using hastily developed, unvalidated tests that are used by policymakers in ways that violate professional standards and are frequently inaccurately scored

The "achievement gap" is more accurately a *test score gap*. It's also an *opportunity gap*. And, a visit to an affluent white suburban school and one to an urban primarily minority school will illustrate there is a *resources gap*, and that same visit will also reveal an *income gap*. Focusing on the test score gap without attention to these other gaps will do little to alleviate the inherent racism in educational opportunity and achievement.

COLLEGE ENTRANCE TESTS

In the face of great odds, children of color and living in poverty do complete high school and aspire to attend postsecondary education where they encounter another

Table 5.2
2002 College Bound Seniors SAT Scores

	Verbal	Math	Total	
Ethnic Group				
African American or Black	430	427	857	
Mexican or Mexican American	446	457	903	
Puerto Rican	455	451	906	
Other Hispanic or Latino	458	464	922	
American Indian or Alaskan Native	479	483	962	
White	527	533	1060	
Asian, Asian American, Pacific Islander	501	569	1070	
Other	502	514	1016	
Family Income				
Less than $10,000/year	417	442	859	
$10,000–$20,000/year	435	453	888	+29
$20,000–$30,000/year	461	470	931	+43
$30,000–$40,000/year	480	485	965	+34
$40,000–$50,000/year	496	501	997	+32
$50,000–$60,000/year	505	509	1014	+17
$60,000–$70,000/year	511	516	1027	+13
$70,000–$80,000/year	517	524	1041	+14
$80,000–$100,000/year	530	538	1068	+27
More than $100,000/year	555	568	1123	+55
All Test-Takers	504	516	1020	
(Approximately 1.3 million)				

Source: College Board, *College-Board Seniors National Report,* 2002.

potential setback in the form of college entrance tests. Based on a lack of validity and the differential performance of minority and poor children (see Table 5.2 and Table 5.3) there has been increasing criticism and rejection of both SAT and ACT scores for college admissions.[16] Still, many colleges expect students to take these admissions tests, and Tables 5.2 and 5.3 illustrate the disadvantage for minority students and the impact of income on test scores. Sacks concludes, "there is little doubt that the prevailing paradigm about merit has consistently reproduced social and economic advantages for the "dukes of the system," the relatively few who conform to widely held views of merit."[17]

College admissions scores are used for more than admissions, however. Scholarship awards are also based on SAT or ACT scores. In a letter to Florida's Governor Jeb Bush, Fairtest, MALDEF, and others outline the problems:

While African Americans comprised 14.4 percent of all SAT and ACT takers, they received only 3 percent of all Academic Scholars Awards (100% funding) and only 8.3 percent of Merit Scholarship Awards (75% funding). Latinos, who made up 13.7 percent of all test takers, earned only 8.7 percent of the Academic Scholars Awards

Table 5.3
2002 College Bound Seniors ACT Scores

Ethnicity		
African American/Black	16.8	
American Indian/Alaskan Native	18.6	
Mexican American/Chicano	18.2	
Puerto Rican/Hispanic	18.8	
Other	19.2	
Multiracial	20.9	
Asian American/Pacific Islander	21.6	
Caucasian American/White	21.7	
Household Income		
Less than $18,000/year	17.8	
$18,000–$24,000/year	18.6	+0.8
$24,000–$30,000/year	19.4	+0.8
$30,000–$36,000/year	19.9	+0.5
$36,000–$42,000/year	20.4	+0.5
$42,000–$50,000/year	20.8	+0.4
$50,000–$60,000/year	21.3	+0.5
$60,000–$80,000/year	21.8	+0.5
$80,000–$100,000/year	22.4	+0.6
More than $100,000/year	23.3	+0.9
All Test-Takers	20.8	
(1.1 million test-takers)		

Source: ACT High School Profile Report: H.S. Graduating Class of 2002 National Report.

and 12.3 percent of Merit Scholarships. White students, by contrast, comprised 53.4 percent of test takers, yet received 76.3 percent of the Academic Scholars Awards and 71.5 percent of Merit Scholarships.

The use of SAT and ACT score cut-offs to determine eligibility is a major reason why proportionately few African American and Latino students received these lucrative scholarships. Students must score 1270 or higher on the SAT, or 28 or higher on the ACT, in order to qualify for Academic Scholars; the Merit Scholarship Award eligibility is set at a SAT of 920 or an ACT of 20. Yet in Florida, the average SAT score was 857 for African Americans and 952 for Latinos, both of which are more than 300 points below the cut-off for the Academic Scholars Award. For whites in Florida, the average score was 1044. Other measures of academic preparation, such as grades, do not demonstrate such a great racial disparity. It is the high test score minimums, particularly for the Academic Scholars program, that put receipt of these awards far out of the reach of many students of color.[18]

The move away from needs-based and toward merit-based scholarships, such as in the Florida example, is happening in all parts of the country with similar results. In the Introduction to their edited collection, Heller and Marin parody the deleterious effects of such scholarships:

> Imagine someone reacting to higher education's current situation by saying that what we needed were large new programs to subsidize white and middle- to upper-income students to attend college, and that it was not necessary to raise need-based aid even enough to cover new tuition increases. We would give some minority students entering awards because of their relatively high grade point averages from inferior segregated schools. However, we will take their aid away when they cannot get a "B" average in a vastly more competitive college setting and blame them for not being up to the task. A huge amount of money would go into this new program, far more than was spent for the need-based scholarships in some states. We would get the money from an extremely regressive tax-a-state lottery that drew money disproportionately from poor and minority players. In other words, poor blacks and Latinos would end up paying a substantial part of the cost of educating more affluent white students, who would have gone to college even if they had not had the additional financial incentive. And to add insult to injury, colleges would cut their own financial aid funds, or shift these resources to give more money to high scoring students. In cases where the financial aid made more students eager to go to a particular institution in the state, rather than an out-of-state school where they would have to pay tuition, the in-state institution could raise its selectivity ratings by excluding students with lower scores, students who would usually be minority and from less affluent families.[19]

CONCLUSION

There is every reason to believe that access and quality of schooling is differentiated in this country and that differentiation is along race and class lines. Standardized testing plays a substantial role in maintaining this differentiation beginning in kindergarten on through school and into access to professions and jobs. This issue is one that must be addressed as a K-16 issue, not one isolated in either public schools or higher education. This K-16 alliance also includes parents, and the rise of grassroots organizations that combine the knowledge and resources of educators, researchers, and parents are on the rise.[20] Researchers are now beginning to see the common threads that can support a critique of testing as it is employed across the K-16 educational spectrum. Elsewhere I have described the hegemony of accountability that is test-driven and illustrated how this is manifest in both K-12 and postsecondary contexts.[21]

There is little reason to believe that current test based reforms in precollegiate, collegiate, and professional education will redress the inequities between white and minority students and between those living in poverty and those not. Indeed this testing has the potential to further deepen and divide Americans along race and class lines.

NOTES

* This chapter is a slightly revised version of an article of the same name previously published in *Workplace: A Journal for Academic Labor*, July 2003. Available at http://www.cust. educ.ubc.ca/workplace/issue5p2/mathison.html.

1. V. E. Lee, and D. T. Burkham (2002). *Inequality at the starting gate*. Washington, DC: Economic Policy Institute.

2. Association for Childhood Education International (1991). On standardized testing: A position paper of the Association for Childhood Education International. *Childhood Education* (Spring), 130–142.

3. *Quality Counts* 2006. (2006). *Education Week* [Online]. Available at http://www.edweek.org/sreports/qc06/.

4. S. F. Reardon and C. Galindo (2002). Do high stakes tests affect students' decision to drop out of school? Evidence from NELS. Paper presented at the annual meeting of the American Educational Research Association, New Orleans, April 2002.

5. *Quality Counts* 2006.

6. S. Dorn (2003). High-stakes testing and the history of graduation. *Education Policy Analysis Archives*, 11(1) [Online]. Available at http://epaa.asu.edu/epaa/v11n1/.

7. A. L. Amrein and D. C. Berliner (2002). High-stakes testing, uncertainty, and student learning. *Education Policy Analysis Archives*, 10(18) [Online]. Available at http://epaa.asu.edu/epaa/v10n18.

8. K. Gayler, N. Chudowsky, N. Kober, and M. Hamilton (2003). *State high school exams put to the test*. Washington, DC: Center on Education Policy.

9. Ibid., p. 31.

10. G. J. Marchant and S. E. Paulson (January 21, 2005). The relationship of high school graduation exams to graduation rates and SAT scores. *Education Policy Analysis Archives*, 13(6). Retrieved on January 3, 2006 from http://epaa.asu.edu/epaa/v13n6/.

11. *Quality Counts* 2006.

12. Reardon and Galindo, Do high stakes tests affect students' decision to drop out of school?

13. W. Haney (2000). The myth of the Texas miracle in education. *Education Analysis Policy Archives*, 8 (41) [Online]. Available at http://epaa.asu.edu/epaa/v8n41/.

14. These data are based on the *Quality Counts* 2001 report, as *Quality Counts* 2006 does not provide similar data.

15. See the following references for more detailed discussions of the impact of high stakes testing on teaching, teachers, and learning.

Amrein and Berliner, High-stakes testing, uncertainty, and student learning.

M. Clarke, A. Shore, K. Rhoades, L. Abrams, J. Miao. and J. Li (2003). *The perceived effects of state mandated testing programs on teaching and learning: Findings from interviews with educators in low-, medium-, and high-stakes states*. Boston: NBETTP [Online]. Available at http://www.bc.edu/research/nbetpp/reports.html.

G. Hillocks, Jr. (2002). *The testing trap: How state writing assessments control learning*. New York: Teachers College Press.

G. Madaus (1998). The distortion of teaching and testing: High-stakes testing and instruction, *Peabody Journal of Education*, 65, 29–46.

S. Mathison, E. W. Ross and K. D. Vinson (2001). Defining the social studies curriculum: The influence of and resistance to curriculum standards and testing in social studies. In E. W. Ross (Ed.), *The social studies curriculum: Purposes, problems, and possibilities*. Albany, NY: SUNY Press.

L. M. McNeil (2000). *Contradictions of school reform: Educational costs of standardized testing*. New York: Routledge.

J. Pedulla, L. Abrams, G. Madaus, M. Russell, M. Ramos, and J. Miao (2003). *The perceived effects of state mandated testing programs on teaching and learning: Findings from a national survey of teachers.* Boston: NBETTP [Online]. Available at http://www.bc. edu/research/nbetpp/reports.html.

K.D. Vinson, R. Gibson, and E. W. Ross (2001). High-stakes testing and standardization: The threat to authenticity. *Monographs of the John Dewey Project on Progressive Education,* 3(2) [Online]. Available at http://www.uvm.edu/˜dewey/monographs/ProPer3n2.html.

16. P. Sacks (2000). *Standardized minds: The high price of America's testing culture and what we can do to change it.* Perseus Books.

17. Sacks, *Standardized minds*, p. 264.

18. FairTest (2001, December). Letter to Governor Jeb Bush [Online]. Available at http: //fairtest.org/pr/Bright_Futures_lttr.html.

19. D. E. Heller and P. Marin (2002) (Eds.). *Who should we help? The negative social consequences of merit aid scholarships.* Harvard Civil Rights Project [Online]. Available at http: //www.civilrightsproject.harvard.edu/research/meritaid/fullreport.php.

20. See http://www.eval.org/hstlinks.htm for a list of grassroots organizations, many of which are regional or state based, but some are national in scope, such as the Rouge Forum or the fledgling ACT NOW, Advocates for Children and Teachers National Organizing Workshop.

21. S. Mathison, and E. W. Ross (2002) The hegemony of accountability in schools and universities. *Workplace: A Journal of Academic Labor* [Online]. Available at http://www. louisville.edu/journal/workplace/issue5p1/mathison.html

FAMILY AND OTHER BASELINE CORRELATES OF GED VERSUS OTHER ACADEMIC ATTAINMENT STATUSES AMONG ADOLESCENTS

Richard K. Caputo

Over the past 30 years in the United States, the earning capacity of those both with and without benefit of a high school degree has deteriorated, particularly more so for the latter, such that the progress made against poverty in the post–World War II period ceased.[1] In 2004, 12.7 percent of all people (except unrelated individuals under age 15) of all educational levels fell below the U.S. official poverty thresholds (37.0 million persons) compared to 21.8 percent (or 10.2 million persons) of those without a high school diploma based on highest grade completed.[2] For those under 25 years of age compared to those 25 years of age or older, 17.9 percent and 10.0 percent respectively of all educational levels were poor compared to 18.7 percent and 23.9 percent respectively of those without a high school diploma. In 1992 among those 25 years of age or older, 11.0 percent of all educational levels fell below the U.S. official poverty thresholds compared to 25.8 percent of those without a high school diploma.[3] Throughout the 1970s and 1980s, increasing percentages of the high school dropouts among noninstitutionalized males 20–29 years of age reported no earnings, from 6.5 percent in 1973 to 13.0 percent in 1987, while the real annual earnings of black male dropouts and graduates respectively fell 44 percent and 36 percent.[4] Increases in unemployed young black males, that is, with no annual earnings, were reported to have occurred more recently as well.[5]

In light of socioeconomic disadvantages associated with dropping out of high school and in an effort to increase the efficacy of early intervention efforts, the present study examines distal family processes, parental styles, peer activities, and other background measures as predictors of obtaining General Equivalency Degree (also known as General Educational Development or GED) certificates versus other academic achievements among adolescents. This study focuses on GED recipients because they are more likely than conventional high school graduates to be poor and they have been found to have less favorable outcomes over the life course in such areas as cognition, depression, physical illnesses, and household income.[6] Given that economic status has been found to be strongly correlated across generations,[7] obtaining a traditional high school diploma rather than an alternative such as the GED takes on added importance. In addition, GED recipients are often classified with conventional high school graduates,[8] perhaps to their detriment.[9] This lumping continues to occur even though nonequivalency of the GED certificate and traditional high school diploma has been observed and noted since the 1980s,[10] albeit with some exceptions.[11] To the extent that many studies, reports, and government statistics lump high school graduates and GED recipients together, they may be remiss. In Philip Gleason and Mark Dynarski's and Gary D. Sandefur, Sara McLanahan, and Roger A. Wojtkiewicz's studies of dropout risks, for example, it would have been helpful to know if the lack of predictive validity of most risk factors was similar for conventional high school completers and for GED recipients.[12]

There has also been some concern about educational policies enacted by the Federal Government resulting in higher dropout rates and less investment in human capital by dropouts. The Goals 2000: Educate America Act passed in 1994[13] and The No Child Left Behind Act of 2001[14] are cited as examples.[15] Both acts stress the importance of test-taking, which may encourage educators to jettison marginal students from their ranks, while enabling states to count GED recipients as graduates.[16]

Russell W. Rumberger long ago called for a comprehensive model of factors associated with dropping out of high school, one that incorporates distal and proximate measures.[17] The author contends that intervention efforts relying primarily or exclusively on proximate factors and processes associated with adolescents' academic achievement may be less successful because such efforts would begin too late and have insufficient time to take effect. There is some empirical support for reliance on distal factors associated with academic achievement, including the classic study by James Samuel Coleman et al., which highlighted the importance of socioeconomic background.[18]

The focus on GED is also important in light of ongoing questions regarding the merits of the GED,[19] the increased proportion of contemporary high school students, especially among males and racial/ethnic minorities, who leave prior to completing all their courses successfully,[20] and the decreased labor force participation rates of high school dropouts 16–24 years old since 1990.[21] Given their higher rates of poverty and increased social marginalization, high school dropouts present a formidable challenge to educators, social workers, and others concerned about the well-being of these individuals as well as on their ability to meet the country's workforce needs of the twenty-first century.[22] This is the case especially in the United States where cash assistance for low-income single parents, many of whom participate in the welfare-to-work program known as Temporary Assistance for Needy Families (TANF) and have adolescent children with serious emotional and behavioral problems,[23] is increasingly dependent on labor force participation and where an aging population will in all likelihood become increasingly dependent on the Social Security contributions of younger workers.[24]

This chapter proceeds with a brief description of today's GED. Historical treatment can be found elsewhere.[25] The related literature regarding adolescents' academic achievements primarily through high school is then reviewed. The major research issue and hypotheses are then presented. Study methods, results, and a discussion of practice and policy implications in light of findings follow accordingly.

TODAY'S GED

Over one million adults worldwide took one or more of the five GED tests in 2001, a record number, with nearly 70 percent receiving the credential; the number of test takers, however, dropped to 603,019 in 2002 but rose to 703,512 in 2003.[26] In 2003, the U.S. total was 552,396, with 387,470, slightly more than 70 percent, passing the battery of tests; it should be noted, however, that in 2003 only 2 percent of the U.S. population of adults without a high school degree were tested, 1.7 percent of those adults completed the battery of tests, and 1.2 percent passed.[27]

Approximately 95 percent of U.S. colleges and universities admit students with GED certificates on the same basis as traditional high school graduates.[28] The scope of the GED can also be assessed in dollars. In fiscal year 1999–2000, federal funds targeted for adult education programs authorized by the Adult Education and Family Literacy Act of 1998 totaled $365 million.[29] They increased to $587 million in 2003, with projected expenditures of $2.5 billion for 2004–2008,[30] although they declined to $569.7 million in fiscal year 2005.[31] The main beneficiaries of these funds were GED preparation programs offered by public high schools, community colleges, community-based organizations, and prisons. No formal training, however, was required to take the test. Hence, there was little if any socialization component to the GED. By design, the GED was meant to distinguish dropouts with high-level cognitive skills, rather than institutionalize workplace norms.

LITERATURE REVIEW

The empirical literature in regard to academic achievement, especially of high school dropouts, is extensive, spanning several decades, and it is not easily summarized. What follows is a review of recent studies (within the past 10 years) whose findings about correlates of academic achievement in general and GED attainment in particular were used as guides to variable selection and for the theoretical organization of salient family background, baseline, and other measures used in the present study. In general among those 16–24 years of age, men have been more likely to drop out of high school than women since the mid-1980s and more recently those of Hispanic origin about twice as likely as those of non-Hispanic black origin who in turn are twice as likely to drop out as those of non-Hispanic white origin.[32] In addition, the lower income "event" drop out rate has stabilized since 1990 and remains about 10–13 percent compared to 4–6 percent for middle-income youth and 1–3 percent for upper-income youth.[33]

Robert Haveman and Barbara Wolfe have summarized much of the earlier studies regarding determinants of children's educational choices.[34] Their review of seven high school graduation and eight educational attainment studies[35] published between 1982 and 1994 showed that the human capital of parents, typically measured by the number of years of schooling attained, was statistically significant and quantitatively important to children's educational attainment no matter how it was defined. Family structure was also found to influence high school completion and educational attainment. Growing up in a one-parent family was inversely related to educational attainment and being raised in an intact family increased the odds of graduating from high school. Theoretically, the presence of both parents increased the human capital available to children, especially as mothers' educational levels increased, in addition to devoting more time and other resources to children than would be the case in single-parent families. Other factors found to influence either high school graduation or educational attainment included the number of siblings, religiousness, school-related parenting practices, and the presence of reading materials in the home.

Most of the studies Haveman and Wolfe examined, also found that race was not associated significantly with educational attainment when accounting for family income and other background measures. Social investment measures such as unemployment rates, quality of the neighborhood, region of country, suburban vs. urban residence, and the like were also reported to be correlated with children's educational attainment, but of marginal statistical significance when controlling for other factors. Among the high school graduation studies only one[36] made explicit reference to the GED as educational attainment, but GED certificate holders were lumped with high school graduates.

Several recent studies focused only on high school dropout rates. Karen A. Randolph, Roderick A. Rose, Mark W. Fraser, and Dennis K. Orthner, for example, focused on children in single female-headed families receiving cash income from the Aid to Families with Dependent Children (AFDC) program in 1993 and 1994.[37] They reported that unstable labor force participation of mothers increased the hazard rate at which the children dropped out of high school. With the exceptions of first-grade retention, race and sex, all measures of this study were proximate, for example, suspension, truancy, participation in extracurricular activities and the like while in high school. Given the restricted sample of the Randolph et al. study, generalizations across schools, school districts, urban areas, or states were limited. Rumberger had noted similar limitations in an earlier review of high school dropout studies.[38]

Beth Spenciter Rosenthal studied nonschool correlates of high school dropouts.[39] Taking an ecological approach that organized such measures along macro, mezzo, and micro dimensions, Rosenthal reported that SES was the best documented, with students from lower socioeconomic status much more likely to drop out of school. Minority group status disappeared when controlling for family background characteristics such as SES. Men were more likely to drop out than women. Community characteristics associated with dropouts included urban residency, living in the South and West, living in poor areas (indexed by per capita income, percentage of school families receiving public assistance, and average wage levels), living in areas with higher percentages of female-headed, non-white, and foreign-born communities. Social support for remaining in school, measured by parents' level of education, amount of reading materials in the home, and percent of friends who remain in school, were also associated with likelihood of dropping out. Family processes also influenced likelihood of dropping out of high school. Students whose parents were more involved in and monitored their everyday activities were less likely to drop out. Dropouts had poorer relationships with their parents compared to completers and they saw their parents as more punitive. Parents of dropouts were found, however, to use a more permissive parenting style but were also more likely to use extrinsic punishments.

In their study of the effects of family type on high school graduation, Sandefur, McLanahan, and Wojtkiewicz showed that living, at age 14, with someone other than both parents had negative consequences for children's high school graduation (regardless of whom they lived with) and that such effects persisted when controlling for income and for some psychological attributes of the adolescents.[40] Similar intergenerational religious affiliation, which provides a greater sense of shared experiences, though not directly linked to educational attainment, has been shown to affect adolescents' delinquent behavior, which in turn may influence children's educational attainment.[41]

Haveman and Wolfe's[42] and Rosenthal's[43] theoretical frameworks, which incorporate children's, parental, and social investments in education, guide the present study. Economic and social psychological bodies of theory and research underlie their framework. Economic theory treats children's educational attainment or human capital as a function of household production and parental investment in time and money.[44] Haveman and Wolfe also note the importance of social investments such as school-related government expenditures, residential tax bases, neighborhood quality, and the like to the development of human capital. Social psychological theory views children's educational attainment in part as a consequence of parents' ability to instill the requisite motivation and skills in their children and in part as a function of peer influence. Rosenthal stressed the importance of separating social supports affecting students' social-psychological makeup into two clusters of measures: family support and peer support. In addition to identifying the major categories of measures used in this study (personal characteristics, responding parent characteristics, family structure, and community environment), economic and social psychological theories also provide the selection criteria of main-interest vis-à-vis control measures within each category.

At issue for purposes of this study is the extent to which family structure and parental involvement in children's elementary school years are better predictors of adolescents' obtaining GED certificates than community environment when controlling for a variety of parental background, personal, and other baseline measures. Specifically, this study addresses the following questions:

1. To what extent are family structures and parental involvement while their children are in elementary school robust predictors of GED receipt?

2. How does community environment during a child's elementary school years affect the likelihood of obtaining a GED certificate independently of the aforementioned family structure and parental involvement?

3. How do age, gender, race/ethnicity, SES, and other family background measures affect the likelihood of GED receipt among adolescents?

Answers to these questions are important in part because findings can suggest viable avenues of early, preventive interventions by human service providers and by policymakers. For example, educators, school social workers, and others who work with elementary school children can benefit from knowing how a child's family structure and parental involvement are likely to affect that child's likelihood of obtaining GED certificates vis-à-vis dropping out of high school, completing high school, or going beyond high school by the time they get to high school. To the extent such distal factors such as family structure and parental involvement during children's elementary school years matter, early school-based intervention strategies can be designed accordingly. In addition, to the extent that distal community factors such as peer-group activities and presence of gangs matter more or less than family structure and parental involvement during children's elementary school years, policymakers may want to direct more resources to equalize opportunities for children who might be adversely affected by these factors over which school-based initiatives have little or no influence. Further, to the extent that dropping out of high school and GED receipt have stigmatizing effects and other adverse outcomes that last well into adulthood,[45] identification of distal predictors for purposes of prevention and early intervention to ensure better academic achievement becomes that much more important.

This study goes beyond previous studies in several significant ways. First, it relies on a nationally representative sample of youth obtained from a recent cohort. Second, it distinguishes GED recipients from those who completed high school with or without the GED, as well as from those whose highest level of academic achievement was the high school degree and from those who obtained neither the GED nor a high school degree. Third, it incorporates measures of activities in which adolescents report their peers partake, thereby making possible separate treatment of family versus peer support as Rosenthal had recommended.[46]

METHODS

Data and Subjects

Data were obtained from the 1997 National Longitudinal Survey of Youth (NLSY97) the purpose of which was to collect information on youth labor force experiences and investments in education. The NLSY97 is a nationally representative sample of 8,984 people living in the United States in 1997 who were born during the years 1980–1984. Two subsamples comprised the NLSY97. The first was a cross-sectional sample (6,748) designed to be representative of people living in the United States during the initial survey round and born between January 1, 1980 and December 31, 1984. The second probability sample comprised a set of supplemental samples (2,236) designed to over-sample Hispanic and black people living in the United States during the initial survey round and born during the same period as the cross-sectional sample. Data are particularly suited for this study because participants were asked specifically about enrollment in or completion of GED certificate programs. Additional information about sampling design and fielding procedures can be found in the *NLSY97 User's Guide*.[47]

The study sample ($n = 2,433$) was restricted to those enrolled in elementary schools in survey year 1997. It comprised only those respondents whose enrollment status was obtained in survey year 2003, the most recent year of available data, and about whom information on all study measures was reported, and for whom mutually exclusive categories of race/ethnicity (white, black, or Hispanic) could be determined. Questions about family processes in the initial 1997 round were asked only of respondents 12–14 years of age.

Measures

Academic achievement status, the study's outcome measure, was obtained from a survey question regarding a respondent's enrollment status at the time of interview in survey year 2003. Four mutually exclusive categories were created: (1) high school dropouts with no GED or other terminal degree; (2) GED recipients whose certificate was their terminal degree; (3) traditional high school graduates for whom this degree was the terminal degree and who did not have GED certificates; and (4) traditional high school graduates who pursued additional years of schooling and who did or did not have GED certificates.

Correlates or predictors of academic achievement status were grouped into two main categories, namely main-interest measures and control measures. Main-interest correlates were classified into five domains: (1) personal characteristics of respondents; (2) responding parents' background characteristics; (3) family structural characteristics; (4) family involvement characteristics; and (5) community environment characteristics. Personal characteristics of respondents while in elementary school included ability, behavioral problems, delinquency, ever repeated a grade, participated in Head Start, number of schools attended, and use of abusive substances. The Peabody Individual Achievement Test (PIAT) Math Assessment, administered to all respondents who had completed less than 9 years of schooling in 1997, was used to measure elementary school ability. PIAT is among one of the most widely used brief assessments of academic achievement, with demonstrably high test-retest reliability and concurrent validity. The version used in this study is PIAT-Revised (PIAT-R).[48] A behavior and emotional problem scale was created by Child Trends, Inc., an organization involved in the NLSY97 questionnaire design process. Documentation of detailed descriptions, which includes results of reliability and validity tests conducted by Child Trends, Inc., of this and other scales and indices used in this study as noted below were found in Appendix 9 of the *NLSY97*.

Codebook Supplement Main File Round 1[49]

The behavior and emotional problem scale was constructed from four 3-point (0–2, not true to often true) items asked of responding parents about the youths. Scores of the behavior and emotional problem scale ranged from 0 to 8, with higher scores signifying more behavioral problems (alpha = .65 for boys and .57 for girls). Whether youths participated in a Head Start program when they were children was obtained from a question to that effect asked of responding parents. This measure was included in light of on-going policy as well as scholarly concerns regarding the well-being of Head Start participants vis-à-vis other children as they go through elementary and high school.[50]

The substance abuse index was constructed from three yes-no items asked of youth in regard to whether they ever smoked cigarettes, had a drink of an alcoholic beverage, or used marijuana. Scores ranged from 0 to 3, with higher scores signifying more instances of substance abuse.

Personal characteristic control measures included age, ethnicity/race, health, and sex. Health was obtained from a question asked of parents about the youth and when unavailable from the parents from the youths' reports. The reported item asked to rate the youth's health on a five-point scale, which was recoded such that 1 = poor health and 5 = excellent health. Higher scores signified better health.

Main-interest responding parents' background characteristics included measures of whether they had completed high school, lived with both their parents at age 14, and type of residence where they grew up (center city, suburban, or other). These measures were included to capture parents' socioeconomic backgrounds. Completion of high school and growing up in the suburbs vis-à-vis elsewhere was meant to signify the potential human capital parents had to offer their children. Living with both parents was meant to capture the benefits of purportedly transmitted social capital from the parents to their children. Such social capital has often been attributed to intact family structures vis-à-vis growing up in single-parent households.[51]

Responding parents' background control measures included whether responding parents were born in the United States, ever had health problems since the birth of respondents, and ever received public cash assistance. Whether households were three-generational was used as a control measure for family structural characteristics. Parent-youth religious agreement was used as a control measure for family involvement characteristics. Community environment control measures included the area of residence unemployment rate and the region of country of residence.

Main-interest family structural characteristics of the youth in 1997 included measures of number of adults aged 18 and over in the household, presence of mother and father in the household, and socioeconomic status (SES). The first two measures were meant to capture potential social support. SES signifies parents' potential human capital. It was constructed by Center for Human Resource staff from all sources of income, accounted for family size, and relied on U.S. poverty threshold indices to determine whether youth lived in poor families.

Whether youths lived in three-generation households and enriched home environment were used as controls for family structural characteristics. Child Trends, Inc. developed the enriching environment index from three items (each coded 1 for enriching and 0 for not enriching) asking youths whether their home had a computer or a dictionary and whether they spent any time within the week prior to survey taking extra classes or lessons such as music, dance, or foreign language lessons. Scores ranged from 0 to 3, with higher scores signifying a more enriching environment.

Main-interest family involvement characteristics included measures of responding parent's involvement in youth's school, parental style, and quality time. Parents' involvement in youth's schools index was created from two items asking responding parents if they attended PTA meetings or volunteered to help out in classrooms. Responses to each of the two (yes = 1, no = 0) responses were summed and averaged, yielding scores with a range of 0–1. Child Trend, Inc. created a measure of parenting styles from several items asked of youth in regard to how they perceived their parents treating them throughout childhood. Questions were asked about each parent in the family. For purposes of this study, responses reflect those about mothers in all families where they were present and about fathers in those families where mothers were not present. This measure comprised four mutually exclusive categories: (1) Uninvolved (permissive and not very or somewhat supportive); (2) Authoritarian (strict and not very or somewhat supportive); (3) Permissive (permissive and very supportive); and (4) Authoritative (strict and very supportive). The Quality Time scale was created from three items asking youth about the number of days per week they ate, had fun, or did something religious with the family (alpha = .51). Responses to each item were summed then averaged, with higher scores signifying more quality time. Parent-youth agreement of religious affiliation was used as a control measure for family involvement.

Main-interest community environment characteristics included measures of positive and negative activities of youths' peers, student–teacher ratio in schools, urban area, and whether gangs were in the school of the neighborhood. Two measures of peer activities were created from ten items asking youth about the percentage of their peers who engaged in activities such as going to church regularly, getting drunk, belonging to gangs, using illegal substances, planning to go to college, and the like. The ten items were subjected to factor analysis (Principal Component Analysis and Varimax rotating procedures) and then loaded into two groupings, one suggesting positive activities (going to church regularly, participating in school activities, planning to go to college, doing voluntary work; eigen value = 1.53, with factor loading ranging from .570 to .833) and the other suggesting negative activities (smoking, getting drunk more than once per month, belonging to gangs, using illegal substances, and cutting classes; eigen value = 3.31, with factor loadings ranging from .523 to .630). Region of residence was used as a control measure for community environment characteristics.

Procedures

Chi-square and, due to an unbalanced design, General Linear Model (GLM) procedures were used on unweighted data to determine statistically significant bivariate relationships between academic achievement status and nominal and continuous level measures accordingly. For purposes of parsimony, only those bivariate measures found to be statistically significant were used in the multivariate analysis. Multinomial regression analysis was used to determine which measures had greater predictive capacity for each academic achievement status outcome vis-à-vis obtaining the GED as the terminal degree. Measures were entered in a forward direction, with main-interest measures entered first followed, accordingly, by control measures in the following order: personal, responding parent, family structure, family involvement, and community involvement.

RESULTS

Of the 2,433 youth in the study, 107 or 4.4 percent (weighted) had obtained the GED as the terminal degree as of survey year 2003; 406 or 14.4 percent were high school dropouts; 586 or 23.2 percent had obtained a traditional high school degree as the terminal degree, but no GED; and 1,334 or 58.2 percent had gone beyond high school, with or without a GED. The youth ranged from 18 to 20 years old. Males and females were equally represented in the study sample and they averaged 19 years of age in survey year 2003. The majority of adolescents were non-Hispanic white (74%). Most responding parents (85%) had completed high school, while 16 percent of the adolescents lived in poor families in 1997.

As can be seen in Table 6.1, most nominal level measures had a statistically significant relationship with academic achievement status. Of particular note for purposes of this chapter were the poverty-related measures and their relationship to academic achievement. Higher percentages of the youth who were Head Start participants were dropouts or GED recipients than were those who were not Head Start participants (28.3% vs. 13.7% and 6.2% vs. 3.9% respectively), as were youth who lived in poor families in 1997 vs. those who did not (33.8% vs. 11.7% and 7.1% vs. 3.6% respectively), and who reported the presence of gangs in their schools or neighborhood (19.5% vs. 14.4% and 4.7% vs. 4.2% respectively). Youths whose parents had completed high school were less likely to drop out of high school or obtain GED certificates than those whose parents had not completed high school (11.8% vs. 35.0% and 3.9% vs. 6.2% respectively), as were youths whose parents had lived with both their parents at age 14 (14.5% vs. 22.6% and 4.3% vs. 4.7% respectively), who were residing with their mothers and fathers in 1997 (13.0% vs. 26.3% and 3.4% vs. 7.1% respectively).

As can be seen in Table 6.2, most ordinal and interval level measures also had a statistically significant relationship with academic achievement status. Keeping to our focus on poverty-related measures, delinquency, use of abusive substances, and negative peer influences distinguished GED recipients and high school dropouts from

Table 6.1
Bivariate Chi-Square Results (Row percents)

			Academic Achievement Status			
Variable	Value Label	Dropouts	GED	High School	>High School	χ^2 Value
Personal characteristics						
Main interest						
Ever repeat a grade	Yes	40.5	9.4	30.1	20.1	223.153***
	No	13.2	3.7	23.2	59.9	
Head Start participant	Yes	28.3	6.2	25.0	40.5	79.724***
	No	13.7	3.9	23.9	58.5	
Control						
Ethnicity/race	Hispanic	21.3	2.9	28.2	47.6	66.323***
	Non-Hispanic Black	22.0	5.5	27.0	45.4	
	Non-Hispanic White	12.8	4.4	21.4	61.3	
Sex	Female	14.2	3.5	20.7	61.6	44.311***
	Male	19.2	5.2	27.4	48.2	
Responding parent						
Main interest						
Completed high school	Yes	11.8	3.9	22.7	61.6	219.046***
	No	35.0	6.2	29.2	29.6	
Lived with both parents at age 14	Yes	14.5	4.3	22.1	59.1	51.660***
	No	22.6	4.7	29.4	43.4	
Type of residence raised	Center City	20.4	5.0	21.8	52.7	24.430***
	Suburb	11.3	3.8	21.1	63.8	
	Other	17.0	4.4	5.7	53.0	
Control						
Born in United States	Yes	16.3	4.8	24.2	54.7	7.701
	No	19.2	1.6	23.1	56.0	
Health problems since birth of respondent	Yes	17.6	6.9	28.2	47.2	7.813
	No	16.6	4.1	23.7	55.6	
Public assistance recipient (ever)	Yes	24.6	6.3	27.7	41.3	221.545***
	No	8.2	2.3	20.2	69.3	

Family structure

Main interest

Presence of mother & father in HH	Yes	13.0	3.4	23.8	59.9	96.562***
	No	26.3	7.1	24.8	41.8	
Socioeconomic status	Poor	33.8	7.1	27.8	31.3	211.615***
	Not Poor	11.7	3.6	23.0	61.7	

Control

Three-generation HH	Yes	19.8	5.9	25.1	49.1	11.626**
	No	15.8	4.0	23.8	56.4	

Family involvement

Main interest

Parenting style	Uninvolved	22.3	4.9	28.3	44.6	35.167***
	Authoritarian	18.9	5.8	24.7	50.6	
	Permissive	16.8	3.6	23.8	55.8	
	Authoritative	13.4	4.0	22.4	60.2	

Control

Parent–youth religious agreement	Agree	15.8	4.3	23.9	56.0	5.603
	Not Agree	19.3	4.7	24.8	51.3	

Community environment

Main interest

Urban residence	Yes	17.0	4.4	23.4	55.3	1.607
	No	16.0	4.5	25.6	53.9	
Whether gangs in school or neighborhood	Yes	19.5	4.7	24.0	51.7	13.426**
	No	14.4	4.2	24.1	57.3	
Region of residence	Northeast	15.1	4.6	20.3	60.0	23.582**
	North Central	16.4	3.4	23.2	57.0	
	South	18.6	6.0	23.9	51.5	
	West	16.7	2.7	27.7	54.9	

*** $p < .001$, ** $p < .01$.

Table 6.2
Bivariate ANOVA Results

Variable	Academic Achievement Status				F-value	Post-Hoc Tests[a]
	Dropouts(DO)	GED	High School(HS)	Beyond HS(BHS)		
Personal characteristics						
Main interest						
Ability (PIAT Math scores)	87.50	92.16	91.88	100.18	129.69***	DO < HS < BHS; DO < GED < BHS; HS, DO
Behavioral problems	2.62	2.18	2.02	1.47	64.16***	DO, GED, HS > BHS; DO > HS
Delinquency	1.83	1.89	1.30	0.91	39.77***	GED, DO > HS > BHS
Schools attended (#)	0.96	1.15	1.10	1.19	12.41***	DO < HS, GED, BHS; HS < BHS
Use of abusive substances	1.07	1.12	0.81	0.65	23.40***	GED, DO > HS > BHS
Control						
Age	18.93	19.09	19.00	19.03	2.00	
Health	4.03	4.10	4.20	4.42	29.35***	DO, GED, HS < BHS; DO < HS
Family structure						
Main interest						
Adults 18+ yrs. old in HH (#)	1.80	1.74	1.92	1.98	8.80***	GED, DO, HS, BHS; GED < BHS; DO < BHS
Control						
Enriched environment	1.30	1.49	1.58	2.00	120.65***	DO, GED, HS < BHS; DO < HS
Family involvement						
Main interest						
Parent involved in school	1.66	1.70	1.73	1.91	26.30***	DO, GED, HS < BHS
Quality time	3.14	3.04	3.13	3.17	0.33	
Community environment						
Main interest						
Negative peer activities	8.85	8.91	7.99	7.64	13.77***	GED, DO > HS, BHS
Positive peer activities	10.28	10.35	10.44	11.15	23.61***	DO, GED, HS < BHS
Student–teacher ratio	2.32	2.13	2.33	2.33	1.24	
Unemployment rate	2.34	2.15	2.34	2.33	1.19	

[a]For post hoc tests, the statistical significance of between group comparisons was determined at the .05 level.
*** $p < .001$.

those who completed high school as the terminal degree and from those who went beyond high school. GED recipients and high school dropouts, for example, reported the highest percentage of peers engaged in negative activities, 8.91 percent and 8.85 percent respectively, which significantly differed from those with terminal high school degrees (7.99%) and those who went beyond high school (7.64%). Dropouts, GED recipients, and terminal degree high school graduates had comparably greater levels of behavioral/emotional problems and lower levels of parental involvement in schools and positive peer influences than did those who went beyond high school. Although GED recipients had about the same ability as traditional high school graduates, signified by their respective PIAT scores (92.16 vs. 91.88), their mathematical ability was below that of youth whose education went beyond high school (100.18), while above that of dropouts (87.5). No relationship was found between academic achievement status and the unemployment rate of their residence in 1997.

As Table 6.3 shows, three measures of interest distinguished GED recipients from dropouts and all three had to do with characteristics of the adolescents: ability, behavioral/emotional problems, and schools attended. Decreased ability increased the likelihood of adolescents dropping out vis-à-vis obtaining the GED certificate (3% for each point lower on PIAT, OR = .097, $p < .01$), as did attending *fewer* elementary schools (37% for each school, OR = .063, $p < .01$), while more behavioral/emotional problems increased the likelihood of their dropping out (OR = 1.21, $p < .01$). One control measure, region of residence, was also found to distinguish GED recipients from dropouts. Living in the North Central part of the United States increased the odds of dropping out of high school by nearly two times that of obtaining a GED certificate (OR = 1.94, $p < .05$). No differences were found between dropouts or GED recipients in regard to race/ethnicity, sex, or SES.

Only one measure of interest distinguished GED recipients from adolescents who completed high school as the terminal degree. Repeating a grade in elementary school decreased the odds of completing high school by 46 percent (OR = .054, $p < .05$). Three control measures were also found to distinguish GED recipients from adolescents who completed high school as the terminal degree: two ethnicity/race measures and region of residence. Being black non-Hispanic or being Hispanic vis-à-vis being white non-Hispanic increased the odds of completing high school (OR = 2.21 and 2.77, $p < .01$ respectively). Living in the North Central part of the United States increased the odds of completing high school by twice that of obtaining a GED certificate (OR = 2.10, $p < .05$).

As Table 6.3 also shows, four measures of interest distinguished GED recipients from adolescents who had gone beyond high school: two personal characteristics of adolescents (ability and repeating a grade), one parental characteristic (having a responding parent who completed high school), and one family structure characteristic (presence of both parents in the household). Ability was positively related to going beyond high school vis-à-vis obtaining a GED certificate (OR = 1.03, $p < .01$), as was having respondent parents who completed high school (OR = 2.04, $p < .01$) and having both parents in the household (OR = 1.83, $p < .05$), while repeating

Table 6.3
Multinomial Regression: Odds Ratios (OR)

Variable	Academic Achievement Status[a]		
	Dropouts	**High School**	**Beyond High School**
Personal characteristics			
Main interest			
Ability	0.972**	0.992	1.030**
Behavioral problems	1.207**	1.062	0.918
Ever repeat a grade	0.834	0.536*	0.267***
Schools attended	0.632**	0.944	1.286
Control			
Ethnicity/race			
Black Non-Hispanic	1.317	2.212**	2.379**
Hispanic	1.887	2.771**	3.129**
White Non-Hispanic (reference)			
Sex (1 = female)	1.095	1.187	2.070**
Responding parent			
Main interest			
Completed high school	0.738	1.333	2.036**
Control			
Public assistance recipient (ever)	0.837	0.599	0.397***
Family structure			
Main interest			
Presence of mother & father in HH	1.025	1.673	1.831*
Control			
Enriched environment	0.791	1.117	1.734**
Community environment			
Control			
Region of residence			
North Central	1.936*	2.096*	2.014*
South (reference)			
West	1.749	2.533**	2.558**
−2 Log Likelihood	4283.85 (χ^2 = 1110.33, df = 93, $p < .001$)		

Note: Only statistically significant measures are shown.
[a] Reference category is GED.
*** $p < .001$, ** $p < .01$, * $p < .05$.

a grade in elementary school decreased the odds of going beyond high school by 73 percent (OR = 0.27, $p < .001$). Six control measures were also found to distinguish GED recipients from adolescents who went beyond high school: two ethnicity/race measures (black non-Hispanic and Hispanic), sex, one parental characteristic measure (receipt of public assistance), one family structure measure (enriched environment), and one region of residence measure (North Central). Being black non-Hispanic or being Hispanic vis-à-vis being white non-Hispanic increased the odds of going beyond high school vis-à-vis obtaining a GED certificate (OR = 2.38 and 3.13, $p < .01$ respectively), as did being female (OR = 2.07, $p < .01$), living in an enriched family environment (OR = 1.73, $p < .01$), and residing in the North Central part of the United States (OR = 2.01, $p < .01$). Having a responding parent who had been a recipient of public assistance decreased the odds of going beyond high school vis-à-vis obtaining a GED certificate by 60 percent (OR = 0.40, $p < .001$).

DISCUSSION

Findings of the study indicate that only a few of the bivariate correlates of academic achievement status found to be statistically significant are robust when distinguishing adolescents who obtain GED certificates from dropouts, high school completers, and those going beyond high school. This does not extinguish the substantive significance of those measures that still serve as useful markers to identify a pool of adolescents at risk. Socioeconomic status, for example, is one of the substantively significant measures whose statistical significance disappears when controlling for a variety of other personal and environmental measures. Nonetheless, it is important for policymakers and professionals who work with adolescents to know that a far higher percentage of youth residing in poor families drop out of high school than those from middle- and upper-income families and among those who do get the GED or graduate certificates from high school, they are also far less likely to pursue additional education. The multivariate findings suggest that poverty may not per se be the cause of such disparities in academic achievement among adolescents, but the bivariate correlation between SES and academic achievement nonetheless points in the direction of where to locate those less likely to reap the benefits that accrue to those who either complete their high school education at the least or go beyond it.

Race/ethnicity and gender are robust measures of academic attainment. Findings indicate, for example, that although non-Hispanic black and Hispanic youth have higher percentages of dropouts than non-Hispanic white youth, they are more likely to complete high school than to obtain a GED. These findings suggest that if ways can be found to reduce the likelihood of dropping out, non-Hispanic black and Hispanic adolescents have a greater likelihood of completing high school rather than obtaining a GED. Given prior evidence that GED recipients have many longer-term adverse outcomes which are similar to high school dropouts vis-à-vis high school completers, as Richard K. Caputo has shown,[52] such findings suggest that drop-out prevention intervention efforts targeting non-Hispanic black and Hispanic adolescents are warranted.

Findings also suggest that ever repeating a grade in elementary school distinguishes adolescents who obtain GED certificates from high school completers, when controlling for other measures. This finding suggests that social workers, high school counselors, and others interested in adolescents' academic achievements can increase the likelihood of adolescents' completing high school as the terminal degree vis-à-vis obtaining GED certificates by focusing primarily on those who had ever repeated a grade in elementary school. Such efforts would be particularly beneficial to non-Hispanic black and Hispanic youth since they are disproportionately more likely to drop out of high school than are white youth.

Findings also suggest that interventions focusing on adolescents' ability, behavioral/emotional problems, and number of elementary schools attended would also increase the likelihood of obtaining GED certificates. As noted above, however, GED recipients have many longer-term adverse outcomes similar to high school dropouts. Findings of this study suggest that educational resources might be better used by focusing on the identification of factors associated with the likelihood of repeating a grade in elementary school and of remaining in the same schools, and then designing program and policy responses accordingly.

Findings of this study also suggest that resources devoted to improving elementary school children's ability and reducing their behavioral/emotional problems if successful would nonetheless be insufficient in regard to increasing the likelihood of completing high school rather than obtaining GED certificates. This is not to say that ability and behavioral/emotional problems in elementary school are not related to the likelihood of repeating a grade. Rather, findings suggest that other factors, not accounted for in this study, that contribute to repeating a grade in elementary school need to be identified and addressed in order to increase the likelihood that adolescents will complete high school. To ensure that elementary school children obtain the requisite developmental, educational, and social skills to complete all grades without repeating any, findings of this study suggest that resources should be devoted to the identification of such factors and to the design and implementation of program and policy responses accordingly.

To the extent social workers, high school counselors, and others interested in adolescents' academic achievements, however, want to increase the likelihood of adolescents' going beyond high school vis-à-vis obtaining GED certificates, findings of this study point to two other main factors of interest (whether adolescents' parents have high school degrees and whether mothers and fathers are present in the household) and one control factor (sex—that is, women are more likely to go beyond high school than to obtain a GED).

Parental completion of high school is a form of human capital that is positively related to children's academic achievement and findings of this study support those of Haveman and Wolfe.[53] Having two parents in the household signifies greater availability of time and attention of children's developmental and educational needs while in elementary school and findings of this study corroborate those of Sandefur, McLanahan, and Wojtkiewicz.[54] Taken together, these two study findings raise family-related policy issues. Clearly, two-parent households are more likely to provide greater levels of human capital to their children than single-parent households. Policymakers may be more inclined to exhort the virtues of two-parent families and devote resources to such unions rather than to place those resources at the disposal of single-parent families with children of high school age. Such policymakers would be remiss, however, if single parents and their children were left adrift. Findings of this study suggest that resources would be wisely spent when devoted to identification of factors associated with and implementing programs designed to reduce the likelihood of poor performance and repeated grades in elementary school regardless of family structure. Elementary school children from single-parent families, many of whom are likely to be poor, might have greater need with more dire long-term consequences in light of more limited human capital than is the case for children of two-parent families. Attention to non-Hispanic black and Hispanic youth and to a lesser extent to men who currently make up less than half of entering college students and graduates is warranted.

In conclusion, this study examined five major categories of characteristics thought to influence children's academic achievement through high school and beyond with a particular focus on the GED. Socioeconomic status was deemed a suitable marker for locating adolescents most likely to drop out of high school or obtain a GED rather than graduate from or go beyond high school. Ability, behavioral/emotional problems, and number of elementary schools attended were found to be robust predictors of adolescent attainment, distinguishing adolescents who obtain GED certificates from high school dropouts. In the multivariate analyses, no differences were found between dropouts or GED recipients in regard to race/ethnicity, sex, or SES. Being black non-Hispanic or being Hispanic vis-à-vis being white non-Hispanic, however, increased the odds of completing high school and women were more likely to go beyond high school than to obtain a GED. Other findings highlighted the importance of focusing on factors that influence the likelihood of repeating grades in elementary school and remedying these in order to increase the likelihood of completing high school. Corroborating other research, family structure was found to be important in this regard, with single-parent families presenting a formidable obstacle to high school completion vis-à-vis two-parent families. Practice and policy implications were discussed.

NOTES

1. Richard K. Caputo, "Presidents, Profits, Productivity, & Poverty: A Great Divide Between the Pre- & Post-Reagan U.S. Economy?" *Journal of Sociology & Social Welfare* 31(3) (2004): 5–30; Edward N. Wolff, "The Stagnating Fortunes of the Middle Class" in *Should Differences in Income and Wealth Matter?* Ed. Ellen Frankel Paul, Fred D. Miller, and Jeffrey Paul, 55–83 (Cambridge, UK: Cambridge University Press, 2002).

2. U.S. Census Bureau, "Years of School Completed by Poverty Status, Sex, Age, Nativity and Citizenship: 2002 Below 100% of Poverty—All Races Table POV29" (2005). Available at http://pubdb3.census.gov/macro/032005/pov/new29_100_01.htm (accessed October 3, 2005).

3. U.S. Census Bureau, "Table 11: Years of School Completed by Persons 25 Years of Age and Over, by Age, Race, Household Relationship, and Poverty Status: 1992," *Poverty in the United States: 1992. Current Population Reports. Series P60–185* (1993). Available at http://www.census.gov/hhes/www/prevcps/p60-185.pdf (accessed on July 23, 2004).

4. Andrew Sum and Neal Fogg, "The Changing Economic Fortunes of Young Black Men in America," *The Black Scholar* 21(1) (1990): 47–55.

5. Bob Herbert, "An Emerging Catastrophe," *The New York Times*, sec. A17, July 19, 2004.

6. Richard K. Caputo, "The GED as a Signifier of Later-life Health and Economic Well-being," *Race, Gender & Class* 12(2) (2005), 81–103; Richard K. Caputo, "The GED as a Predictor of Mid-life Health and Economic Well-being," *Journal of Poverty* 9(4) (2005): 69–93.

7. Samuel Bowles and Herbert Gintis, "Schooling in Capitalist America Revisited," *Sociology of Education* 75(1) (2002): 1–18; Richard K. Caputo, *Advantage White and Male, Disadvantage Black and Female: Income Inequality, Economic Well-being and Economic Mobility Among Families in a Youth Cohort, 1979–1993* (Danbury, CT: Rutledge Books, Inc., 1999).

8. For example, see Avner Ahituv and Mark Tienda, "Employment, Motherhood, and School Continuation Decisions of Young White, Black, and Hispanic Women," *Journal of Labor Economics* 22(1) (2004): 115–158; David Boesel, Nabeel Alsalam, and Thomas M. Smith, *Research Synthesis: Educational and Labor Market Performance of GED Recipients* (Washington, DC: U.S. Department of Education, 1998). Available at http://www.ed.gov/PDFDocs/GED/gedfront.pdf (accessed onDecember 19, 2005); Doris R. Entwisle, Karl L. Alexander, and Linda Steffel Olson, "Temporary as Compared to Permanent High School Dropout," *Social Forces* 82(3) (2004): 1181–1205; Kathryn Hoffman, Charmaine Llagas, and Thomas D. Snyder, *Status and Trends in the Education of Blacks* (Washington, DC: U.S. Department of Education, National Center for Education Statistics, 2003). Available at http://nces.ed.gov/pubs2003/2003034.pdf (accessed on December 19, 2005); Jonathan Jacobson, Cara Olsen, Jennifer King Rice, Stephen Sweetland, and John Ralph, *Educational Achievement and Black-White Inequality.* NCES 2001-061 (U.S. Department of Education, National Center for Education Statistics, 2001). Available at http://nces.ed.gov/pubs2001/2001061.PDF (accessed on October 22, 2005); Steven Klein, Rosio Bugarin, Renee Beltranena, and Edith McArthur, *Language Minorities and Their Educational and Labor Market Indicators—Recent Trends.* Statistical Analysis Report (Washington, DC: U.S. Department of Education, National Center for Education Statistics, 2004). Available at http://nces.ed.gov/pubs2004/2004009.pdf (accessed on December 19, 2005); Timothy Landrum, Antonis Katsiyannis, and Teara Archwamety, "An Analysis of Placement and Exit Patterns of Students with Emotional or Behavioral Disorders," *Behavioral Disorders* 29(2) (2004): 140–153.

9. As suggested in Caputo, "The GED . . . Later-life," 81–103 and "The GED . . . Mid-life," 69–93.

10. Russell W. Rumberger, "High School Dropouts: A Review of Issues and Evidence," *Review of Educational Research* 57(2) (1987): 101–121.

11. For example, see Carl F. Kaestle, Anne Campbell, Jeremy D. Finn, Sylvia T. Johnson, and Larry J. Mikulecky, *Adult Literacy and Education in America: Four Studies Based on the National Adult Literacy Survey* (Washington, DC: National Center for Education Statistics, 2001). Available at http://nces.ed.gov/pubs2001/2001534.pdf accessed on December 19, 2005) which reported literacy equivalence between GED recipients and high school graduates.

12. Philip Gleason and Mark Dynarski, "Do We Know Whom to Serve? Issues in Using Risk Factors to Identify Dropouts," *Journal of Education for Students Placed at Risk* 7(1) (2002): 25–41; Gary D. Sandefur, Sara McLanahan, and Roger A. Wojtkiewicz, "The Effects of Parental Marital Status During Adolescence on High School Graduation," *Social Forces* 71(1) (1992): 103–121.

13. U.S. Congress, "Goals 2000: Educate America Act," *Public Law 103–227* (1994). Available at http://frwebgate.access.gpo.gov/cgi-bin/getdoc.cgi?dbname=103_cong_bills&docid=f:h1804enr.txt.pdf (accessed December 19, 2005).

14. U.S. Congress, "No Child Left Behind Act of 2001," *Public Law 107–110* (2002). Available at http://www.ed.gov/policy/elsec/leg/esea02/index.html (accessed on December 19, 2005).

15. American Council on Education, "GED exam surpasses one million adult test takers in 2001. Start of new exam sparks record participation," *ACE News*, July 31, 2002. Washington, DC: Author http://www.acenet.edu/news/press_release/2002/07july/ged.release.html (accessed July 24, 2004); Richard J. Murane, John B. Willett, and Katheryn Parker Boudett, "Do High School Dropouts Benefit from Obtaining a GED? *Educational Evaluation and Policy Analysis* 17(2) (1995): 133–147.

16. Karen W. Arenson, "More Youths Opt for G.E.D., Skirting High School Hurdle," *New York Times*, May 15, 2004, available at http://www.nytimes.com/2004/05/15/education/15GED.html?pagewanted=print&position= (accessed on December 19, 2005); Dierdre Glenn Paul, "The Train Has Left: The No Child Left Behind Act Leaves Black and Latino Literacy Learners Waiting at the Station," *Journal of Adolescent and Adult Literacy* 47(8) (2004): 648–656; John R. Rachal and Millard J. Bingham, "The Adolescentizing of the GED," *Adult Basic Education* 14(1) (2004): 32–44.

17. Rumberger, "High School Dropouts."

18. James Samuel Coleman, E.Q. Campbell, C.F. Hobson, J.M. McPortland, A.M. Mood, F.D. Weinfeld, and R.L. York, *Equality of Educational Opportunity* (Washington, DC: GPO, 1996). Also, see Judy A. Temple, Arthur J. Reynolds, and Wendy T. Miedel, *Can Early Intervention Prevent High School Dropout? Evidence from the Chicago Child-parent Centers*. Institute for Research on Poverty Discussion Paper No. 1180–98 (1998). Available at http://www.irp.wisc.edu/publications/dps/pdfs/dp118098.pdf (accessed on October 24, 2005), Russell W. Rumberger and Scott L. Thomas, "The Distribution of Dropout and Turnover Rates among Urban and Suburban High Schools," *Sociology of Education* 73(1) (2000): 39–67, and Doris R. Entwisle, Karl L. Alexander, and Linda Steffel Olson, "First Grade and Educational Attainment by Age 22: A New Story," *American Journal of Sociology* 110(5) (2005): 1458–1502.

19. For example, see Anonymous, "GED students' skills above other grads'," *Training & Development* 45(11) (2001): 14; Steven V. Cameron and James J. Heckman, "The Nonequivalence of High School Equivalents," *Journal of Labor Economics* 11(1) (1993): 1–47; Jay P Greene, "GEDs Aren't Worth the Paper They're Printed On," *City Journal* 12(1) (2002): 82–87. Available at http://www.city-journal.org/html/12_1_geds_arent.html (accessed on December 19, 2005).

20. Anonymous, "Minorities Have '50–50' Chance of Graduating High School, Study Finds," *Black Issues in Higher Educatio* 21(3) (2004): 9; J.A. Klerman, and L.A. Karoly, *The Transition to Stable Employment: The Experience of U.S.Yyouth in Their Early Labor Market Career*. MR-564-NCRVE/UCB (Berkeley, CA: National Center for Research in Vocational Education/RAND, 1995). Available at http://www.rand.org/publications/MR/MR564/ (accessed on December 19, 2005); Andrew Sum and Paul Harrington, *The Hidden Crisis in the High School Dropout Problems of Young Adults in the U.S.: Recent Trends in Overall School Dropout Rates and Gender Differences in Dropout Behavior*. (Boston, MA: Center for Labor Market Studies, Northeastern University/Washington, DC: The Business Roundtable, 2003). Available at http://www.businessroundtable.org/pdf/914.pdf (accessed on October 24, 2005); Beth Aronstamm Young, *Public High School Dropouts and Completers from the Common Core of Data: School Year 2000–01* (Washington, DC: U.S. Department of Education, National Center for Education Statistics, 2003). Available at http://nces.ed.gov/pubs2004/2004310.pdf (accessed on December 19, 2005).

21. Anonymous, "The Fate of Dropouts," *Black Issues in Higher Education* 21(9) (2004): 112.

22. Jay D. Teachman, Kathleen Paasch, and Karen Carver, "Social Capital and Dropping Out of School Early," *Journal of Marriage and the Family* 58(3) (1996): 773–783.

23. Brenda J. Lohman, Laura D. Pittman, Rebekah Levine Coley, and P. Lindsay Chase-Lansdale, "Welfare History, Sanctions, and Developmental Outcomes Among Low-income Children and Youth," *Social Service Review* 78(1) (2004): 41–73.

24. John Comings, Stephen Reder, and Andrew Sum, *Building a Level Playing Field: The Need to Expand and Improve the National and State Adult Education and Literacy Systems.* NCSALL Occasional Paper (2001). Available at http://www.ncsall.net/fileadmin/resources/research/op_comings2.pdf (accessed on December 19, 2005).

25. Caputo, "The GED . . . Later-life," and "The GED . . . Mid-life," 69–93.

26. GED Testing Service of the American Council on Education, Trends in the Number of GED Candidates Who Tested, Completed, and Passed GED Tests: 1994–2003. (Washington, DC: Author, 2005). Available at http://www.acenet.edu/AM/Template.cfm?Section=GEDTS&Template=/CM/ContentDisplay.cfm&ContentID=11865 (accessed on December 22, 2005).

27. GED Testing Service, "Table 1: Target Population of Adults without High School Diplomas," *GED Statistical Report 2003.* Available at http://www.acenet.edu/AM/Template.cfm?Section=GEDTS&Template=/CM/ContentDisplay.cfm&ContentID=11506 (accessed on December 22, 2005).

28. American Council on Education, "GED Exam Surpasses One Million Adult Test Takers in 2001. Start of New Exam Sparks Record Participation," *ACE News,* July 31, 2002. Available at http://www.acenet.edu/news/press_release/2002/07july/ged.release.html (accessed on July 24, 2004).

29. John H. Tyler, "Economic Benefits of the GED Lessons from Recent Research," *Review of Educational Research* 73(3) (2003): 369–403.

30. CBO, "S. 1627 Workforce Investment Act Amendments of 2003. Congressional Budget Office Cost Estimate." Available at http://www.cbo.gov/showdoc.cfm?index=4709&sequence=0 (accessed on December 22, 2005).

31. U.S. Department of Education, "Adult Education—Basic Grants to States." Available at http://www.ed.gov/programs/adultedbasic/2005allot.html (accessed on November 27, 2005).

32. National Center for Education Statistics, "Fast Facts." Available at http://nces.ed.gov/fastfacts/display.asp?id=16 (accessed on May 10, 2006.)

33. National Center for Education Statistics, "Event dropout rates by family income, 1972–2001." Available at http://nces.ed.gov/programs/coe/2004/section3/indicator16.asp (accessed on May 10, 2006).

34. Robert Haveman and Barbara Wolfe, "The determinants of children's attainments: A review of methods and findings," *Journal of Economic Literature* 33(4) (1995): 1829–1878.

35. Each of the eight studies relied on the following data files: The Michigan Panel Study of Income Dynamics (PSID), the High School and Beyond Survey (HSB), the Public Use Microdata Sample (PUMS), the National Longitudinal Survey of Youth (NLSY), the Current Population Survey (CPS), and the National Longitudinal Survey (NLS).

36. Sandefur et al., "The Effects of Parental Marital Status During Adolescence on High School Graduation."

37. Karen A. Randolph, Roderick A. Rose, Mark W. Fraser, and Dennis K. Orthner, "Examining the Impact of Changes in Maternal Employment on High School Completion among Low-income Youth," *Journal of Family and Economic Issues* 25(3) (2004): 279–299.

38. Rumberger, "High School Dropouts."

39. Beth Spenciter Rosenthal, "Non-school Correlates of Dropout: An Integrative Review of the Literature," *Children and Youth Services Review* 20(5) (1998): 413–433.

40. Sandefur et al., "The Effects of Parental Marital Status During Adolescence on High School Graduation."

41. Lisa D. Pearce, and Dana L. Haynie, "Intergenerational Religious Dynamics and Adolescent Delinquency," *Social Forces* 82(4) (2004): 1553–1572.

42. Haveman and Wolfe, "The determinants of children's attainments."

43. Rosenthal, "Non-school Correlates of Dropout."

44. Roberto Agodini and Mark Dynarski, *Understanding the Trend Toward Alternative Certification for High School Graduates* (Princeton, NJ: Mathematica Policy Research, 1998). Available at http://www.mathematica-mpr.com/publications/PDFs/dod-ged.pdf (accessed on December 22, 2005).

45. Caputo, "The GED . . . Later-life," and "The GED . . . Mid-life," 69–93.

46. Rosenthal, "Non-school Correlates of Dropout."

47. Center for Human Resource Research, *NLSY97 User's Guide: A Guide to the Rounds 1–5 Data National Longitudinal Survey of Youth 1997* (Columbus, OH: The Ohio State University, 2003).

48. F.C. Markwardt, *Peabody Individual Achievement Test-Revised* (Circle Pines, MN: American Guidance Service, Inc, 1998).

49. Center for Human Resource Research, *NLSY97 Codebook Supplement Main File Round 1* (Columbus, OH: The Ohio State University, 1999).

50. Richard K. Caputo, "Head Start and School-to-Work Program Participation," *Journal of Poverty* 8(2) (2004): 25–42; Richard K. Caputo, "The Impact of Intergenerational Head Start Participation on Success Measures Among Adolescent Children," *Journal of Economic and Family Issues* 25(2) (2004): 199–223.

51. Susan L. Brown, "Family Structure and Child Well-being: The Significance of Parental Cohabitation," *Journal of Marriage and Family* 66(2) (2004): 351–367; Wendy D. Manning, and Kathleen A. Lamb, "Adolescent Well-being in Cohabitating, Married, and Single-parent Families," *Journal of Marriage and Family* 65(4) (2003): 876–893; Teachman et al., "Social Capital and Dropping Out of School Early," 773–783.

52. See note 6.

53. See note 43.

54. See note 15.

CHAPTER 7

BETWEEN THE LINES, ON THE STAGE, AND IN THE CLUB: ADDITIONAL WAYS STUDENTS FIND TO OVERCOME DISADVANTAGE THROUGH SCHOOL

Jason M. Smith

The title of this volume, *The Promise of Education*, conjures particular images—students taking notes in class, studying hard, taking exams, "doing well in school" and thereby improving their social status by graduating, going to college, and so forth. Attention to success through education ordinarily focuses on these academic and cognitive pathways, and well they should. Achievement in grade school and high school is well linked to "success" in life, in terms of further educational attainment, as well as occupational attainment, income, and so forth.

But, as Samuel Bowles and Herbert Gintis note, "[S]chooling does more than enhance cognitive skills."[1] Many scholars have investigated the ways in which schools affect the habits and styles students adopt,[2] and the social networks in which students are embedded.[3] From the work of these authors and others, it can be seen that schools provide sites for the development of knowledge beyond the academic: social skills and relationships, work habits, and hopes for the future. Schools are places where young people come into contact with people who can guide them into successful adult lives by setting positive examples for them to follow; by helping them to develop attitudes and behaviors directed towards achievement and contributing to society in positive ways; and by providing information about opportunities that may be open.

School is also where students are involved with other students, learning from the activities, relationships, attitudes, and knowledge of these peers. The importance of school in the social world of the adolescent has been well established, going back at least to James S. Coleman's work on *The Adolescent Society*.[4] One of the most important lessons from that work is that, in the lives of adolescents, many school-related things are of great importance, but not all of them are academic or classroom-related. Prime among these is the extracurriculum. Students were asked, "If you could be remembered here at school for one of the three things below, which one would you want it to be: brilliant student, athletic star [for boys]/leader in activities [for girls], or most popular?" The most common response for boys was athletic star (44.4%), and for girls it was leader in activities (37.0%).

Like the classroom regimen, participating in extracurricular activities may provide students with advantages noted above and prior scholarship has borne this out. James Shulman and William Bowen's 2001 book, *The Game of Life*,[5] demonstrated how high school athletes receive an admission advantage at some of America's most elite universities, an advantage greater than that of legacies or racial minorities. With the ever-increasing numbers of applicants, and the ever-increasing demands for a college degree to gain entry into the job market, gaining admission to college is becoming more and more competitive. Students from disadvantaged backgrounds face more obstacles than most, from higher rates of dropping out and lower standardized test scores, to less encouragement to attend and poorer preparation for higher education, and a lack of information on or contact with colleges and financial aid.[6]

While prior studies have shown evidence of positive effects of participation, no studies have focused exclusively on students from "high poverty schools."[7] It is possible that the dynamics and benefits of participating in school-sponsored activities may function differently for these students when compared with others. This chapter will pursue this line of inquiry by investigating the effects of extracurricular participation on a student's odds of dropping out of high school, of graduating from high school, and of attending some form of postsecondary education (PSE), focusing exclusively on students from high-poverty schools.

RECENT SCHOLARSHIP ON THE EXTRACURRICULUM

The extracurriculum has garnered renewed interest of late in the sociological literature. As noted, the activities that schools provide students beyond the classroom have long been of interest to social scientists, but recently sociological inquiry into the effects of extracurricular participation has been renewed and expanded. Past studies have shown that participation in the extracurriculum has positive effects on educational aspirations and attainment,[8] occupational aspirations and attainment,[9] and earnings.[10] More recently, the resurgence of interest in the extracurriculum has replicated these findings.[11] Joseph Mahoney[12] and Ralph McNeal[13] separately showed that participation increases the odds of completing (i.e., not dropping out of) high school, while J. Eccles and B. Barber[14] found that participation in extracurricular activities decreased risk-taking behavior.

What is there about participation in extracurricular activities that explains these findings? Extracurricular participation can be a place for learning skills (e.g., teamwork, goal formation), and for forming relationships that surround a student with peers and adults that foster mobility. Michael Hanks and Bruce Eckland[15] found that participation placed students in a peer group that was more college- and achievement-oriented. Andrew Guest and Barbara Schneider[16] employed both community and school contexts, as well as individual identity, to explain the beneficial outcomes of participation in sports and nonsports on both achievement and ambition. They found that a student in a lower- or middle-class school who thinks of him/herself as an athlete is seen by others as a better student, and is more likely to get higher grades and go on to college. They also found that, in schools with higher academic expectations and higher socioeconomic makeup, taking part in nonsport activities leads a participant to be seen as a better student.

Beckett Broh[17] showed strong evidence that social capital may be the mechanism for the positive outcomes of extracurricular participation. Broh notes that social capital is both a mechanism for social control, as well as information and resource dissemination, provided that the people involved have some resource(s) they are willing and able to share. In the case of extracurriculars and educational outcomes, these resources could include information on colleges, advice on application procedures, tips regarding applying for financial aid or taking college entrance exams, or even connections with admissions officers. Participation in school activities generally increases student–parent contact, student–teacher interaction, and parent–school connections, and that this explains much of the positive effect of participation on math and English grades in twelfth grade. Curtis, McTeer, and White[18] also acknowledged the importance of the concept of capital, using ideas of cultural, physical, and social capital in their "General Theoretical Interpretations" section, though they did not include them empirically in their analyses.

In addition to the more developed theoretical and empirical incorporation of social capital, Broh's study also goes beyond the usual sports/nonsports dichotomy to decompose participation into various categories, including interscholastic sports vs. intramural, music groups, drama, student council, journalism, and vocational clubs. This sort of breakdown of activities was first employed (in similar, but slightly different form) in McNeal's analysis of the effects of participation on dropout rates noted above. Activities have different demographics and prestige within the school, and, therefore, put participants into contact with diverse groups of peers and provide differing levels of status within the school. This differential context will cause various activities to have variable effects on participants and their outcomes.

As evidenced by the more theoretically developed approaches of McNeal; Broh; Curtis, McTeer, and White; and Guest and Schneider, the approach social scientists are taking in order to understand the effects of extracurricular participation is improving. However, other shortcomings exist in most of the literature that have not been addressed fully. Most of the previous studies produced results that were not generalizable to the entire high school population, since the data were often regional, and are now quite dated. Furthermore, many of the above studies only included males.

There are numerous problems with the extant literature because of these factors. Getting some form of postsecondary education has come to be a much more necessary part of occupational attainment in the last 35 years, given the restructuring of the U.S. economy. More people are able to attend higher education thanks to Affirmative Action and other legislation. In addition, the athletic enterprise has become much more important and influential in college admissions, thus having been a high school athlete in the last 15 to 20 years is more important than in the early samples studied by previous literature (see Shulman and Bowen's work for an extensive and enlightening discussion of this phenomenon). Furthermore, females have seen greatly increased opportunities to pursue sports. Female athletic opportunities were rather limited until the 1970s with the advent of Title IX in 1972, and even for years after that as institutions failed to implement changes required by that law. Not until the late 1970s to early '80s did the government even begin to pursue seriously enforcement of the statute. Rates of participation, and the lower level of intensity of what participation there was, made it unlikely that any effects for females would exist or be significant (statistically or substantively.) This is likely no longer the case, but the outcomes for girls are not as well documented as for boys in this area of extracurriculars.

Additionally, with the exception of the study by Broh and that by McNeal, most previous studies only consider extracurriculars in terms of sports, equating the effects of playing football and being on the swim team, or only compare sports with non-sports, ignoring the differences between vocational clubs and school music groups. Few of these studies explicitly include other activities like drama, journalism, or music, and when they do these activities usually are considered as an aggregate—extracurriculars in general, or only differentiating between "sport" and "nonsport" activities. As already noted, different types of activities have different demographics and, therefore, differential social influences on participants. Therefore, they may have different effects, and aggregating them all simply as "extracurriculars" can mask the effects of certain endeavors or make others look more (or less) facilitating than they are.

Clearly, research with more recent data from nationally representative samples that analyzes the effects of different types of activities is needed. Furthermore, with the advances of women in the realm of sport, as well as higher education and the labor force, incorporation of females is requisite when attempting to quantify the effects of participation for student outcomes. Such research will be more convincing for policy concerns, giving decision makers direct evidence of programs and activities that improve the life chances of high schoolers. To begin to fill these gaps in the literature, this study employs a nationally representative dataset collected between 1988 and 2000, that includes both males and females, and subdivides participation into more specific categories than "sport vs. nonsport".

The rest of this chapter will focus only on students from schools with at least half of their student bodies eligible for free- or reduced-price lunch. The analyses will investigate whether participants in extracurriculars have different rates of graduating from high school and of attending some form of postsecondary education (PSE). Based on prior research, these analyses can be expected to show that participation is associated with higher rates of graduation, as well as increased rates of postsecondary attendance.

DATA AND MEASURES

The data for these analyses comes from the National Education Longitudinal Study (NELS), with data most recently from 2000. This nationally representative sample

Table 7.1
Descriptive Statistics

Measure	Description	Mean (SD)
Female	Indicator for female students (1 = Yes)	0.498
Hispanic	Indicator for Hispanic students (1 = Yes)	0.31
Black	Indicator for black students (1 = Yes)	0.255
General participation	Participant in any extracurricular activity (1 = Yes)	0.794
Total participation	Total # of categories of activities in which student participated	1.656 (1.34)
High Profile sport	Participant in football, basketball, baseball, softball (1 = Yes)	0.274
Low Profile sport	Participant in soccer, swimming, other team sport, or other individual sport (1 = Yes)	0.215
Cheerleading	Participant in cheerleading, drill, or pompom team (1 = Yes)	0.075
Fine arts	Participant in band, choir, or drama (1 = Yes)	0.26
Academic clubs	Participant In science fair, academic honor society or academic clubs (1 = Yes)	0.272
Student government	Participant in student government (1 = Yes)	0.057
Social clubs	Participant in yearbook/newspaper, service, hobby, or vocational ed clubs (1 = Yes)	0.414
Drop out	Indicates if student dropped out between 10th and 12th grade (1 = Yes)	0.145
HS grade	Indicates if student received high school diploma (1 = Yes)	0.81
Any PSE	Indicates if student attended any postsecondary education (1 = Yes)	0.551
	Total N	1,445

of over 12,000 students follows students from the eighth grade until eight years after high school graduation (or what should have been their year of graduation, in the case of those who did not finish on time or at all.) Data on student background and extracurricular participation in a range of activities are available, as well as school characteristics. The dataset also includes whether or not the student graduated from high school, and what (if any) postsecondary institution they attended.

The full NELS 2000 sample ($n = 12,144$) was reduced to include only those students who had not dropped out before tenth grade, and then subsequently to include only those students who attended a high school where at least 50 percent of the student body was eligible for free or reduced-price lunches (a "high-poverty" school). This left a sample of $n = 1445$ for the analyses. Descriptive statistics of student demographics are in Table 7.1.

The measures for student participation were derived from a number of items in the NELS survey. Students were asked to self-report participation in a variety of school-based activities, ranging from various team and individual sports (e.g., football, swimming) to other activities like drama club or science fair. For the current research, participation was categorized into seven areas:

1) High Profile Sports—including interscholastic baseball (softball for females), basketball, and/or football

2) Low Profile Sports—including any other sport, either team or individual; e.g., soccer, swimming, etc.

3) Cheerleading/Drill Team/PomPom Squad

4) Fine Arts—any sort of band, choir, or drama group

5) Academic Activities—academic clubs, honor societies, science fair, etc.

6) Student Government

7) Social and Occupational Activities—journalism/yearbook club, vocational education clubs like Future Teachers of America, plus service clubs and hobby groups

If a student participated in any one (or more) of the activities listed under the category, that student was coded as "1" for that variable. Variables for General ("Did the student participate in *any* activity?" Yes = 1) and Total participation (the number of the above categories in which a student participated) were also included. For example, a female student who played basketball, softball, and golf, as well as being in the drama club and serving as vice-president of her class would be a "Yes" for the general extracurricular participation variable (she was involved in the extracurriculum), a "4" on the total extracurricular participation variable (she was involved in High Profile Sports, Low Profile Sports, Fine Arts activities, and Student Government), and a "Yes" for each of those individual categories as well.

The outcome measures are dichotomous variables (1 = Yes) for Graduating from High School, and for attending some form of Postsecondary Education (PSE). Graduating from high school does *not* include obtaining a GED, since labor market studies have shown that the outcomes for GED holders are more akin to dropouts than holders of the diploma.[19] As they note in their abstract, "Exam-certified high school equivalents are statistically indistinguishable from high school dropouts." For this study, PSE includes *any* form of formal education completed after high school (except military training), from short courses at a local vocational/technical college to attendance at a 4-year university. The underlying idea is that participation in extracurriculars helps bond students to the educational system, encouraging and enabling them to persist within it to higher levels of attainment.

RESULTS

The results show a remarkable level of consistency. Across the board, graduation rates and rates of attendance in Postsecondary education are nearly always higher for those who participated in the extracurriculum than for those who do not participate at all. Whether these rates are analyzed by gender, race, or both simultaneously, being involved in school-related activities has positive effects on the percentages of

Table 7.2
Graduation and PSE Attendance Rates by Gender and Extracurriculars

	Boys	**Girls**
A. Graduation Rates		
No participation	72.3	69.2
Some participation		
1+ activities	82.1	85.3
1 category	79.5	81.5
2–3 categories	83.3	88.0
4+ categories	85.7	87.1
Categories		
High profile sport	82.4	80.4
Low profile sport	88.0	87.4
Cheerleading	77.3	81.4
Fine arts	87.2	88.1
Academic clubs	84.1	88.4
Student government	74.4	93.0
Social activities	78.4	84.9
n	725	720
B. PSE Attendance Rates		
No participation	43.2	44.1
Some participation		
1+ Activities	53.5	62.6
1 Category	42.3	55.0
2–3 Categories	58.2	68.6
4+ Categories	68.6	64.3
Categories		
High oprofile sport	56.7	52.3
Low profile sport	67.8	63.8
Cheerleading	63.6	67.4
Fine arts	59.1	68.1
Academic clubs	56.9	65.8
Student government	64.1	76.7
Social activities	50.5	60.3
n	725	720

students who graduate from high school and continue their educations after high school.

Tables 7.2A and 7.2B show the rates of high school graduation and postsecondary attendance separately for male and female students, based on their participation in the extracurriculum. For graduation rates, approximately 70 percent of both male and female nonparticipants graduated from high school, 69.2 percent for girls and 72.3 percent for boys. These rates increase to 85.3 percent and 82.1 percent, respectively, for students who took part in at least one extracurricular activity. Being involved in multiple categories of extracurriculars further increases the rates of graduation, to a high of 88.0 percent for girls in 2 or 3 categories, and to 85.7 percent for boys in 4 or more categories. Each category of activities also graduates a higher proportion of its participants than the rate for those who do not participate in extracurriculars. For girls, these rates range from a low of 80.4 percent of High Profile Sport athletes, to a high of 93 percent for those in Student Government; for boys, the range is from 74.4 percent for Student Government to 88.0 percent for Low Profile Sports.

For Postsecondary Attendance, 44.1 percent of nonparticipant girls and 43.2 percent of nonparticipant boys go on to some form of formal educational training after high school. These rates are also increased appreciably for those who take part in the extracurriculum. Of the girls who were involved in any activity, 62.6 percent graduated; for boys the corresponding figure is 53.5 percent. Again, breadth of participation further enhances the rates of attendance, to a high of 68.6 percent for girls in 2–3 categories, and to 68.6 percent for boys in 4+ categories. As with graduation, PSE attendance is greater for those in each of the extracurricular categories than for nonparticipants. The lowest rate of PSE attendance for girls is in High Profile Sport (52.3%), and the highest is for Fine Arts (68.1%). For boys, 50.5 percent of those in Social Activities attend some form of PSE, while 67.8 percent of those in Low Profile Sports continued their educations after high school.

Tables 7.3A and 7.3B present the same set of outcomes, this time broken down by student race. White students not involved in the extracurriculum graduate 70.1 percent of the time, while the general participant graduation rate for whites is 87.3 percent. For blacks, 67.2 percent of nonparticipants and 78.9 percent of general participants graduate, while 74.7 percent of Hispanic nonparticipants and 81.7 percent of participants graduate. As with the gender-based analyses, being involved in a broader set of activities (i.e., multiple categories of extracurriculars) is positively associated with graduation rates. White and black students involved in 4 or more categories have the highest rates of graduation, 92.2 percent and 85.0 percent, respectively. For Hispanics, the highest rate is for those in 2–3 categories, 88.0 percent. For the various categories of activities, the graduation rates of participants are all measurably higher than the rate for nonparticipants (with one exception). White students range from 87.0 percent graduates (in Social Activities) to 92.0 percent (Student Government). Black students involved in the extracurriculum vary between 75.5 percent graduates (Social Activities) and 82.5 percent (Fine Arts), while Hispanic students fall between 71.4 percent for cheerleaders (the exception to the pattern), and 89.1 percent for Fine Arts.

In terms of attendance in PSE, 42.1 percent of white non-participants attend, compared to 59.7 percent of those involved in at least one activity. Non-participating black students attend PSE 37.5 percent of the time, while more than half—51.3 percent—of those black students active in the extracurriculum further their education after high school. Hispanic students who do not take part in any school-related activities attend PSE 46.5 percent of the time, outpaced by participants who go on in school 59.0 percent of the time. As before, those involved in more categories of activities have higher rates of PSE attendance, paralleling the results for graduation

Table 7.3
Graduation and PSE Attendance Rates by Race and Extracurriculars

	Whites	Blacks	Hispanics
A. Graduation Rates			
No participation	70.1	67.2	74.7
Some participation			
1+ Activities	87.3	78.9	81.7
1 Category	83.7	76.4	76.0
2–3 Categories	88.8	79.6	88.0
4+ Categories	92.2	85.0	74.1
Categories			
High profile sport	88.1	77.1	79.3
Low profile sport	89.5	82.2	88.8
Cheerleading	88.6	77.1	71.4
Fine arts	90.8	82.5	89.1
Academic clubs	88.6	82.4	86.0
Student government	92.0	76.0	80.0
Social activities	87.0	75.5	77.0
n	484	368	448
B. PSE Attendance Rates			
No participation	42.1	37.5	46.5
Some participation			
1+ Activities	59.7	51.3	59.0
1 Category	45.2	40.6	51.3
2–3 Categories	67.6	56.7	65.9
4+ Categories	70.6	60.0	59.3
Categories			
High profile sport	60.3	47.5	57.8
Low profile sport	73.3	50.7	68.4
Cheerleading	74.3	60.0	71.4
Fine arts	66.7	63.5	62.0
Academic clubs	63.8	55.1	62.4
Student government	76.0	60.0	70.0
Social activities	57.9	51.6	51.3
n	484	368	448

with white and black students in 4+ categories having the highest rates, and 2–3 categories showing the highest rates for Hispanics. Also reflecting the overall pattern of results discussed so far, the rates of PSE attendance vary between the different kinds of activities, but all exceed the rates for nonparticipants. Among white students, those in Student Government attend PSE most often, 76.0 percent, while the lowest rate is for those in Social Activities, 57.9 percent—still well above the 42 percent of nonparticipants. The highest rate among black students is for those in Fine Arts

Table 7.4
Graduation and PSE Rates by Race & Extracurriculars—Boys Only

	Whites	Blacks	Hispanics
A. Graduation Rates			
No participation	70.5	70.6	77.3
Some participation			
1+ Activities	85.1	77.7	80.4
1 Category	81.4	76.4	74.3
2–3 Categories	84.8	79.5	86.4
4+ Categories	96.0	78.3	72.7
Categories			
High profile sport	86.8	78.9	80.0
Low profile sport	88.1	85.4	88.5
Cheerleading	50.0	81.8	83.3
Fine arts	88.9	81.0	93.5
Academic clubs	88.4	78.5	84.3
Student government	92.3	60.0	71.4
Social activities	85.1	67.2	71.7
n	256	191	207
B. PSE Rates			
No participation	41.0	35.3	45.5
Some participation			
1+ Activities	58.5	43.3	55.2
1 Category	37.1	32.7	45.7
2–3 Categories	69.7	46.2	60.5
4+ Categories	72.0	60.9	72.7
Categories			
High profile sport	63.7	48.9	57.6
Low profile sport	77.6	52.1	69.2
Cheerleading	50.0	54.5	100.0
Fine arts	66.7	56.9	54.8
Academic clubs	62.8	44.6	61.4
Student government	69.2	53.3	85.7
Social activities	57.9	38.8	45.0
n	256	191	207

(63.5%), and the lowest is 47.5 percent for High Profile Sport athletes—a full 10 percent above the nonparticipant rate. Hispanic students show similar differences in PSE attendance rates, ranging from a high of 71.4 percent (for Cheerleaders) to a low of 51.3 percent (for those in Social Activities).

Tables 7.4 and 7.5 (each with parts A and B) disaggregate participants by both race and gender. As before, with only minor exceptions, participants in the extracurriculum

Table 7.5
Graduation and PSE Rates by Race & Extracurriculars—Girls Only

	Whites	Blacks	Hispanics
A. Graduation Rates			
No participation	69.6	63.3	72.7
Some participation			
1+ Activities	89.6	80.3	82.8
1 Category	86.2	76.5	77.4
2–3 Categories	93.3	79.7	89.5
4+ Categories	88.5	94.1	75.0
Categories			
High profile sport	91.4	71.4	77.4
Low profile sport	92.1	76.0	89.1
Cheerleading	93.5	75.0	68.2
Fine arts	92.0	83.8	86.9
Academic clubs	88.9	85.9	87.4
Student government	91.7	100.0	84.6
Social activities	89.2	81.5	80.4
n	228	177	241
B. PSE Rates			
No participation	43.5	40.0	47.3
Some participation			
1+ Activities	61.0	59.9	62.4
1 Category	53.8	49.0	56.0
2–3 Categories	65.2	67.1	70.9
4+ Categories	69.2	58.8	50.0
Categories			
High profile sport	51.4	42.9	58.1
Low profile sport	65.8	48.0	67.4
Cheerleading	77.4	62.5	63.6
Fine arts	66.7	69.1	65.6
Academic clubs	64.6	64.8	63.2
Student government	83.3	70.0	61.5
Social activities	57.8	60.9	55.4
n	228	177	241

graduate and attend PSE at higher rates than nonparticipants, regardless of race or gender, whether we consider extracurricular participation in general, by total number of categories, or by individual categories. For both boys and girls, of any race, being involved in the extracurriculum, especially in a variety of different types of activities, increases the odds of both graduating from high school and of continuing one's education at the postsecondary level.

DISCUSSION AND CONCLUSIONS

Students from high-poverty schools face challenges above and beyond those of av-erage adolescents. Outcomes associated with going to such disadvantaged schools in-clude poorer graduation rates and a lower likelihood of continuing education beyond the secondary level. Low high-school completion rates are a persistent and pernicious problem in high-poverty areas, which, when coupled with the ever-increasing need for further education to garner success in the labor force, only serves to further the disadvantage suffered by those in areas serviced by these schools. Many programs and public policies aim to trump these obstacles and improve the educational attainment of students from these types of schools, and the findings from this analysis contribute to that effort. Each of the above analyses has indicated the value of extracurricular participation for students of either gender, and of various racial backgrounds. Those who participate in extracurricular activities have higher graduation rates and higher rates of attendance in postsecondary education programs than those students who do not take part in school-based activities. Each category of extracurriculars also showed these patterns.

Why this occurs has been explored, if indirectly, in previous research. Hanks and Eckland note that students who plan to go to college, who routinely associated with college-oriented peers, and who discussed their plans with teachers were more likely to take part in the extracurriculum. This suggests a possible explanation for the pattern of results found here. Being involved in extracurriculars puts one in contact with a more academically oriented peer group, which in turn "rubs off" and serves to focus a person more on their studies as well. This perspective is supported by Otto and Alwin's study, where the positive effects of athletic participation on educational aspirations and attainment primarily operated through the influence of significant others. Broh's work demonstrated the positive impact of participation on social capital between students, parents, and teachers, which helped explain the positive effects on grades, which are also correlated with attainment. Furthermore, the desire to play a sport, or be involved in the school play, or participate in a particular school club with one's friends may motivate a student to stay in school to continue those activities. Past scholarship is supported by the findings here, replicating the positive effects of participation on graduation and postsecondary attendance, and extending that work, showing that these patterns exist even in the more challenging context of schools with impoverished student bodies.

This chapter demonstrates that, for students in high-poverty schools, there are positive effects to participation in extracurricular activities on educational outcomes, specifically earning a high school diploma, as well as attaining postsecondary edu-cation. Combining these results with those of other educational research makes the findings clear: the extracurriculum plays an important role in integrating students into their school, keeping them enrolled as opposed to dropping out, surrounding them with more academically oriented peers, getting them to earn their diploma, and fostering the continued attainment of education beyond the high school setting. With the obstacles faced by this student population, any programs and policies that can be adopted to encourage such attainment are vital to the quest for upward mobility out of the ghettoes and disadvantaged neighborhoods for which so many public policies and politicians aim.

The policy implications are also clear. With yearly budget battles and funding shortfalls in these schools, cutting extracurricular activities clearly further disadvantages the students in these schools in terms of the outcomes of this analysis, not to mention the health (both physical and mental) and social benefits that one derives from participation in such activities. With so many obstacles already in these students' paths, public policy must seek to maintain the programs that help them clear these hurdles (pun intended) and aid them in attaining the education and human and social capital they need to find their way out of disadvantage. Priority must be placed on preserving the few assets students in these schools do have that can assist them in achieving their future goals and realizing their potential. Without such prioritizing, the already widening gap between the haves and have-nots will only grow more quickly. Extracurricular programs clearly have benefits for students in high-poverty schools; policymakers must endeavor to preserve these benefits.

DEDICATION

Dedicated to my mother, Becky A. Gonzalez, who passed away during the writing of this chapter.

NOTES

1. Samuel Bowles and Herbert Gintis. 2002. "Schooling in capitalist America revisited." *Sociology of Education* 75: 1–18.

2. See Paul Dimaggio. 1982. "Cultural capital and school success: The impact of status culture participation on the grades of U.S. high school students." *American Sociological Review* 47: 189–201; George Farkas. 1996. *Human capital or cultural capital? Ethnicity and poverty groups in an urban school district.* New York: Walter de Gruter. 2003. "Cognitive skills and noncognitive traits and behaviors in stratification processes." *Annual Review of Sociology* 29: 541–562; and Anne Swidler. 1986. "Culture in action: Symbols and strategies." *American Sociological Review* 51: 273–286.

3. See Andrew A. Beveridge and Sophia Catsambis. 2002. "Vital connections for students at risk: Family, neighborhood and school influences on early dropouts." In *American Educational Research Association Annual Meeting.* New Orleans, LA; Pierre Bourdieu. 1986. "Forms of capital." In *Handbook of theory and research for the sociology of education,* edited by J. Richardson. New York: Greenwood Press; Beckett A. Broh. 2002. "Linking extracurricular programming to academic achievement: Who benefits and why?" *Sociology of Education* 75: 69–95; Frank F. Furstenberg Jr. and Mary Elizabeth Hughes. 1995. "Social capital and successful development among at-risk youth." *Journal of Marriage and the Family* 57: 580–592; and E. M. Horvat, E. B. Weininger, and A. Lareau. 2003. "From social ties to social capital: Class differences in the relations between schools and parent networks." *American Educational Research Journal* 40: 319–351.

4. James S. Coleman. 1961. *The adolescent society: The social life of the teenager and its impact on education.* New York: Free Press.

5. James Shulman and William Bowen. 2001. *The game of life: College sports and educational values.* Princeton, NJ: Princeton Press.

6. Paul H. Carmichael. 1997. "Who receives federal title I assistance? examination of program funding by school poverty rate in New York state." *Educational Evaluation and Policy Analysis* 19: 354–359; Martin E. Orland. 1990. "Demographics of disadvantage: Intensity of childhood poverty and its relationship to educational achievement." In *Access to knowledge: An agenda for our nation's schools,* edited by J. I. Goodlad and P. Keating. New York: College Entrance Examination Board; Kevin J. Payne and Bruce J. Biddle. 1999. "Poor school funding, child poverty, and mathematics achievement." *Educational Researcher* 28: 4–13.

7. "High poverty schools" are usually defined as those schools where more than 50% of the student body is eligible for free- or reduced-price lunch. See James S. Kim and Gail L. Sunderman. 2005. "Measuring Academic Proficiency Under the No Child Left Behind Act: Implications for Educational Equity." *Educational Researcher* 34: 3–13; G. Orfield and C. Lee. 2005. *Why segregation matters: Poverty and educational inequality.* Cambridge, MA: The Civil Rights Project, Harvard University; and Steven W. Raudenbush. 2004. *Schooling, statistics, and poverty: Can we measure school improvement?* Princeton, NJ: Educational Testing Service.

8. M.P. Hanks and B.K. Eckland. 1976. "Athletics and social participation in the educational attainment process." *Sociology of Education* 49: 271–294; F. Howell, A. Miracle, and C.R. Rees. 1984. "Do high school athletics pay? The effects of varsity participation on socioeconomic attainment." *Sociology of Sport Journal* 1: 15–25; H. Marsh. 1993. "The effects of participating in sport during the last two years of high school." *Sociology of Sport Journal* 10: 18–43; L.B. Otto. 1976. "Social integration and the status attainment process." *American Journal of Sociology* 81: 1360–1383; L.B. Otto and D.F. Alwin. 1977. "Athletics, aspirations, and attainments." *Sociology of Education* 50: 102–113.

9. Marsh, "The effects of participating in sport during the last two years of high school."; Otto, "Social integration and the status attainment process."; Otto and Alwin, "Athletics, aspirations, and attainments."

10. F. Howell, A. Miracle, and C.R. Rees. 1984. "Do high school athletics pay? The effects of varsity participation on socioeconomic attainment." *Sociology of Sport Journal* 1: 15–25; Otto, "Social integration and the status attainment process"; J.S. Picou, V. McCarter, and F. Howell. 1985. "Do high school athletics pay? Some further evidence." *Sociology of Sport Journal* 2: 72–76.

11. John M. Barron, Bradley T. Ewing, and Glen R. Waddell. 2000. "The effects of high school athletic participation on education and labor market outcomes." *Review of Economic Statistics* 82: 409–421, J. Curtis, W. McTeer, and P. White. 2003. "Do high school athletes earn more pay? Youth sport participation and earnings as an adult." *Sociology of Sport Journal* 20: 60–76; R. Eide and N. Ronan. 2001. "Is participation in high school athletics an investment or a consumption good?" *Economics of Education Review* 20: 431–442; Shulman and Bowen, *The game of life.*

12. J.L. Mahoney. 2000. "School extracurricular activity participation as a moderator in the development of antisocial patterns." *Child Development* 71: 502–516.

13. Ralph B. McNeal. 1995. "Extracurricular activities and high school dropouts." *Sociology of Education* 68: 62–81.

14. J.S. Eccles and B.L. Barber. 1999. "Student council, volunteering, basketball, or marching band: What kind of extracurricular involvement matters?" *Journal of Adolescent Research* 14: 10–43.

15. Hanks and Eckland, "Athletics and social participation in the educational attainment process."

16. Andrew Guest and Barbara Schneider. "The Adolescents' extracurricular participation in context: The mediating effects of schools, communities, and identity." *Sociology of Education* (April 2003) 76 No. 2 89–109.

17. Broh, "Linking extracurricular programming to academic achievement: Who benefits and why?"

18. Curtis, McTeer, and White, "Do high school athletes earn more pay?"

19. S.V. Cameron and J.J. Heckman. 1993. "The nonequivalence of high school equivalents." *Journal of Labor Economics* 11: 1–47.

CHAPTER 8

TO WORK OR NOT TO WORK? THE ROLE OF POVERTY, RACE/ETHNICITY, AND REGIONAL LOCATION IN YOUTH EMPLOYMENT

Constance T. Gager, Jacqueline C. Pflieger, and Jennifer Hickes Lundquist

Paid work has become a common and expected part of the lives of many youth in the United States. Recent data show that 2.9 million youth aged 15 to 17 were employed during the school year, and 4 million were employed during the summer months. The likelihood of employment for youth increases markedly through the progression of adolescence. For example, according to the U.S. Department of Labor, 9 percent of 15-year-olds reported working for pay, whereas 39 percent of 17-year-olds were working for pay in 2000.[1] Youth employment also varies by other individual as well as family characteristics, including race/ethnicity, gender, family income/poverty level, family structure, and regional location.[2,3] Yet a lack of recent research has focused on how youths' participation in paid labor may vary by the needs of their families. For example, youth in single-parent families may share a larger burden of housework or of caring for siblings than youth from two-parent families, which may constrain their available time for paid employment. In contrast, youth in single-parent families are more likely to live in poverty; thus, we might expect to see earlier entry into employment given family financial need. In this chapter, we describe how youth participation in paid work varies by these key youth and family characteristics, focusing especially on important contextual measures, including family income/poverty level, family structure, and regional location, while controlling for individual youth characteristics including gender, race/ethnicity, and time use. In sum, we will focus on the context of youth employment, specifically with regard to socioeconomic status.

On the macro level, several economic and social factors affect youth employment, including discrimination and social disadvantage as well as cyclical and structural trends in the economy. On the micro level, youths' individual and family characteristics as well as their regional location influence their labor force participation. Although one might expect that youth from poor families are more likely to work in order to help support their families, the data show a quite different pattern. First, employed youth are more likely to be middle class, Caucasian, and to live in suburban areas.[4] This is attributable to the fact that most youth work in service-sector jobs, which are highly concentrated in suburban areas, where Caucasian, middle-class youth and their families are more likely to reside. Second, youth employment rates mirror those for adults with regard to race/ethnicity, with employment rates lowest among African American and Latino youth.[5] Last, working youth of today contribute little of their earnings to support their families. Research has shown that youth spend the majority of their earnings on their own needs and activities.[6,7] Although historically, children from poor families were more likely to be employed and to economically contribute to their family,[8] working youth of today are less likely to be poor and they contribute little of their earnings to their families.

LITERATURE REVIEW

Although the U.S. public believes that work is valuable for children and adolescents—teaching them needed skills that will ease the transition from school to work—much debate in research and policy arenas focuses on the adverse outcomes of youth employment. The debate has primarily concentrated on (1) how much work is too much; (2) whether paid work deters youth from other more developmentally beneficial activities; and (3) the effect of early paid work on youths' educational and later labor market outcomes. Thus, the literature on youth employment, similar to the literature on youth development in general, has been plagued by a tendency to emphasize negative outcomes, especially in regard to youth employment.[9]

Considerable research attention has focused on the adverse consequences of employment on youth development.[10,11] Specifically, researchers argue that adolescent employment, particularly that over 20 hours a week or "high intensity," may have negative consequences.[12] Researchers have found that youth paid employment decreases opportunity costs in terms of academic achievement,[13] increases the likelihood to engage in problematic behaviors,[14] reduces time in extracurricular activities for Caucasian males,[15] and reduces time spent with family.[16,17]

On the positive side, researchers have suggested that youth employment may help ease the transition to adulthood. Glen H. Elder, Jr.'s pioneering research sheds light on the relationship between employment and subsequent achievement, finding that work experience among rural farm youth had lasting benefits, such as instilling positive values and building confidence.[18] Similarly, Katherine S. Newman's moving portrayal of inner-city youth employed in low-skilled jobs suggests such experience leads to improved occupational outcomes.[19] Doris R. Entwiste, Karl L. Alexander, and Linda Steffel Olson note that both the beneficial and adverse consequences of early work experience may vary for minority youth.[20] As Jeylan T. Mortimer, Jeremy Staff, and Sabrina Oesterle argue, little research or policy attention has focused on whether youth involvement in paid work might act as a mechanism through which youth "acquire knowledge about the labor force, form occupational values, learn how to behave appropriately, and acquire skills that will facilitate their adaptation to work."[21] In other words, early work experience may provide youth with a special advantage when they compete for full-time jobs, thus easing the transition to adulthood.

Research on youth employment has been conducted in a variety of disciplines, including sociology, psychology, child development, geography, and economics. Although many of these studies operate in isolation from research in the other disciplines, most of this research broadly examines similar issues—barriers to and predictors of youth employment. Sociologists have focused on the social deterrents of employment resulting from social isolation of minorities in urban areas due to a lack of exposure to regularly employed middle-class role models and/or social networks that lead to knowledge of and access to job opportunities.[22] Douglas S. Massey and Nancy A. Denton have persuasively argued that although both urban African Americans and Latinos experience high levels of residential segregation, African Americans are subject to "hypersegregation," which crystallizes inequality by constraining educational opportunities and may lead to the development of a distinct culture outside the mainstream.[23] Testing this theory, Katherine M. O'Regan and John M. Quigley find that living in a neighborhood with a high concentration of poverty or with an African American population reduces the likelihood of youth employment.[24] Research by geographers and economists has highlighted the "spatial frictions" faced by minorities who are concentrated in urban areas, as employment opportunities are located in suburban areas. Many of these studies have focused on locational constraints on employment options. For example, the costs of commuting or housing discrimination might deter urban minorities from access to employment in suburban areas.[25, 26] In sum, a spatial mismatch exists between where workers live and where jobs are available. Although debates continue over the magnitude of this mismatch,[27] the majority of published reviews of the spatial mismatch literature conclude that there exists strong or moderate support for the hypothesis in the empirical literature on adult employment[28–30] (for an exception see Christopher Jencks and Susan E. Mayer, 1990).[31]

Concerns over simultaneity between employment and residential location led researchers to focus on employment among youth living with their parents, as their residential location would be exogenously determined by their parents or guardians. A growing body of research has examined the role of spatial mismatch in youth employment.[32–34] Youth are an especially interesting group to study from this perspective, as the majority of youth are employed in retail and service sector jobs, which are more highly concentrated in suburban areas.[35, 36] While urban African American and Latino youth experience high levels of residential segregation, they have little control over the choice of their residence. In addition, they may face fewer transportation options compared with adults, as they have a lower likelihood of possessing a driver's license and of owning a car. In sum, youth are especially susceptible to spatial mismatch.[37] However, the evidence to date on youth experiencing lower employment rates due to spatial mismatch is inconclusive.

In addition, regional location, especially the urban/suburban dichotomy, is highly correlated with family poverty status, family structure, and joblessness. Inner city urban neighborhoods, as compared with suburban neighborhoods, are characterized by higher concentrations of poverty, female-headed households, and unemployment. For example, in 2000, the poverty rate in central cities was 18.4 percent, more than twice of that in the suburbs (8.3 percent), although the central city/suburban gap has decreased by .5 percent since 1990. In cities that experienced the greatest decline in poverty rates, child poverty rates declined even more sharply. Conversely, cities in the northeast and Southern California experienced increased rates of poverty and higher rates of child poverty, although at a smaller increase than overall poverty rates.[38] Thus, higher rates of overall poverty and child poverty continue to persist in urban versus suburban regions.

These higher rates of poverty are attributed to high levels of joblessness, especially in the manufacturing sector, as work has "disappeared" or moved to suburban or overseas locations.[39, 40] This change is exacerbated by spatial changes in the growth of new service sector jobs. The majority of these new jobs are concentrated in suburban areas; thus, urban areas are left with fewer job opportunities.[41] The changing job structure is especially salient for youth who are likely to be employed in service sector jobs, which are concentrated in suburban locations.

Family structure also contributes to high rates of poverty, especially in urban areas. According to recent estimates from the Current Population Survey, 8.8 percent of married couples with two children live below the poverty line, whereas 43.8 percent of female-headed families with two children live in poverty.[42] Thus, children growing up in female-headed families are nearly 5 times more likely to experience childhood poverty than are children in married-couple families. Although small in number, children growing up in single-father families are twice as likely to live in poverty as children with married parents.[43] Family structure may influence youth employment, as single parents may rely more on youth for assistance with caring for siblings and household labor because they do not have a second parent on whom to rely. As discussed above, it would intuitively seem children from socially and economically disadvantaged families might enter employment to provide financial support for struggling families; however, recent evidence shows that these youth are actually less likely to be employed.[44] Thus, our analysis will provide evidence as to whether this is the case or not.

Further, individual characteristics of youth, including age, gender, and race/ethnicity, are related to youth employment. In this chapter, we focus on youth during middle-to-late adolescence (ages 14 to 18). As adolescence is a period of developmental growth characterized by distinct physical, cognitive, social, and behavioral transformations, there is much variability during this span of time. One of the most pronounced characteristics of adolescence is the need for independence from parents in order to establish one's own identity. Erik Erikson characterized this stage of life as "identity versus role confusion."[45] Often, conflict with parents over the desire for independence is a central marker of this developmental period. One way in which adolescents can establish their individual selves is through outside employment.

In addition to age, youths' gender and race/ethnicity are linked with youth employment. For example, researchers find significant time-use differences between boys and girls, and that these differences increase with age.[46, 47] Specifically, Constance T. Gager, Teresa M. Cooney, and Kathleen Thiede Call find that girls spend more time in paid work than do boys in the ninth grade, although this difference disappears by the twelfth grade.[48]

Youths' race/ethnicity also are important to consider because youth employment rates have been shown to mirror those of adults.[49] Newman finds that young African American workers seeking employment face a double disadvantage.[50] Specifically, she found that African Americans seeking jobs at a national fast food restaurant chain in Central Harlem faced disadvantages in the hiring process compared with their Latino counterparts. African American applicants were rejected at a higher rate than Latinos. Eighty-five percent of African American applicants were rejected, whereas 65.2 percent of Latino applicants were rejected. Her research also suggests that youth labor markets in the inner city are evaporating because urban employers have the option of hiring adults, whereas suburban employers in tighter labor markets do not. Again, applicants to the chain restaurant she studied who were under age 22 were rejected at a higher rate compared with their older adult counterparts. Thus, age and race/ethnicity are important factors in youth employment.

The main goal of this chapter is to recognize *both* the individual and structural factors that may influence youth involvement in paid employment, with a specific focus on how poverty, urban location, and family structure are related to youth employment. In sum, we examine who works and who does not work and how employment varies by youth and family socioeconomic characteristics as well as geographic location. Based on our synthesis of theoretical approaches from multiple disciplines, we identify the most important correlates of youth employment. These correlates include characteristics of youth, such as age, race/ethnicity, and gender, and/or characteristics of their families, such as family socioeconomic status, family structure, and regional residence. Family socioeconomic status is measured by family income and Temporary Assistance for Needy Families (TANF) or food stamp recipiency. Family structure is measured as living in a two-parent married structure versus a single-mother or single-father family. Last, regional residence is measured as living in an urban or suburban neighborhood.

In addition, we address several data shortcomings in previous research examining general youth time-use, and specifically, involvement in paid work. First, much of what we know about youth time-use has come from studies that lack complete and accurate estimates of youths' time-use activities.[51, 52] For example, studies often rely on adult estimates of children's involvement, rather than on reports from children themselves.[53–56] Second, many studies on involvement in paid work utilize a regional sample (although longitudinal) of mostly Caucasian, suburban, middle-class youth[57] or of African American, urban, lower-class youth[58, 59] without examining a comparison group. Thus, we do not know the degree to which involvement varies by race/ethnicity, income level, or regional residence. Although the few studies that do include comparison groups are informative, they often rely on non-representative samples that cannot be generalized to a national population.[60–62] Thus, we present data to show the degree to which involvement in paid labor varies by race/ethnicity, income level/poverty status, or regional residence by using a nationally representative sample.

DATA AND METHODS

This chapter will summarize data from the Survey of Adults and Youth (SAY), collected as part of the Urban Health Initiative (UHI) and funded by the Robert Wood Johnson Foundation (prior to 2005, The Survey of Adults and Youth (SAY) was referred to as The Survey of Parents and Youth (SPY). The UHI seeks to ameliorate the health, safety, and well-being of children and youth living in America's most economically distressed cities. The sample is a probability sample of the entire United States, in which UHI purposely over-sampled urban areas and six economically distressed cities, thereby resulting in higher percentages of African American and urban families. Thus, the SAY survey was administered to a nationally representative population and over-samples parents and youth living in urban areas in six cities: Baltimore, MD; Chicago, IL; Detroit, MI; Oakland, CA; Philadelphia, PA; and Richmond, VA. SAY, a random digit-dialed survey, includes 4,441 parents and 7,778 youth. Telephone interviews were conducted every 3 years beginning in 1998 and commencing in 2005.[63, 64] The present study utilizes data from the first wave of data collected between October 1998 and May 1999.

SAY is unique in that it includes interviews with adults, parents, and youth ages 10 to 18. Most importantly, SAY surveys youth about their involvement in school and nonschool related activities, including paid work, thereby presenting a complete picture to better understand how youth divide their time. Youth were asked to report on their time spent in paid work, housework, and extracurricular activities as well as their demographic characteristics. The parent survey generates information on family socioeconomic status, including family income, welfare recipiency, family structure, and regional location. Our data analysis combines information collected from both the youth and the parental interviews.

Parents were interviewed first, and then youth were interviewed upon permission from their parents. The youth survey lasted approximately 30 minutes, and the parent survey lasted about 20 minutes. The response rate for parents was 89 percent, and the response rate for parents who granted permission to interview a child was 74 percent. The current analysis is limited to youth ages 14 to 18, with an effective sample size of 3,441 parent-child pairs, for whom there are no missing data. No differences between responders and nonresponders were found with regard to urbanicity, region of country, race/ethnicity, and family income.

Variables

The youth employment variable is based on the question, "During the last week, have you earned any money at any job besides housework: yes or no." Additional individual youth variables in this study are age (14 to 18 years), gender (0 = male, 1 = female), and race/ethnicity. Race/ethnicity of the respondent was coded as

1 = Caucasian, 2 = non-Hispanic African American, 3 = Asian, 4 = Hispanic, and 5 = other race/ethnicity.

Family characteristics include income, welfare recipiency, family structure, and regional residence. Parents were asked, "What was your total family income last year?" The response categories include 1 = less than $20,000, 2 = $20,001 to $30,000, 3 = $30,001 to $50,000, and 4 = over $50,000. The use of social welfare services was measured by two questions. The first question regards government assistance and asked, "In the past 12 months, did you or anyone in your family receive assistance from AFDC or TANF?" They also were asked, "In the past 12 months, did you or anyone in your family receive food stamps?" They responded either "yes" or "no" to each question. Due to small sample sizes, we coded family structure as 1 = two-parent married families (may be either biological or stepparent structures), 2 = mother-only families, and 3 = father-only families. Last, regional location was measured as families who live in urban areas versus suburban areas.

We will present descriptive statistics, including means and frequencies, to describe the characteristics of our total SAY sample. Next, we will describe how employed and unemployed youth differ by demographic and socioeconomic characteristics. We perform a Pearson Chi-Square analysis to determine if significant associations exist between youth employment status and each youth/family characteristic.

RESULTS AND DISCUSSION

In Table 8.1, we present descriptive statistics for our main variables. Thirty-eight percent of our sample reported that they had earned money at a job in the past week, and of those, the mean hours of work reported were 15.8 hours.

In terms of individual youth characteristics, the average age of youth in our sample was 15.8 years, and the sample was evenly split between males and females. Forty-three percent of youth in our sample were Caucasian, 39.8 percent were African American, 10.3 percent were Latino, 2.3 percent were Asian American, and 4.6 percent were in the other category. The other category comprises youth who considered themselves Native American, who identified with more than one racial or ethnic category, or who chose the category "other." Approximately 67 percent of the youth we surveyed lived in two-parent, intact families. Most of the youth in our sample were from families who did not receive food stamps or AFDC/TANF in the past year (88% and 93%, respectively). Approximately 20.2 percent of families had incomes below $20,000, whereas 37.5 percent reported incomes above $50,000. Most of the youth lived in urban areas (69.3%), as the SAY survey purposely over-sampled urban areas.

In the next section, we describe how youth employment status varied by key demographic and socioeconomic characteristics. The likelihood of youth employment status varied most by youth age and regional residence, as can be seen in Figures 8.1 and 8.2. In Figure 8.1, for example, we see that age is a key correlate of youth employment status. At age 14, only 24.8 percent of youth reported that they worked at a paid job last week, whereas by age 18, that percentage increased to 60.5 percent.

Table 8.1
Descriptive Statistics of Variables Used in Analysis

Variable	N	%	Mean
Paid work (last week)			
Not employed	2130	61.9	
Employed	1309	38.0	15.8 hours
Age			15.8 years
Gender			
Female	1736	50.5	
Male	1705	49.5	
Race			
Caucasian	1479	43.0	
African American	1370	39.8	
Asian American	80	2.3	
Latino	355	10.3	
Other	157	4.6	
TANF/AFDC			
Yes	240	7.1	
No	3159	92.9	
Food Stamps			
Yes	396	11.6	
No	3031	88.4	
Total Family Income			
Less than $20,000	694	20.2	
$20,001–$30,000	518	15.1	
$30,001–$50,000	729	21.2	
More than $50,000	1291	37.5	
Family Structure			
Two parent married	2039	67.2	
Mother only	831	27.4	
Father only	164	5.4	
Residence			
Suburban	1057	30.7	
Urban	2384	69.3	

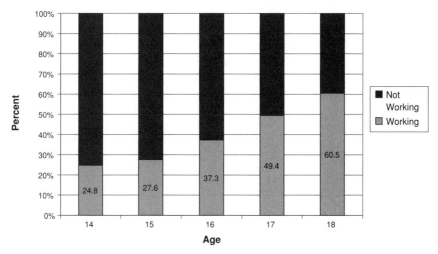

Figure 8.1
Youth Employment Status by Age

Thus, older youth are significantly more likely to be employed compared to their younger peers ($\chi^2 = 235.75$, $p \leq .001$).

Mirroring trends among the adult population, we find that the likelihood of youth employment varied by race/ethnicity ($\chi^2 = 59.94$, $p \leq .001$). Forty-five percent of Caucasian youth were employed, whereas only one-third of African American and Latino youth were employed, respectively. In contrast to rates reported by the Bureau

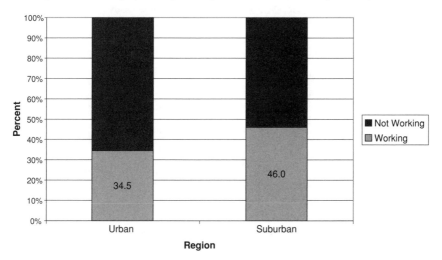

Figure 8.2
Youth Employment Status by Regional Residence

of Labor Statistics, Asian youth in our sample had the lowest employment rates at 28.8 percent.[65]

Our analyses found no significant differences in employment likelihood by gender among the youth in our survey. For both girls and boys, employment rates were approximately 38 percent. However, we did find an interaction between gender and race/ethnicity. Latina girls were significantly less likely to be employed compared with their male peers. Whereas over 62 percent of Latino boys were employed, only 38 percent of Latina girls were involved in paid employment. In contrast, we found greater parity between both African American and Caucasian girls and boys (ranging from 48 to 52 percent); thus, Latino boys had the highest employment rates. This finding is in tandem with recent data from the Bureau of Labor Statistics.[66]

Moving to family characteristics, we found a relationship between youth employment status and family income. A clear positive trend emerges between youth employment and family income. Youth from poor families were less likely to be employed than children from families with higher incomes ($\chi^2 = 15.72$, $p \leq .01$). Thus, although intuitively, we expected youth from economically disadvantaged families would be employed in order to help support their families financially, employed youth were more likely to be from more economically advantaged families.

Next we examined the association between welfare recipiency and youth employment status. Similar to the findings for family income, we found that youth who lived in more economically disadvantaged families, as measured by TANF or food stamp recipiency, were less likely to be employed as compared to youth from families who did not receive these forms of government assistance. Receiving TANF was significantly and negatively associated with youth employment ($\chi^2 = 4.94$, $p \leq .05$). In addition, food stamp receipt was negatively associated with the likelihood of youth employment ($\chi^2 = 7.15$, $p \leq .01$). In sum, youth from more economically disadvantaged families were less likely to be employed than their less economically disadvantaged peers.

We suggested that children from single-parent families may be less likely to work for pay if their parents relied on them for assistance with household labor and care of siblings. We compared youth from two-parent married families (combining stepparents and biological parents) with youth living in mother-only and father-only family structures. Although the data showed a trend toward greater labor force participation among youth from single-parent families, the relationship was not statistically significant ($\chi^2 = 4.42$, $p \leq .10$). It is also interesting to highlight that youth from father-only versus mother-only families did not significantly differ in their labor force participation rate. In sum, we found no association between family structure and youth employment status.

Last, we examined the association between regional location and youth employment rates. As we summarized above, research has suggested a spatial mismatch between youth residence in urban areas and job availability (i.e., service-sector jobs, which are concentrated in suburban areas). This is especially salient for youth who may lack the transportation options of adults (i.e., they are not old enough to have a license and are less likely to own a car). In addition, youth usually do not choose their place of residence. We found a significant association between regional residence and youth employment status. Whereas 46 percent of the youth living in suburban neighborhoods were employed, only 34.5 percent of urban youth were involved in paid labor ($\chi^2 = 40.92$, $p \leq .001$). Thus, suburban youth were more likely to work for pay as compared to urban youth.

Overall, we found high variation in youth employment status by race/ethnicity and regional location, which begs the question: Which effect better predicts youth employment? In additional research using this data set and multivariate methods, we have examined the simultaneous effects of these individual and family characteristics on youth employment status. Our analyses showed that regional location trumped race/ethnicity in predicting the likelihood of youth employment. In other words, suburban/urban residence was the strongest predictor of youth employment.[67] While we know urban neighborhoods, especially in the cities surveyed, have higher concentrations of African Americans, our findings suggest that location matters more than race, as African American youth living in suburban areas in our sample were no less likely to be employed as compared to their Caucasian counterparts.

CONCLUSION

In this chapter, we have highlighted the important correlates of youth employment status. Guided by spatial mismatch theory and previous research, we have described how individual and family characteristics of youth are associated with their likelihood of paid employment. We found that youth employment was more likely among older adolescents, Caucasians, and Latino boys. In terms of family characteristics, we demonstrated that low family income, and TANF and foods stamp recipiency were associated with a lower likelihood of participation in paid work among youth. However, we did not find that gender or family structure was significantly associated with youth employment status. Most notably, we found that living in an urban setting was associated with a lower likelihood of youth employment.

Our findings support previous research on spatial mismatch and labor market outcomes for youth.[68,69] For example, Steven R. Holloway and Stephen Mulherin found that growing up in a poor neighborhood during adolescence can lead to lifetime labor market disadvantage.[70] They suggest that such disadvantage is partially attributable to limited opportunity to accumulate early paid work experience. The disadvantage attributable to spatial mismatch between urban youth residence and suburban job opportunities has implications for policy regarding youth employment, especially in the era of welfare reform. Over the past few decades, policymakers have attempted to ameliorate urban/suburban differences by stimulating development within urban neighborhoods in the form of empowerment zones and spatially targeted job training programs. Policy also has focused on dispersing concentrations of urban poverty through programs such as Moving to Opportunity (MTO). Despite some successes in reducing the concentration of urban poverty during the 1990s, our data suggest that urban/suburban inequality persists in the area of youth employment.

Recent changes enacted through the reauthorization of welfare reform in 2005 may exacerbate the problem of spatial mismatch, as the Federal government has renewed the 50 percent requirement. Under reauthorization guidelines, 50 percent of TANF families must participate in a combination of work and other activities that lead to self-sufficiency. New guidelines also propose that this percentage will increase annually by 5 percentage points until it reaches 70 percent in 2007.[71] As adults on TANF, many of whom are concentrated in economically disadvantaged, urban neighborhoods, face greater pressure to secure employment, the prospects for youth in these same neighborhoods will likely decline. Therefore, policies are needed that specifically target job training for youth, especially those in urban neighborhoods.

First, interventions at the local, state, and federal levels must address the limited transportation options of inner-city youth. Recent demonstration projects have shown that providing direct transportation is essential for connecting inner-city residents with suburban job opportunities.[72] However, transportation alone cannot solve the many issues involved in moving youth to job opportunities far from home. Private companies, especially those who employ large numbers of service workers, such as fast-food restaurants, retail stores, and hotels, can intervene by recruiting and investing in young workers. The recent ordinance passed by the Chicago city council that "Big Box" stores must pay workers hourly rates greater than minimum wage is an interesting example of how local government can force private companies to invest in their workers.[73] Thus, we suggest that interventions are needed from both public and private entities in order to close the wage gap and better prepare youth for future employment.

NOTES

1. "Report on the Youth Labor Force." Available at http://www.bls.gov/opub/rylf/rylfhome.htm (accessed April 26, 2006).

2. Ibid.

3. Diane C. Keithly and Forrest A. Deseran. "Households, Local Labor Markets, and Youth Labor Force Participation." *Youth and Society* 26, no. 4 (June 1995): 463–492.

4. Ibid.

5. "Report on the Youth Labor Force."

6. Lloyd D. Johnston, Jerald G. Bachman, and Patrick M. O'Malley. *Monitoring the Future: Questionnaire Responses from the Nation's High School Seniors, 1981*. Ann Arbor, MI: ISSR, 1982.

7. Laurence Steinberg, Suzanne Fegley, and Sanford M. Dornbusch. "Negative Impact of Part-Time Work on Adolescent Adjustment: Evidence from a Longitudinal Study." *Developmental Psychology* 29, no. 2 (March 1993): 171–180.

8. Glen H. Elder, Jr. *Children of the Great Depression: A Social Change in Life Experience*. Chicago: University of Chicago Press, 1974.

9. Frank F. Furstenberg. "The Sociology of Adolescence and Youth in the 1990s: A Critical Commentary." *Journal of Marriage and the Family* 62 (2000): 896–910.

10. Jerald G. Bachman, Lloyd D. Johnston, and Patrick M. O'Malley. "Smoking, Drinking, and Drug use among American High School Students: Correlates and Trends, 1975–1979." *American Journal of Public Health* 71, no. 1 (1981): 59.

11. Herbert W. Marsh. "Employment during High School: Character Building Or a Subversion of Academic Goals?" *Sociology of Education* 64, no. 3 (July 1991): 172–189.

12. National Research Council and Institute of Medicine, Committee on the Health and Safety Implications of Child Labor. *Protecting Youth at Work: Health, Safety, and Development of Working Children and Adolescents in the United States*. Washington, DC: National Academy Press, 1998.

13. Marsh, "Employment during High School."

14. Bachman, Johnston, and O'Malley, "Smoking, Drinking, and Drug use among American High School Students."

15. Ronald D'Amico. "Does Employment during High School Impair Academic Progress?" *Sociology of Education* 57 (1984): 152–164.

16. Ellen Greenberger and Laurence Steinberg. *When Teenagers Work: The Psychological and Social Costs of Adolescent Employment*. New York: Basic Books, 1986.

17. Laurence Steinberg and Sanford M. Dornbusch. "Negative Correlates of Part-Time Employment during Adolescence: Replication and Elaboration." *Developmental Psychology* 27, no. 2 (March 1991): 304–313.

18. Elder, Jr., *Children of the Great Depression*.

19. Katherine S. Newman. *No Shame in My Game: The Working Poor in the Inner City*. New York: Russell Sage Foundation, 1999.

20. Doris R. Entwisle, Karl L. Alexander, and Linda Steffel Olson. "Early Work Histories of Urban Youth." *American Sociological Review* 65 (2000): 279–297.

21. Jeylan T. Mortimer, Jeremy Staff, and Sabrina Oesterle. "Adolescent Work and the Early Socioeconomic Career." in *The Handbook of the Life Course*. Edited by Jeylan T. Mortimer and Michael J. Shanahan. New York: Plenum Press, 2003.

22. Jeylan T. Mortimer, Jeremy Staff, and Sabrina Oesterle. *The Truly Disadvantaged: The Inner City, the Underclass, and Public Policy*. Chicago: University of Chicago Press, 1987.

23. Douglas S. Massey, and Nancy A. Denton. *American Apartheid: Segregation and the Making of the Underclass*. Cambridge, MA: Harvard University Press, 1993.

24. Katherine M. O'Regan and John M. Quigley. "Teenage Employment and the Spatial Isolation of Minority and Poverty Households." *Journal of Human Resources* 31 (1996): 692–702.

25. John F. Kain. "The Spatial Mismatch Hypothesis: Three Decades Later." *Housing Policy Debates* 3 (1992): 371–462.

26. John F. Kain. "Housing Segregation, Negro Employment, and Metropolitan Decentralization." *The Quarterly Journal of Economics* 82 (1968): 175–197.

27. Keith R. Ihlanfeldt and David L. Sjoquist. "The Spatial Mismatch Hypothesis: A Review of Recent Studies and their Implications for Welfare Reform." *Housing Policy Debate* 9 (1998): 849–892.

28. Kain, "The Spatial Mismatch Hypothesis."

29. Keith R. Ihlanfeldt. *Job Accessibility and the Employment and School Enrollment of Teenagers*. Kalamazoo, MI: W. E. Upjohn Institute for Employment Research, 1992.

30. Phillip Moss and Chris Tilly. *Why Black Men are Doing Worse in the Labor Market: A Review of Supply-Side and Demand-Side Explanations*. New York: Social Science Research Council, 1991.

31. Christopher Jencks and Susan E. Mayer. "The Social Consequences of Growing Up in a Poor Neighborhood." in *Inner-City Poverty in the United States*. Edited by Lynn Lawrence, Jr., and Michael McGeary. Washington, DC: National Academy of Sciences Press, 1990.

32. Douglas Massey and Nancy Denton, *American Apartheid: Segregation and the Making of the Underclass*. 1993 Cambridge MA: Harvard University Press.

33. Steven R. Holloway. "Job Accessibility and Male Teenage Employment, 1980–1990: The Declining Significance of Space?" *Professional Geographer* 48, no. 4 (1996): 445.

34. Thomas Larson and Madhu Mohanty. "Minority Youth Employment, Residential Location, and Neighborhood Jobs: A Study of Los Angeles County." *The Review of Black Political Economy* 27, (1999): 33–62.

35. "Report on the Youth Labor Force."

36. William J. Wilson. *When Work Disappears: The World of the New Urban Poor.* New York: Knopf, 1997.

37. Larson and Mohanty, "Minority Youth Employment, Residential Location, and Neighborhood Jobs."

38. Alan Berube and William H. Frey "A Decade of Mixed Blessings: Urban and Suburban Poverty in Census 2000." http://www.brookings.edu/es/urban/publications/berubefreypoverty.pdf (accessed April 26, 2006).

39. Mortimer, Staff, and Oesterle, *The Truly Disadvantaged.*

40. Wilson, *When Work Disappears.*

41. Ibid.

42. U.S. Census Bureau. "Current Population Survey: 2005 Annual Social and Economic Supplement." U.S. Census Bureau. Available at http://pubdb3.census.gov/macro/032005/pov/new04_100_01.htm (accessed April 26, 2006).

43. Ibid.

44. "Report on the Youth Labor Force."

45. Erik Erikson. *Childhood and Society.* New York: Norton, 1963.

46. Constance T. Gager, Teresa M. Cooney, and Kathleen Thiede Call. "The Effects of Family Characteristics and Time use on Teenagers' Household Labor." *Journal of Marriage and the Family* 61, no. 4 (November 1999): 982–994.

47. Timmer, Susan Goff, Jacquelynne Eccles, and Kerth O'Brien. "How Children use Time." in *Time, Goods, and Well-being.* Edited by F. Thomas Juster, Frank P. Stafford. Ann Arbor, MI: Institute for Social Research, 1985.

48. Gager, Cooney, and Call, "The Effects of Family Characteristics and Time use on Teenagers' Household Labor."

49. U.S. Department of Labor. "Employment and Unemployment among Youth Summary." http://www.bls.gov/news.release/youth.nr0.htm (accessed April 26, 2006).

50. Newman, *No Shame in My Game.*

51. Asher Ben-Arieh and Anat Ofir. "Opinion, Dialogue, Review: Time for (More) Time-use Studies: Studying the Daily Activities of Children." *Childhood* 9, no. 2 (May, 2002): 225–248.

52. Constance T. Gager and Laura A. Sanchez. "Whose Time is it?: The Effect of Gender, Employment, and work/family Stress on Children's Housework." San Francisco, CA: American Sociological Association, 2004.

53. Sampson Lee Blair. "Children's Participation in Household Labor: Child Socialization Versus the Need for Household Labor." *Journal of Youth and Adolescence* 21, no. 2 (April 1992): 241–258.

54. Sampson Lee Blair. "The Sex-Typing of Children's Household Labor: Parental Influence on Daughters' and Sons' Housework." *Youth and Society* 24, no. 2 (December 1992): 178–203.

55. David H. Demo and Alan C. Acock. "Family Diversity and the Division of Domestic Labor: How Much have Things really Changed?" *Family Relations* 42, no. 3 (July 1993): 323–331.

56. Reed W. Larson and Suman Verma. "How Children and Adolescents Spend Time Across the World: Work, Play, and Developmental Opportunities." *Psychological Bulletin* 125, no. 6 (November 1999): 701–736.

57. Jeylan T. Mortimer. *Working and Growing Up in America.* Cambridge, MA: Harvard University Press, 2003.

58. Entwisle, Alexander, and Olson, "Early Work Histories of Urban Youth."

59. Tama Leventhal, Julia A. Graber, and Jeanne Brooks-Gunn. "Adolescent Transitions to Young Adulthood: Antecedents, Correlates, and Consequences of Adolescent Employment." *Journal of Research on Adolescence* 11, no. 3 (2001): 297–323.

60. Randall Brown and William P. Evans. "Extracurricular Activity and Ethnicity: Creating Greater School Connection among Diverse Student Populations." *Urban Education* 37, no. 1 (January 2002): 41–58.

61. Robin L. Jarrett, Patrick J. Sullivan, and Natasha D. Watkins. "Developing Social Capital through Participation in Organized Youth Programs: Qualitative Insights from Three Programs." *Journal of Community Psychology* 33, no. 1 (2005): 41–55.

62. Annette Lareau. "Invisible Inequality: Social Class and Childrearing in Black Families and White Families." *American Sociological Review* 67, no. 5 (October 2002): 747–776.

63. T. Mijanovich and B. C. Weitzman. "Which "Broken Windows" Matter?: School, Neighborhood, and Family Characteristics Associated with Youths' Feelings of Unsafety." *Journal of Urban Health: Bulletin of the New York Academy of Medicine* 80, (2003): 400–415.

64. M. Modi. "Survey of Parents and Youth. Surveys Measuring Well-being." Available at http://www.wws.princeton.edu/~kling/surveys/SPY.htm (accessed April 26, 2006).

65. "Report on the Youth Labor Force."

66. U.S. Department of Labor. "Employment and Unemployment among Youth Summary."

67. Constance T. Gager and Jennifer Hickes Lundquist. "To Work Or Not to Work? A Reevaluation of Correlates of Adolescent Employment." Boston, MA, Population Association of America, April 2004.

68. Steven R. Holloway and Stephen Mulherin. "The Effect of Adolescent Neighborhood Poverty on Adult Employment." *Journal of Urban Affairs* 26, no. 4 (2004): 427–454.

69. Katherine M. O'Regan and John M. Quigley. "Teenage Employment and the Spatial Isolation of Minority and Poverty Households." *Journal of Human Resources* 31, (1996): 692–702.

70. Holloway, and Stephen, "The Effect of Adolescent Neighborhood Poverty on Adult Employment."

71. The White House. "Working Toward Independence: The President's Plan to Strengthen Welfare Reform." The White House. Available at http://www.whitehouse.gov/news/releases/2002/02/welfare-reform-announcement-book.pdf (accessed April 26, 2006).

72. Mark Elliott, Beth Palubinsky, and Joseph Tierney. *Overcoming Roadblocks on the Way to Work: Bridges to Work Field Report.* Public private ventures report, 1999. Available at http://www.ppv.org/ppv/publications/assets/102_publication.pdf (accessed August 21, 2006).

73. Erik Eckholm. "Chicago Orders 'Big Box' Stores to Raise Wage." *The New York Times*, July 27, 2006. Available at http://www.nytimes.com/2006/07/27/us/27chicago.html?ex=1311652800&en=807bb2062a8d6a5a&ei=5088&partner=rssnyt&emc=rss (accessed August 21, 2006).

CHAPTER 9

MORAL CAPITAL: SINGLE MOTHERHOOD, EDUCATIONAL ATTAINMENT, AND PERSONAL RESPONSIBILITY

Judith Hennessy

The American dream that we were all raised on is a simple but powerful one—if you work hard and play by the rules you should be given a chance to go as far as your God-given ability will take you

–Bill Clinton 1993

Recent decades have witnessed dramatic changes in women's lives including higher employment rates among mothers and more women pursuing college degrees. A related change, with significant consequences for low-income and impoverished women is the 1996 welfare reform. The Personal Responsibility and Work Opportunity Reconciliation Act (PRWORA) abolished Aid to Families with Dependent Children (AFDC) and created Temporary Assistance to Needy Families (TANF). In establishing TANF, legislators ended low-income mothers' entitlement to public assistance, required paid work in exchange for continued state assistance, and restricted support for postsecondary education.[1]

Prior to the 1996 PRWORA legislation, mothers of small children were exempt from working as a condition of receiving welfare assistance, and cash assistance was available to students enrolled in postsecondary education through the Job Opportunities and Basic Skills (JOBS) program. In contrast, the shift to a "workfare" policy emphasizes moving recipients into the workforce as quickly as possible, lowers the child age exemption to infants as young as 3 months in some states, limits job skills training and education to specific employment categories and imposes time limits on education.[2]

Research on the workforce participation and earnings of low-income women finds that poor single mothers often leave welfare for low-wage jobs and experience considerable hardship both on and off welfare.[3] Other research illustrates the struggles of welfare recipients to pursue higher education under TANF. These studies note that the emphasis on increased participation in paid work and restrictions on educational attainment hamper poor mothers' ability to reach long-term self-sufficiency and instead trap them in low-wage jobs.[4]

Studies documenting the struggles of poor women to make ends meet have rightfully taken a prominent place in research on impoverished and working-class women. However, this research has largely overlooked the moral dilemmas facing low-income single mothers. I address this understudied, albeit important aspect of low-income single mothers' struggles to raise children in an era of changing work and family relations and shifts in public assistance for impoverished families. I use interview data to examine the broadly shared, normative, cultural models salient to a group of student and nonstudent mothers in the wake of welfare reform. We see how low-income mothers, who are solely responsible for providing and caretaking, use widely shared understandings about work, family, and educational attainment to make decisions about work and family and resist stigmatized identities of poor single mothers on public assistance.

MORALITY AND WORK AND FAMILY DECISIONS

Despite the growing number of women who participate in paid work, few studies have explicitly attended to the *moral dimension* of combining paid work with caring for children. The few studies that do focus on the moral facets of work and family decisions explicitly posit that people's worldviews and actions regarding work and family responsibilities are not only or even primarily economic, strategic, or reactive but rather are imbued with moral significance and emotional salience.[5] However, research on the moral dimension of work and family has focused on middle-class cultural models.[6] This literature has not given systematic attention to the moral identities and dilemmas of single mothers struggling to provide for their children with low-wage jobs and/or welfare assistance nor those who find their path out of poverty obstructed by restrictions on educational attainment.

However, morality is no stranger to studies of poor women on welfare. A few influential works on welfare policy and poverty portray the problems of the poor as individual idiosyncrasies or pathologies.[7] Much of this literature blames the poor for their disadvantage and fuels racially charged stereotypes of poor single mothers. The dominant image of the "welfare mother" is that she resists supporting her children through paid work and "chooses" to remain on welfare, thereby transmitting her lack of initiative and motivation to her children, Moreover, the public response to poor single mothers' decisions about work and family differs markedly from the widespread social approval of middle-class mothers who "opt out" of careers to care for their children.[8] For low-income and impoverished mothers, reliance on public assistance to support one's family represents moral failings, while participating in paid labor is a sign of personal responsibility.[9]

Studies show that poor mothers may resist stigmatized identities and maintain status as good mothers by drawing upon dominant cultural models of motherhood where children's needs must come first.[10] However, poor single mothers raising children do not derive the moral credit earned by middle-class mothers through their self-sacrificing devotion to children. Indeed, with the advent of welfare reform, poor mothers are *required* to work and find their pursuit of education obstructed by welfare policies that privilege "any job" over a college degree. For mothers on welfare, "good mothers" put their children in daycare and go to work.[11]

Thus, the moral imperative imposed upon poor women is labor force participation (rather than caregiving or education) that designates them as worthy of state support. As we shall see, when paid work becomes an obstacle to responsibility for children, and/or a college degree, many mothers resist this definition of moral worth. In contrast to the rhetoric and assumptions of welfare policymakers, poor mothers find moral worth in responsibility for children and long-term self-sufficiency through education.

Moral Dimension of Paid Work

The strong work ethic that characterizes U.S. culture—anyone who is willing to work hard can get ahead and reward is commensurate with effort—remains a widely shared, powerful, and moral imperative.[12] The flip side of this ideology is that those who fail to get ahead—poor single mothers—are blamed for their own misfortune presumably because they lack attachment to mainstream values.[13] Thus, attaining self-sufficiency through paid work not only provides the material means to alleviate poverty but also signals membership in a moral community.[14]

Even though few families in today's society consist of a stay-at-home caregiver and male breadwinner it still resonates as a dominant cultural ideal.[15] In contrast to men's male provider role, women's moral obligation, indeed *sacred calling*, has rested in motherhood and marriage.[16] For women with children, excessive devotion to a career is a sign of self-centeredness and failure to be a good mother.[17] This presents a particularly cruel paradox for poor mothers on welfare. Poor single mothers who reject jobs that conflict with caring for children are punished under TANF by mandated reductions in cash and other welfare benefits. Thus, waged work, not child rearing is the socially approved path to membership among the deserving for poor women.[18]

Moral worth constructed in these terms imposes the masculine family ethic of good provider on poor women as their means of fulfilling a positive family role.[19] Paid work, long a symbol of men's moral obligation to their families, is now a sign of virtue for low-income mothers who rely on the state to meet their family obligations.

Education as a Cultural Ideal /American Dream

Educational opportunity reinforces the dominant ideology of the work ethic in U.S. society: the opportunity for all to succeed through their own efforts. This ideal—the American dream—is reinforced by the U.S. public's expectation that the educational system provides the means for all to believe in and pursue this ideal.[20] As Senator Olympia Snowe of Maine asks: "Who would dispute that education is the great equalizer in our society that can give every citizen in our nation—regardless of race, gender, income or geographic background—the same opportunity to succeed?"[21]

However, welfare reform policies hinder the achievement of this ideal through increased work hours and restrictions on educational activities for recipients who desire to pursue postsecondary education.[22] Women's' advocates oppose TANF's mandatory work participation rates and argue for giving states flexibility to design programs that allow more education and training opportunities.[23] A few states, notably Maine's Parents as Scholars program (PaS), use state funds to allow welfare recipients to continue postsecondary education, freeing them from compliance with restrictive federal rules. The result is increased wages and economic well-being for former welfare recipients.[24]

Moreover, the benefits of postsecondary education extend beyond income. Postsecondary education is associated with enhanced self-esteem and self-confidence and increased gains in the educational attainment of children.[25] Former welfare recipients with college degrees are also more likely to stay employed and not return to welfare[26] underscoring the contradictions in proposals for increased mandatory work hours and limits to postsecondary degree programs.[27]

In the analysis that follows, educational attainment figures prominently in constructions of personal responsibility and moral worth as a group of low-income single mothers articulates work and family responsibility and the promise of education according to widely shared cultural ideals.

METHODS AND DATA

Participants in this study are low-income single mothers, both on and off TANF who received social welfare services from a local Community Action Center in 1998–1999, the first 2 years of welfare reform. Eight mothers were currently attending college in pursuit of undergraduate or graduate degrees. All respondents had earned a GED or high school diploma. The women range in age from 20 to 47 years (mean 31), and the racial and ethnic characteristics of the sample include one Latina, one Black, and 18 whites. Only two respondents had never received AFDC or TANF. Eight respondents were receiving TANF cash benefits at the time of the interview, and four had left welfare within a year of the interview.

The data consist of semistructured interviews that ranged from 45 minutes to an hour and a half and were conducted in the fall of 1999 through January 2000. Interviews were tape recorded and then transcribed verbatim and coded into appropriate theoretical categories. All names used are pseudonyms and any identifying information was omitted to respect the confidentiality of respondents.

This study focuses on an understudied group: poor, predominantly white single mothers that reside in a rural Northwestern United States college town. The mothers in this study face few of the problems associated with the urban poor and single motherhood: waiting lists for subsidized housing, unsafe neighborhoods, low-quality child care and substandard schools. Moreover, the state that is the site of this study is characterized by a history of relatively generous public assistance.[28] Therefore, this sample stands out as a relatively "privileged" group compared to other studies of women on welfare in terms of resources. This group of poor single mothers—college students and noncollege students—can be examined as a "best case scenario" of low-income women who confront work and family decisions with greater resources than the urban poor, yet fewer resources than middle-class women.

My initial research goal was to investigate the material well-being of low-income women in the early days of the reform. I was interested in whether poor women were better off under TANF than the AFDC program. The "success" of welfare was widely promoted by policymakers due to the drop in the welfare caseload and the rising employment rates of former welfare recipients. As I listened to participants, what emerged was a far more complex story of how low-income single mothers view "success" in their ability to meet their work and childrearing responsibilities. I hope, through this rather unique group of women, to make visible the powerful, normative cultural models—so taken-for-granted as to appear invisible—that shape and constrain the "choices" of low-income women as they raise their children, go to work, and pursue educational goals. These findings are not intended to be statistically generalizable to a larger population, but may offer insight into similarly situated cases.

FINDINGS

Two Groups of Mothers: Employed Non-student and Student Mothers.

I first examine how non-student mothers make sense of their experiences as workers and mothers within the constraints of poverty and public assistance.

Personal Responsibility

Most of the women in this sample had extensive work histories. They provided ample evidence of the existence of a strong work ethic without the "push to work" provided by TANF.

Nancy is a 24-year-old never-married single mother of two small boys, ages 7 years and 18 months. Nancy currently works for a local telephone call center and described her job as, "There is no where to go. It is just right now paying the bills"

In this interview Nancy makes it clear that her participation in paid work is not the result of any incentives provided by the state. She is not a recent convert to personal responsibility and always worked except for a short period of time. Nancy, although not a student mother, includes educational attainment as a means of shouldering personal responsibility in opposition to reliance on public assistance.

I have *never* not worked. Except for the time when my mom sold her business until he [her youngest child] was 4 months and that was the only time I had never not worked since I was 16 years old, and it was terrible. I had never been that broke in my life and now it is like, all right, I am working and paying my bills, and I am still broke but my bills are paid. And before I was broke and my bills weren't paid . . . You have to work 20 hours per week in Washington, but I would not just not work. I'd go nuts. I don't want to be on assistance. My goal is to finish school and you know, to have a degree.

According to Robert Wuthnow, "most people work in order to give a culturally legitimate account of themselves, only one possibility of which is to say they are attempting to earn money."[29] I found this in Nancy's account of her work history. Without work "she would go nuts" but work is also defined in opposition to public assistance. Work for Nancy, although she is "still broke" creates a positive moral identity in opposition to mothers on welfare.

Responsibility for Children

Tammy, a 32-year-old mother of two school-age sons, receives TANF and works as a hotel maid. She told me how she had been separated from her children for about 6 months when she and her husband were living in a car and were "into drugs and alcohol." Four years ago she left her husband and moved here from another state with her children to be close to family. She told me that she has "been totally clean for four years . . . I have come a long way from where I was."

Tammy struggled with her desire to model the importance of paid work for her children and her belief that children need the supervision of a parent.

> I don't know, but I just think it is really hard when people say that [the children are old enough to care for themselves]. I mean they need more space, but they also need mom there too, and if it is just a single parent they need somebody there to say you know, this is wrong, this is right. . . .

Both caring for and providing for children are part of Tammy's worldview of her moral obligation as a mother. Tammy feels a need to be home with her children to provide moral guidance and she had reported earlier that her participation in paid work provides a good example for them. Her reliance on welfare and single motherhood status amplify the moral salience of personal responsibility through paid labor. Employment outside the home establishes an identity in contrast to the "welfare mother." Yet Tammy also sees her responsibility to her children in light of her view that to be a "good mother" is to be there for children when they get home from school. Tammy resists the notion that her primary obligation to her children is to provide financially—she is instead torn between two conflicting models of what responsible mothers *should* do.

STUDENT MOTHERS

I now turn to student mothers who combine work, school, and motherhood. This group of women although burdened by additional demands on time, receives additional resources from their pursuit of education. Student mothers derive symbolic resources given the ideological currency of pursuing educational attainment, and material resources from loans, grants, work-study, and university facilities. Drawing on moral capital obtained from widely shared approval of education, student mothers use this to display superior character, forging identities as good mothers and individuals who are trying to get ahead. As they apply new interpretations of moral worth they distance themselves from welfare policymakers and redefine their situation in opposition to welfare policies that restrict their access to education and their ability to reach self-sufficiency and care for their children.

The widely shared value of education in addition to the added burden in terms of time commitment and constraints by the welfare system generates resistance to work requirements. Here we see how high regard for the promise of education shapes student mother's choices about work and motherhood, identities as deserving, and undermines the legitimacy of the welfare system.

Student Status As Moral Capital

Betty a 25-year-old never married student mother was in her last semester of college courses. She found that trying to fulfill the work requirement was very difficult with the demands of school and family. She expressed the distinction between students and others as those who are "trying" and those who are not and would benefit from work requirements.

> I actually think that this new program [TANF] is beneficial except for us students. It did not take into effect those students who are going to school, are single moms and are supposed to work . . . I think that they need to reevaluate the Work First part of it as far as the students go. I think that it really is beneficial for those who aren't working. I think that they need to take into consideration those who are already *trying to be self-reliant* and they are punishing those people more than anything.

Betty clearly believes that student status demonstrates her moral worth and the fact that she is complying with the spirit and substance of welfare reform's call for personal responsibility in her quest to become self-reliant. Her pursuit of education sets her apart from others who are not trying to get ahead.

With so many mothers in the labor force, many mothers experience difficulty balancing work and family responsibilities. Therefore, requiring single mothers to work seems more "normative" than constraints on education. In fact, as more mothers entered the workforce, welfare assistance to poor mothers was increasingly perceived as a benefit not available to other working families who struggle with work and family conflict.[30] Thus, reference to the difficulty of combining single motherhood with work does not provide the same degree of moral currency as does a desire to make a better life for oneself and children through education.

Betty expresses the sentiments of many mothers with the conflict between her choice to complete her education and the requirements of public assistance. Here Betty relates a conversation with her caseworker about having to go to the welfare office for an eligibility meeting and a conflict with her class schedule.

> And I have had to call and say I can't make it because I have class. Well she told me you have to have your priorities in order. Well I'm sorry. Welfare is not my priority, school is. This is what is going to get me off the system, not coming to a meeting.

Personal Responsibility through Education

As I listened to mothers talk about their educational goals, they were very aware of the relationship between educational attainment and their ability to financially support themselves and their children in the long run. As Vivyan Adair argues "post-secondary education can unlock the door to economic opportunity and thus enable disadvantaged women to live lives of dignity, supporting and nurturing their children."[31] The lack of support for postsecondary education by the welfare system presented a direct challenge to respondents' efforts to obtain a better life.

Student mothers also distinguished between good jobs that would allow them to "get ahead" and provide for their families and low-wage work that was often seen as an obstacle to that goal. Their current work situations were secondary to their educational goals, and the twenty-hour work requirement was often described as impeding the promise of upward mobility through education. Carol, 37 years, divorced with a 6-year-old daughter expressed her frustration with the work requirement.

> When you are a single parent having to work that 20–25 hours that is tough when you are a single mom trying to go to school. I think that thing should be done away with. I mean if you are going to school and you are really trying I don't think you should be penalized because you are trying to get ahead. ... You can't support a family on minimum wage, you know so that is what they are doing, they are forcing all these women ...

For Carol and others, work requirements force women to "choose" low-wage jobs. Student mothers must at times choose between family and school commitments. Here Betty, in language almost identical to the way she described her allegiance to her educational goals, discusses her need to miss class to care for her ill daughter.

> It is rough sometimes especially when she is sick. Most of my instructors have been pretty okay with it but sometimes they are just like, "you have to figure out your priorities." And well I did, and it's her and I am not going to be in class today.

Betty does not hesitate when asked to choose between her priorities. Yet, her educational commitments and family commitments are not as separate as they appear, as ultimately her educational attainment will allow her to get a job and create a good life for herself and daughter. But when asked directly Betty defers to the moral imperative demanded of mothers that children's needs come first.[32]

Mary is 36, a full-time student, and mother of two elementary school-age children. The welfare office cut Mary's cash assistance because she did not work the required 20 hours. Mary has "chosen" to reject the welfare office's insistence on waged labor. She exposes the contradiction in definitions of personal responsibility for poor mothers when insistence on paid work hinders education and a single mother's ability to care for children. As a student mother, worn down by the multiple demands of work, school, and motherhood, Mary stakes a position of moral worth above policy makers who "can't understand."

> I can't do all three, I can't be a mom, and school and work. I just can't. So I deal with the lower payment, with a lower grant, as best I can and wait until the next financial aid comes through . . . They [policymakers] can't understand what it is like to do something like that. . . . I would switch places with them for a day, or a week, in a heartbeat. I go to class for 4–5 hours a day, I come home I sleep for a couple of hours before I pick up the kids at day care, I have 4 hours with them, then their homework, feeding them, cleaning up the house, and then my home work and then up at 7 to get them to school.

Mary also expresses the frustration of many others regarding the lack of support for education.

> For DSHS [Department of Social and Health Services] to not take into account a university education, it is very counterproductive, exceedingly. If you can't get help to get educated. I mean a decent living instead of just a subsistence living, what is the point? You know? I can't help but wonder, what are they thinking?

Generating Moral Capital

Melanie, a 33-year-old single mother of two young children was also a full-time student who returned to school after working as a salesperson in a woman's clothing store. She received a TANF grant and combined that with work-study funds. Melanie viewed the changes brought about by TANF and the behavior of caseworkers as adversaries to her educational goals.

> They [caseworkers] were saying that my education does not mean anything, that it does not count for anything, and that it really isn't going to do you anything, that it is not going to benefit. . . . They are telling me I have to have a job. Education is not counted as job related . . . and that is like excuse me! And that really made me angry, and I wasn't going to let them take that from me

Melanie's decision to go on welfare and complete a college degree was based on her inability to support her two young children on her earnings. In addition, she relied on her mother to care for her children and rarely saw them.

> My son had to stay with my mom because I couldn't afford child care and there was no child care help at all. I really very seldom got to see my son. And you know what is the point of working if you can't be around your kids?

Melanie views her education as fulfilling her family responsibility and frames welfare assistance in moral terms. She borrows from the rhetoric of welfare proponents who insist that poor single mothers meet their family responsibilities through paid work. However, she argues that reliance on welfare—not work—has allowed her to care for her children and model responsibility for them as she pursues a college education.

> I will be able to show my children, you know. I am on the system to get myself an education and for no other reason. . . . It is to get me where I need to be in order to support myself and my children, *forever.*

Melanie reinterprets welfare assistance as a means of demonstrating for her children the eventual long-term payoff from education. Her goal of self-sufficiency parallels the American dream where individuals are rewarded for their hard work and individual achievement. Melanie uses the high regard for education to reshape personal responsibility to include her ability to support her children with assistance from the state. In contrast to the negative assumptions about welfare dependency, Melanie turns to widely shared understandings about education, caring for children, and paid work to demonstrate her moral worth as a positive role model for her children. In doing so, she like other mothers, sets herself above policymakers in a hierarchy of moral worth based on taken-for-granted ideals that she shares with others in contemporary U.S society.

DISCUSSION AND CONCLUSION

Welfare reform, from the perspective of policymakers, has been successful in moving poor women off the welfare rolls into the workforce. The policy, in practice, emphasizes workforce participation that may or may not lift a mother and children out of poverty, restricts educational pursuits, and insists that poor mothers' responsibility to children lies in their role as providers not homemakers.[33]

This study took place in the first few years following the implementation of TANF as welfare recipients were negotiating the constraints and opportunities of the reformed welfare policy. As we have seen, decisions that poor women make about commitments to paid work and children are ultimately moral decisions that resonate with broadly shared cultural ideals. These ideals include the belief that mothers should be devoted to children, paid work establishes identities free from the stigma of welfare, and educational attainment makes it possible for even the disadvantaged—poor single mothers—to get ahead if they apply themselves and work hard.

The low-income single mothers in this study, students and nonstudents, illustrate how broadly shared, taken for granted understandings about responsibility for children, workforce participation, and education shape poor mothers' work and family decisions. The "choice" to work, pursue educational goals, and/or care for a sick child are not only constrained and enabled by available resources, but also by moral criteria.

The mothers in this study, along with others in U.S. society, share the belief in the promise of education that characterizes the American Dream. Yet, welfare policies challenge this dream by privileging low-wage work over mothers' responsibility for children and hopes for obtaining a college education. When welfare policies penalize recipients for pursuing this dream, they undermine the legitimacy of the system and generate resistance. Student mothers emphasized their long-term educational goals and responsibility for children in opposition to work requirements that hindered their ability to reach the self-sufficiency promised by welfare reform. Thus, student mothers were able to resist the stigma of welfare, placing themselves above welfare policy makers and other less deserving welfare mothers. I found that poor mothers are not passive recipients of an oppressive social policy environment. Moreover, their resistance is grounded in dominant cultural ideals that the majority of Americans share.

I focus on educational attainment in the early days of the reform because of its salience within this group of women and its power in shaping moral identities and generating resistance. However, as important as education was in the lives of the mothers in this study, we also saw that at times student status conflicted with the demands of motherhood. Dominant cultural models that comprise the moral dimension of poor women's work and family decisions are not gender neutral. When mothers feel their choice is between their responsibility to children and work, or time in the classroom, motherhood almost always wins. However, student mothers also include educational goals as part of their responsibility as mothers to provide for the long-term welfare of children, thus maintaining their status as good mothers buttressed by the moral capital earned through student status.

Greater visibility and explicit recognition of the moral underpinnings of expanding educational opportunity complement the efforts by advocates for increased educational opportunities, good jobs, and greater autonomy for low- income women. It also mirrors the belief by the U.S. public that—*if you work hard and play by the rules* you have the right and opportunity to pursue the American dream. Poor single mothers include themselves and their children in that dream.

NOTES

1. In addition to work requirements, PRWORA restricts cash welfare assistance to a maximum lifetime limit of 5 years (fewer at state option). Under the AFDC program, poor families could receive benefits as long as they met eligibility requirements.

2. Nineteen states and the District of Columbia currently allow postsecondary education to count as work for longer than 24 months—Alabama, Arkansas, California, Colorado, Delaware, Georgia, Hawaii, Illinois, Iowa, Maine, Massachusetts, Missouri, Montana, New Jersey, North Carolina, South Carolina, Vermont, Wisconsin, and Wyoming. Georgia is the only state that allows recipients to enroll in graduate programs. Most states require that students be enrolled in a program that leads to employment, that they maintain a certain GPA and make satisfactory progress toward a degree within a specific period time frame. "From Poverty to Self-Sufficiency: The Role of Postsecondary Education in Welfare Reform," *Center for Women Policy Studies Fact Sheet April 2003.* http://216.146.235.184/report.cfm?ReportID-77 (accessed on February 3, 2006).

3. Heather Boushey and Bethney Gundersen, *When Work Just Isn't Enough: Measuring Hardships Faced by Families after Moving from Welfare to Work* (Washington, DC: Economic Policy Institute, 2001); Mary Corcoran, Sandra K. Danziger, Ariel Kalil, and Kristin S. Seefeldt, "How Welfare Reform Is Affecting Women's Work," *Annual Review of Sociology* 26 (2000):

241–269; Kathryn Edin, and Laura Lein, *Making Ends Meet: How Single Mothers Survive Welfare and Low-Wage Work* (New York: Russell Sage, 1997); Judith Hennessy, "Welfare, Work, and Family Well-Being: A Comparative Analysis of Welfare and Employment Status for Single Female-Headed Families Post-TANF," *Sociological Perspectives* 48 (1) (Spring 2005): 77–104.

4. Valerie Polakow, Sandra S. Butler, Luisa Stormer Deprez, and Peggy Kahn, eds. *Shut Out: Low-Income Mothers and Higher Education in Post-Welfare America* (Albany, NY: State University of New York Press, 2004).

5. Mary Blair-Loy, *Competing Devotions: Career and Family among Women Financial Executives* (Cambridge, MA: Harvard University Press 2003); Judith Hennessy, Learning to Love Labor: Low-Income Women, Work Family Balance and Public Assistance. Dissertation, Washington State University, Pullman, Washington (2005a).

6. Examples of these culturally constructed models of primarily middle-class motherhood are respectively, Sharon Hays, *The Cultural Contradiction of Motherhood* (New Haven: Yale University Press, 1996); Mary Blair-Loy *Competing Devotions*; Anita Garey, *Weaving Work and Motherhood* (Philadelphia: Temple University Press, 1999).

7. Charles Murray, *Losing Ground: American Social Policy* 1950–1980 (New York: Basic Books, 1984); Lawrence Mead, *The New Politics of Poverty: The Non-working Poor in America* (New York: Basic Books 1992), "The Rise of Paternalism" in *The New Paternalism: Supervisory Approaches to Poverty*, edited by Lawrence Mead, 1–38. Washington DC: The Brookings Institution, 1997.

8. Recently media attention has focused on professional mother's workforce participation and the benefit to children and home life when mothers curtail or limit work force participation. See Claudia Wallis, "The Case for Staying Home," *Time Magazine*, March 22, 2004, 163, 51–58; Eduardo Porter, "Stretched to Limit, Women Stall March to Work," *New York Times*, March 16, 2006, Front section.

9. Gwendolyn Mink, *Welfare's End* (Ithaca, NY: Cornell University Press, 1998); Sharon Hays, *Flat Broke with Children: Women in the Age of Welfare Reform* (New York: Oxford University Press, 2003); Mechthild U Hart, *The Poverty of Life Affirming Work: Motherwork, Education, and Social Change* (Westport, CT: Greenwood Press, 2002); Sanford F Schram, *After Welfare: The Culture of Postindustrial Social Policy* (New York: New York University Press, 2000).

10. Karen McCormack, "Stratified Reproduction and Poor Women's Resistance." *Gender and Society* 19 (5) (October 2005): 660–679.

11. Philip N Cohen and Suzanne Bianchi, "Marriage, Children, and Women's Employment: What Do We Know?" *Monthly Labor Review* 122 (12) (1999): 22–31.

12. Robert Jackall, *Moral Mazes: The World of Corporate Managers* (New York: Oxford University Press 1989); Martha Albertson Fineman, "Dependencies," in *Women and Welfare: Theory and Practice in the United States and Europe*, ed. Nancy J. Hirschmann and Urike Liebert, 23–37 (New Jersey: Rutgers University Press, 2001); David Shipler, *The Working Poor: Invisible in America* (New York: Knopf, 2004); Nancy J Hirschmann, "A Question of Freedom, A Question of Rights? Women and Welfare," in *Women and Welfare: Theory and Practice in the United States and Europe*, ed. Nancy Hirschmann and Urike Liebert (New Jersey: Rutgers University Press, 2001): 84–110.

13. Shipler, *The Working Poor*, 5.

14. Benjamin K Hunnicutt, *Work Without End: Abandoning Shorter Hours for the Right to Work* (Philadelphia, PA: Temple University Press, 1988); Max Weber, *The Protestant Ethic and the Spirit of Capitalism* (New Jersey: Prentice Hall, Inc, 1958); Robert Wuthnow, *Poor Richards*

Principle: Recovering the American Dream through the Moral Principle of Work, Business, and Money (Princeton, NJ: Princeton University Press, 1996); Katherine Newman, *No Shame in My Game: The Working Poor in the Inner City* (New York: Alford A Knopf, 1999).

15. Wuthnow, *Poor Richards Principle.*

16. Deborah Stone, "Work and the Moral Woman," *The American Prospect* 8 (35) (1997): 79–86.

17. Hays, *Cultural Contradictions of Motherhood.*

18. Anne Crittenden, *The Price of Motherhood: Why the Most Important Job in the World Is Still the Least Valued* (New York: Metropolitan Books, 2001); Nancy Folbre, Who *Pays for the Kids? Gender and The Structure of Constraint* (New York: Routledge, 1994), argue convincingly that all women's caregiving labor is undervalued by U.S. society and that the "most important job in the world" is not counted as work, thus penalizing women who overwhelmingly are responsible for the work involved in raising the next generation. Although, women who interrupt careers for childrearing suffer major financial consequences, they still reap moral credit for their devotion to family. Single mothers who rely on public assistance derive no moral credit from the U.S. public and policy makers for their performance of the "most important job in the world."

19. Jesse Bernard, "The Good Provider Role: Its Rise and Fall," *American Psychologist* 36 (1) 1981): 1–12.

20. Jennifer Hochschild, *Facing Up to the American Dream: Race, Class, and the Soul of the Nation* (New Jersey: Princeton University Press, 1995): 18; Jennifer Hochschild and Nathan Scovronick, *The American Dream and the Public Schools* (New York: Oxford University Press, 2003): 1.

21. Rebekah J. Smith, Luisa S. Deprez, and Sandra Butler, "New Perspective on Labor and Gender: The Miseducation of Welfare Reform: Denying the Promise of Postsecondary Education," *University of Maine School of Law Review* 55 Me. L. Rev 211 (2003): 211–240.

22. Peggy Kahn, Introduction to *Shut Out: Low Income Mothers and Higher Education,* 1–19.

23. Mark Greenberg, Julie Strawn, and Lisa Plimpton, *State Opportunities to Provide Access to Post-secondary Education under TANF* (Washington, DC: Center for Law and Social Policy, 2000). Available at http://www.clasp.org/publications/postsec_revised_2--00.pdf (accessed on February 6, 2006); Janice Peterson, *Feminist Perspectives on TANF Reauthorization: An Introduction to Key Issues for the Future of Welfare Reform* (Washington, DC: Institute for Women's Policy Research, 2002); Smith, Deprez, and Butler, "New Perspectives on Labor and Gender,""From Poverty to Self-Sufficiency," *Center for Women's Policy.*

24. Smith, Deprez, and Butler, "New Perspectives on Labor and Gender."

25. "From Poverty to Self-Sufficiency," *Center for Women's Policy.*

26. "From Poverty to Self-Sufficiency," *Center for Women's Policy.*

27. HR 4241 *Deficit Reduction Act of 2005*, The Library of Congress (November 7, 2005), http://thomas.loc.gov/cgi-bin/query/z?c109:H.4241; The final bill signed into law on February 8, 2006 requires 30 hours of work participation rates for mothers with children over the age of 6, rather than 40 hours as some legislators had proposed; see Kahn, Introduction (7) and Afterword (237–240) in *Shut Out: Low Income Mothers and Higher Education.*

28. Sharon K Long, Sandra J. Clark, Caroline Ratcliffe and Krista Olson, "Income Support and Social Services for Low-Income People in Washington," *Assessing the New Federalism* (Washington, DC: The Urban Institute, 1998).

29. Wuthnow, *Poor Richards Principle,* 332.

30. Hays, *Flat Broke with Children*.

31. Vivyan Adair, "Fulfilling the Promise of Higher Education," in *Reclaiming Class: Women Poverty and the Promise of Higher Education*, ed. Vivyan Adair and Sandra Dahlberg, 24 (Philadelphia, Temple University Press 2003).

32. Hays, *Cultural Contradictions*.

33. Hays, *Flat Broke with Children*.

INDEX

Academic achievement status, 1, 86;
athletics and, 103–13; community
factors in, 91–94; extracurricular
participation and, xii, 103–14; family
and, x, 30, 50–52, 83, 89–97; gender
and, 106; health and, 26, 52; income
and, 27; measuring, 56–60; personal
factors in, 90, 92–97; poverty and, viii,
x, 1, 26, 56, 59–62, 95, 113;
race/ethnicity and, 26, 83, 93–95, 97,
109–12; resources for improving,
96–97; SES and, ix–xi, 83, 95, 97;
unemployment and, 26; violence and,
26
Academic Scholars, 75–76
Achievement gap, 74
ACT, 75–76
Adair, Vivyan, 139
The Adolescent Society (Coleman), 102
AFDC. *See* Aid to Families with
Dependent Children
Affirmative Action, education
and, 104
African Americans: academic achievement
status of, 93–95, 109–12; colleges and,
74–77; extracurricular participation in,
109–12; high school dropout rate of, 82;
kindergarten mathematics scores by, 36,

38–39; residential segregation in, 119;
school segregation of, 12–13, 16–22;
standardized test scores by, 66–67,
69–73, 75–77; youth employment
among, 118, 120–21, 125–27
Aid to Families with Dependent Children
(AFDC), 83, 132, 142 n.1
Alexander, Karl L., 118
Alwin, D.F., 113
Amrein, A.L., 69
Annie Casey Foundation, 52
Annual School Reports, 16
Asians: kindergarten mathematics scores
by, 36; school segregation of, 12–13,
16–22; youth employment of, 126
Athletics: academic achievement status of,
103–13; colleges and, 104–5; gender
and, 105

Barber, B., 103
Berliner, David, 49–50, 52, 69
Blacks. *See* African Americans
Bordieu, Pierre, x
Bowen, William, 103
Bowles, Samuel, x, 102
Broh, Beckett, 104–5, 113
Bryk, Anthony, 62
Burkam, D.T., 66

About the Editors and Contributors

Barbara A. Arrighi is associate professor of sociology at Northern Kentucky University. Her research interests include work and family, as well as issues related to race, class, and sexism. Her books include: *America's Shame: Women and Children in Shelter and the Degradation of Family Roles* and *Understanding Inequality: The Intersection of Race/Ethnicity, Class, and Gender*. Professor Arrighi has published in the *Journal of Family Issues and elsewhere*.

David J. Maume is professor of sociology, and Director, Kunz Center for the Study of Work and Family, at the University of Cincinnati. His teaching and research interests are in labor market inequality and work-family issues, with recent publications appearing in the *Journal of Marriage and Family*, *Work and Occupations*, and *Social Problems*. He is currently researching gender differences in providing urgent child care in dual-earner families, gender differences in the effects of supervisor characteristics on subordinates' job attitudes, and the effects of shift work on the work and family lives of retail food workers (funded by the *National Science Foundation*).

Richard K. Caputo, PhD, is professor of social policy and research, and Director of the Doctoral Program, Wurzweiler School of Social Work, Yeshiva University, New York City. He has authored four books and edited a fifth. Dr Caputo has many peer-reviewed articles. He also serves on the editorial boards of the *Journal of Family and Economic Issues*, *Families in Society*, *Journal of Poverty*, *Sociology & Social Welfare*, and *Marriage and Family Review*. He has written extensively in the areas of economic well-being of families, adolescent behavior and educational attainment, poverty, aging, and social justice.

Dylan Conger is assistant professor at the George Washington University, School of Public Policy and Public Administration. Her research focuses on social and educational policy, with a particular interest in immigrant students as well as racial and socioeconomic inequality. In addition to studying racial segregation within schools, she is currently examining the school performance of immigrant students in New York City public schools. She has published in such journals as *Educational Evaluation and Policy Analysis, Youth Violence and Juvenile Justice, Child Welfare,* and *The Journal of Negro Education.* Dr. Conger received her BA in Ethnic Studies from the University of California at Berkeley, her MPP from the University of Michigan, and her PhD in public policy from New York University.

Constance T. Gager, a sociologist, is an assistant professor in the School of Social and Family Dynamics at Arizona State University and a founding member of the Center for Population Dynamics. Broadly, her research explores the intersection of family, work, gender, and race. Her research area is twofold. The first area centers on predictors of relationship quality including perceptions of fairness, happiness, sexual frequency, and divorce. Her second research area focuses on time use among youth, including the time they spend in paid work, housework, and extracurricular activities; and how participation varies by family structure, gender, race, and regional residence. She completed her PhD at the University of Pennsylvania and her NICHD-funded postdoctoral training at the Office of Population Research at Princeton University.

Annie Georges is a Senior Research Scientist at the National Center for Children and Families at Teachers' College, Columbia University. Her interests are in policy-relevant research that focuses on family and classroom influences on the academic outcomes of low-income children, and quantitative research methods. The findings presented in his chapter are based upon work supported by the National Science Foundation under grant No. 0439756. Any opinions, findings, and conclusions or recommendations expressed in this material are those of the author and do not necessarily reflect the views of the National Science Foundation.

Judith Hennessy is an assistant professor of sociology and social services at the Central Washington University, Ellensburg. Her research interests are social welfare policy, specifically TANF and the welfare to work transition, and the moral and cultural context of paid work and family attachments for impoverished and low-income women.

Jennifer Hickes Lundquist is an assistant professor in the Department of Sociology and Faculty Research Associate with the University of Massachusetts at Amherst's Social and Demographic Research Institute. A social demographer with an emphasis on race and ethnic stratification, family formation patterns and immigration, she evaluates racial disparities along a variety of demographic outcomes, including marriage, family stability, fertility, and health. She received a joint PhD in Demography and Sociology in 2004 from the University of Pennsylvania.

Sandra Mathison is a professor of Education at the University of British Columbia. Her research is in educational evaluation and focuses especially on the potential and limits of evaluation to support democratic ideals and promote justice. She is currently doing research on the effects of government-mandated testing on teaching and learning in elementary and middle schools. She is editor of the *Encyclopedia of Evaluation* and coeditor of *Defending Public Schools: The Nature and Limits of Standards-Based Reform and Assessment*.

Jacqueline C. Pflieger is a fourth-year graduate student in the School of Social and Family Dynamics at Arizona State University. She teaches and conducts research on adolescence. Her research explores the influence of family on the development of romantic relationship competencies with a focus on the parent–child relationship during adolescence. She completed her MS in Human Development and Family Studies at Auburn University and holds a BA in Psychology from James Madison University.

Deborah A. Phillips, PhD, is currently professor of psychology and associated faculty in the Public Policy Institute at Georgetown University. She is also codirector of the University's Research Center on Children in the United States. Prior to this, she was the first Executive Director of the Board on Children, Youth, and Families of the National Research Council's Commission on Social and Behavioral Sciences and the Institute of Medicine. She also coedited: *From Neurons to Neighborhoods. The Science of Early Child Development*. Her research focuses on the developmental effects of early childhood programs, including both child care and pre-k settings. Current studies are focusing on how children who differ in temperament are differentially affected by child-care experiences and on an evaluation of the Tulsa Oklahoma pre-k program as it affects both cognitive and social-emotional development. As a Congressional Science Fellow of the Society for Research in Child Development, Dr. Phillips served as an analyst at the Congressional Budget Office and on the personal staff of Congressman George Miller. She was a mid-career fellow at Yale University's Bush Center in Child Development and Social Policy, and director of the Child Care Information Service of the National Association for the Education of Young Children. She has served on numerous task forces and advisory groups, including the Carnegie Corporation's Task Force on Meeting the Needs of Young Children and the Secretary's Advisory Committee on Head Start Quality and Expansion of the U.S. Department of Health and Human Services. Dr. Phillips is a fellow of the American Psychological Association and the American Psychological Society.

Edward B. Reeves, PhD, is professor of sociology and director of educational research in the Institute for Regional Analysis and Public Policy at Morehead State University in Morehead, Kentucky. Reeves serves as a member of the Kentucky School Curriculum, Assessment, and Accountability Council, a state policy advisory body. His research interests include education reform and educational research methodology. More specifically, he studies how social factors contribute to school performance and improvement as well as to individual student achievement and attainment. Reeves' recent research publications have appeared in *Rural Sociology* and the *International Journal of Learning*.

Jason M. Smith is with the Department of Sociology at the University of Alabama in Huntsville. He received his PhD in Sociology and Demography from The Pennsylvania State University, and his current research centers on the educational system as a means for social mobility, the educational effects of social capital, and the effects of neighborhoods and schools on educational outcomes. He can be reached at Department of Sociology, University of Alabama in Huntsville, Huntsville, AL 35899, (256) 824-6190.

Marcy Whitebook, PhD is currently director and senior researcher, Center for the Study of Child Care Employment, Institute of Industrial Relations, University of California at Berkeley. Her research focuses on issues of child-care employment with specific attention to its relationship to children's development, school readiness, and its implications for higher education programs and policies. Her most recent book is entitled *By a thread: How centers hold on to teachers; How teachers build lasting career.*